LATIN AMERICAN AND
LIBRARY RESOURCES IN
THE BRITISH ISLES

A DIRECTORY

LATIN AMERICAN AND CARIBBEAN LIBRARY RESOURCES IN THE BRITISH ISLES

A DIRECTORY

Alan Biggins

and

Valerie Cooper

Institute of Latin American Studies
School of Advanced Study, University of London

and

Advisory Council on Latin American and Iberian Information
Resources (ACLAIIR)

Institute of Latin American Studies
School of Advanced Study
University of London

British Library Cataloguing-in-Publication Data
A catalogue record for this book is available
from the British Library

ISBN   1 900039 38 9

©Institute of Latin American Studies
  University of London
  and
  Advisory Council on Latin American and Iberian
  Information Resources (ACLAIIR), 2002

CONTENTS

Foreword   vii

Introduction   ix

Abbreviations   xiii

List of libraries   xv

Libraries included in earlier editions which have closed, merged with other libraries, or which no longer have significant Latin American or Caribbean collections   xxiii

Descriptions of libraries and collections   1

Index   313

FOREWORD

The Institute of Latin American Studies is very pleased to publish this volume on behalf of the Advisory Council on Latin American and Iberian Information Resources (ACLAIIR). As its compilers explain in their Introduction, the present text effectively constitutes a third edition of similar directories published by the Institute in 1975 and 1988. However, the huge advances in information technology since the second edition have meant that this work possesses important new features, and it will likely be used by many readers and researchers in a different fashion to its predecessors.

There is a particular need for precise and accurate guides such as this in an era when, it is sometimes said, we suffer from 'information overload'. It is equally in recognition of important new initiatives in Europe that the geographical scope of the present work is, like that of the first edition, limited to the British Isles. This is not only in keeping with the Institute's national responsibilities but also consonant with the need to sustain the highest level of local knowledge in an increasingly global context. I am confident that the third edition, which has been prepared with most diligent professionalism, will be just as useful to international scholarship as the earlier volumes, and I very much hope that it enables exploration of a region in which much still remains to be discovered.

James Dunkerley
Institute of Latin American Studies

INTRODUCTION

This volume is the third edition of the *Directory of Libraries and Special Collections on Latin America and the West Indies*, first compiled by Bernard Naylor, Laurence Hallewell and Colin Steele and published in 1975. The second edition, *Libraries and Special Collections on Latin America and the Caribbean: a Directory of European Resources*, was compiled by Roger Macdonald and Carole Travis and published in 1988. This new edition has been undertaken on behalf of the Advisory Council on Latin American and Iberian Information Resources (ACLAIIR).

The second edition was extended to cover holdings in Europe, and the compilers hoped that further international co-operation would be enlisted to produce a fuller survey of those European libraries. A year after the appearance of the second edition, and prompted by it, a European association of libraries and documentation centres with collections on Latin America was formed. The Red Europea de Información y Documentación sobre América Latina (REDIAL) was set up with the aim of delivering Europe-wide information resources on Latin America, and, since one of its projects was to stimulate the production of national directories of libraries and from them create a European database of libraries on Latin America, this third edition has been limited to the British Isles.

Foremost among the numerous developments that have occurred since the appearance of the second edition are those relating to electronic resources and remote access via the Internet. In 1988 most library holdings were still indexed in manual catalogues. In the intervening years retroconversion projects have transformed the situation and the majority of the libraries in this edition have fully automated catalogues. Moreover, in the case of at least the national and university libraries, these catalogues can be accessed remotely through the Internet. The development of the World Wide Web has brought other changes with it: in 1988, printed guides to library collections were listed; in 2000, these have been largely superseded by electronic versions available on the libraries' web sites, and researchers increasingly have access to both these and the library catalogues from their offices and in their own homes. The expansion of electronic mail means that an enquiry can be submitted almost instantaneously from the web page to the library. Similarly, telex has been replaced by facsimile transmission, which is much more widely available, and documents can be delivered to the researcher's desk either by fax or by e-mail.

In addition, telephone numbers have changed substantially in the past twelve years. It is certain that the next edition of this directory will be made available in electronic format, and it is possible that this edition will eventually appear on the Internet.

Methodology

As in the case of the previous two editions, information was gathered largely by means of a questionnaire. In addition to contacting libraries included in the previous two editions, substantial efforts were made to identify additional resources. These were gleaned from other library directories, from a survey of resources on the environment made in 1994, from personal knowledge, and from resource lists of non-governmental organisations available on the Internet. An approach was also made to a number of academic institutions that were known to teach on Latin America and the Caribbean and which had not been included in earlier editions.

Once libraries had been identified, questionnaires were sent out by post, and, in the case of libraries included in the second edition, a copy of their existing entry was included for comment and updating. The returns were used to create the entries for this third edition and substantial use was made of the Internet to check and expand the details. The new draft entries were then sent to libraries for checking (by e-mail, whenever possible). A list has been made of libraries which have closed since the previous edition, collections which have been transferred to other libraries and organisations which have merged or been renamed.

Scope

Latin America has been interpreted as including the whole of the mainland south of the Río Grande together with the reasonably adjacent islands, and libraries were asked to state whether their collections related to the area as a whole or were limited to any part of it. As before, no limitations were placed on subject coverage or type of library, and collections covered include those of national, government, university, public, society and charitable libraries, as well as those of international organisations. The main emphasis is on printed materials, although other categories of material listed include maps, slides, films, CD-ROMs, and audio and video recordings. Although the existence of manuscript collections is indicated, we have not attempted full coverage in this specialised area, and the directory should therefore not be seen as comprehensive in this respect.

Arrangement and content

The entries in the directory are arranged alphabetically by the city or town in which the libraries are situated, and then by the name of each library or the name of its parent institution. The method of alphabetical filing is letter by letter rather than word by word.

The preliminary information provided includes the name and full postal and e-mail addresses of each institution, telephone and fax numbers, telnet address for the library catalogue (if applicable) and the World Wide Web address, the name of the chief librarian and any specialist member of staff responsible for the Latin American and Caribbean collections.

The main body of the entry attempts to describe briefly the history of the collection, to indicate any special subject or area interests, or strengths in particular types of materials held, and includes information on access to the shelves. Although an effort has been made to provide precise figures for holdings, these may frequently be regarded only as general approximations; it should be noted that it is the strongest libraries which find it most difficult to make a numerical assessment of their holdings.

The entries also describe access to collections and services, including information on hours of opening, enquiries, admission procedure, lending to non-members, form of catalogue, classification scheme, facilities for microcomputing, on-line searching and Internet access, the availability of CD-ROM and microform services, and provision for the use of portable computers. Readers should be prepared to find restrictions on the photocopying of fragile and rare materials, and that access to electronic resources may often be limited to members of the home institution. 'Union record' indicates the joint records of the holdings of several libraries, published or unpublished, in which the particular library's holdings are included; a key to abbreviations is provided. Finally, in listing publications, we have limited ourselves principally to publications of or about the library, especially published catalogues of the collections.

Index

A full index is provided, covering libraries, institutions, subjects and named special collections. Specialist materials such as official publications, photographs, audio-visual materials, etc., are indexed by form headings. It is assumed that books and pamphlets are covered in each entry; they are therefore not listed separately in the index. Similarly, it is assumed that most collections will include periodicals, so only large or subject-specific collections are indexed. In most instances, cross-references have been provided between subjects and countries, and are also used to direct the user's attention to alternative subject terms used or to related material.

Acknowledgments

We are deeply indebted to the compilers of the first two editions for laying the foundations on which this edition has been constructed, and to all the correspondents who took the trouble to complete questionnaires and update their entries. A special word of thanks is due to Barry Taylor, British Library, who read the manuscript and made many helpful suggestions. As with the previous edition, ACLAIIR will publish changes to the entries in its newsletter, and we therefore hope that users of this directory will draw our attention to any alterations or additions that should be made. We are particularly grateful to the Institute of Latin American Studies, School of Advanced Study, University of London, which has again supported the publication of this work.

Alan Biggins
Valerie Cooper
Institute of Latin American Studies

ABBREVIATIONS

ALA	Associate of the Library Association
ALCID	Academic Libraries Co-operation in Dublin
ANGLES	Anglian Libraries Information Exchange Scheme
ARLIS	Art Libraries Society http://arlis.nal.vam.ac.uk/
BLCMP	Birmingham Libraries Co-operative Mechanisation Project http://www.blcmp.org.uk/
BLDSC	British Library Document Supply Centre (see no. 10)
BUCLA	British Union Catalogue of Latin Americana (see no. 121)
BUCOP	*British Union Catalogue of Periodicals* (London: Butterworth, 1955–58), 4 vols. *Supplement to 1960* [1962]. *New Periodical Titles, 1960–68* [1970]; *1969–73* [1976]; annual vols, 1974–80 [1974–81]. Superseded by *Serials in the British Library*, annual cumulation and quarterly issues [to 1986 includes British Library together with 16 other libraries; 1987– only British Library].
CALIM	Consortium of Academic Libraries in Manchester http://www.calim.ac.uk
CC–IW	Cydfenthyca Cymru / Interlending Wales
COLALAS	Committee on Latin America, *Latin American Serials* (1969–77) 3 vols: vol. 1. *Economic and Social* (London: Bingley, 1969), 189 pp.; vol. 2. *History with Politics* (London: Gregg International, 1973), 165 pp.; vol. 3. *Literature with Language, Art and Music* (London: COLA, 1977), 253 pp.
CURL	Consortium of University Research Libraries http://www.curl.ac.uk/
ELF	Edinburgh Libraries Federation
EMRLS	East Midlands Regional Library System
FLA	Fellow of the Library Association
GLASS	Greater London Audio Specialisation Scheme
IMLC	Irish Medical Libraries Consortium
IRIS	an Irish joint OPAC
LADSIRLAC	Liverpool and District Scientific & Industrial Research Library Advisory Council
LASER	London & South Eastern (Library) Region
NLSLS	National Library of Scotland Lending Scheme

NRLS	Northern Regional Library System
NWRLS	North Western Regional Library System
OCLC	Online Computer Library Center
	http://www.oclc.com/home/
OLIS	Oxford Libraries Information System
	http://library.ox.ac.uk/
RIDING	RIDING Consortium of Academic and other Libraries in Yorkshire and Humberside
	http://www.riding.ac.uk
RLG	Research Libraries Group
	http://www.rlg.ac.uk/
SALSER	Scottish Academic Libraries Serials Database
SCOLCAP	Scottish Libraries Co-operative Automation Project
SUSPER	Union List of Periodicals held in Sussex
SWRLS	South Western Regional Library System
	http://www.swrls.org.uk/
UNITY	The Combined Regions Database
	http://www.thecombinedregions.com
WLSP	*World List of Scientific Periodicals,* 4th ed. (London: Butterworth, 1963–65), 3 vols.
WMRLS	West Midlands Regional Library System
WRLS	Wales Regional Library Service
YHJLS	Yorkshire & Humberside Joint Libraries Service

LIST OF LIBRARIES

1.	ABERDEEN	University of Aberdeen
2.	ABERYSTWYTH	National Library of Wales / Llyfrgell Genedlaethol Cymru
3.	ABERYSTWYTH	University of Wales Aberystwyth / Prifysgol Cymru Aberystwyth. Hugh Owen Library
4.	BANGOR	University of Wales Bangor / Prifysgol Cymru Bangor
5.	BELFAST	Queen's University
6.	BIRMINGHAM	Birmingham Department of Leisure and Community Services, Library and Learning Division
7.	BIRMINGHAM	Research Unit for New Religions and Churches (RUNERC), Centre for Missiology and World Christianity, Department of Theology, University of Birmingham, Selly Oak. Harold Turner Collection
8.	BIRMINGHAM	South American Mission Society (SAMS)
9.	BIRMINGHAM	University of Birmingham
10.	BOSTON SPA	British Library Document Supply Centre
11.	BRACKNELL	National Meteorological Library and Archive
12.	BRADFORD	Development and Project Planning Centre, University of Bradford. DPPC Collection, J.B. Priestley Library
13.	BRIGHTON	Brighton Public Library
14.	BRIGHTON	Institute of Development Studies, University of Sussex. British Library for Development Studies
15.	BRIGHTON	University of Sussex
16.	BRISTOL	Bristol City Libraries. Bristol Reference Library, Central Library
17.	BRISTOL	University of Bristol
18.	BRISTOL	University of the West of England (UWE). Bolland Library
19.	CAMBRIDGE	BirdLife International
20.	CAMBRIDGE	Cambridge University Library
21.	CAMBRIDGE	Centre of Latin American Studies, University of Cambridge
22.	CAMBRIDGE	Faculty of Archaeology and Anthropology, University of Cambridge. Haddon Library

23.	CAMBRIDGE	Faculty of Economics and Politics, University of Cambridge. Marshall Library of Economics
24.	CAMBRIDGE	Faculty of History, University of Cambridge. Seeley Historical Library
25.	CAMBRIDGE	Faculty of Modern and Medieval Languages, University of Cambridge
26.	CAMBRIDGE	Institute of Criminology, University of Cambridge. Radzinowicz Library of Criminology
27.	CAMBRIDGE	Scientific Periodicals Library, Cambridge University Library
28.	CAMBRIDGE	Scott Polar Research Institute, University of Cambridge
29.	CANTERBURY	University of Kent at Canterbury. Templeman Library
30.	CARDIFF	Cardiff University / Prifysgol Caerdydd
31.	CARDIFF	International Bee Research Association. Eva Crane IBRA Library
32.	CHATHAM	Natural Resources Institute, Medway Campus, University of Greenwich
33.	COLCHESTER	University of Essex. Albert Sloman Library
34.	CORBY	Institute of Logistics and Transport
35.	CORK	University College Cork. Boole Library
36.	COVENTRY	University of Warwick
37.	DENBIGH	ASTIC Research Associates
38.	DUBLIN	Dublin City University
39.	DUBLIN	Trinity College Dublin Library
40.	DUBLIN	Trócaire
41.	DUBLIN	University College Dublin
42.	DURHAM	Durham University
43.	EDINBURGH	Edinburgh University
44.	EDINBURGH	National Library of Scotland
45.	EGHAM	CABI Bioscience UK Centre
46.	EGHAM	Royal Holloway, University of London
47.	EXETER	Devon County Council. Devon Library and Information Services
48.	EXETER	University of Exeter
49.	GALWAY	National University of Ireland, Galway. James Hardiman Library
50.	GLASGOW	Department for International Development (DFID)
51.	GLASGOW	Glasgow City Libraries and Archives. Mitchell Library

52.	GLASGOW	Royal Scottish Geographical Society
53.	GLASGOW	University of Glasgow
54.	GLASGOW	University of Strathclyde. Andersonian Library
55.	GODALMING	World-Wide Fund for Nature–UK (WWF–UK)
56.	GUILDFORD	University of Surrey. George Edwards Library
57.	HARPENDEN	Institute of Arable Crops Research–Rothamsted
58.	KEW	Royal Botanic Gardens
59.	KEYWORTH	British Geological Survey
60.	KINGSTON-UPON-HULL	Hull City Council. Hull Local Studies Library
61.	KINGSTON-UPON-HULL	University of Hull. Brynmor Jones Library
62.	KINGSTON-UPON-THAMES	Kingston University
63.	KINGSTON-UPON-THAMES	Sue Cunningham Photographic
64.	LEEDS	Leeds Library Service. Central Library
65.	LEEDS	Trinity and All Saints College, University of Leeds
66.	LEEDS	University of Leeds. Brotherton Library
67.	LEICESTER	University of Leicester
68.	LIMERICK	University of Limerick
69.	LIVERPOOL	The Athenaeum Library
70.	LIVERPOOL	Liverpool Libraries and Information Services. Central Library
71.	LIVERPOOL	University of Liverpool. Sydney Jones Library
72.	LONDON	ActionAid
73.	LONDON	Amnesty International, International Secretariat
74.	LONDON	Andes Press Agency
75.	LONDON	Anti-Slavery International
76.	LONDON	Association of Commonwealth Universities
77.	LONDON	Bank of England. Information Centre
78.	LONDON	Birkbeck College, University of London
79.	LONDON	British Broadcasting Corporation (BBC). Information and Archives Research Services, Music
80.	LONDON	British Film Institute (BFI). BFI National Library

81.	LONDON	British Film Institute (BFI). National Film and Television Archive
82.	LONDON	British Film Institute (BFI). BFI Stills, Posters and Designs
83.	LONDON	British Library, National Sound Archive
84.	LONDON	British Library, Newspaper Library
85.	LONDON	British Library, Reader Services & Collection Development
86.	LONDON	British Museum. Department of Ethnography Library
87.	LONDON	British Standards Institution (BSI)
88.	LONDON	Catholic Central Library
89.	LONDON	Catholic Institute for International Relations (CIIR)
90.	LONDON	Centre for Information on Language Teaching and Research (CILT)
91.	LONDON	Chartered Institute of Bankers
92.	LONDON	Chartered Insurance Institute
93.	LONDON	Christian Aid
94.	LONDON	Commonwealth Institute. Commonwealth Resource Centre
95.	LONDON	Commonwealth Parliamentary Association. Parliamentary Information and Reference Centre
96.	LONDON	Commonwealth Secretariat Library & Archives
97.	LONDON	Corporation of London City Business Library
98.	LONDON	Corporation of London Guildhall Library
99.	LONDON	Council for Education in World Citizenship
100.	LONDON	Department for International Development (DFID)
101.	LONDON	Department of Trade and Industry. British Trade International, Trade Partners UK
102.	LONDON	Development Planning Unit (DPU), University College London, University of London
103.	LONDON	The Fawcett Library: the National Library of Women
104.	LONDON	Folklore Society Library
105.	LONDON	Foreign and Commonwealth Office (FCO)
106.	LONDON	Goldsmiths College, University of London
107.	LONDON	Healthlink Worldwide (formerly AHRTAG)

108.	LONDON	Helpage International
109.	LONDON	Heythrop College, University of London
110.	LONDON	Hispanic and Luso-Brazilian Council. Canning House Library
111.	LONDON	Horniman Museum and Gardens. Horniman Library
112.	LONDON	Hulton|Archive
113.	LONDON	Hutchison Picture Library
114.	LONDON	Inland Revenue, International Division
115.	LONDON	Institute of Advanced Legal Studies, School of Advanced Study, University of London
116.	LONDON	Institute of Commonwealth Studies, School of Advanced Study, University of London
117.	LONDON	Institute of Contemporary History and Wiener Library
118.	LONDON	Institute of Education, University of London
119.	LONDON	Institute of Historical Research, School of Advanced Study, University of London
120.	LONDON	Institute of International Visual Arts (inIVA)
121.	LONDON	Institute of Latin American Studies, School of Advanced Study, University of London
122.	LONDON	Institute of Linguists
123.	LONDON	Institute of Petroleum
124.	LONDON	Institute of Race Relations
125.	LONDON	Institution of Civil Engineers
126.	LONDON	Institution of Mechanical Engineers
127.	LONDON	Institution of Mining and Metallurgy
128.	LONDON	International Coffee Organization (ICO)
129.	LONDON	International Institute for Strategic Studies
130.	LONDON	International Labour Office (ILO)
131.	LONDON	International Planned Parenthood Federation (IPPF)
132.	LONDON	International Rubber Study Group
133.	LONDON	International Sugar Organization
134.	LONDON	King's College London (KCL), University of London
135.	LONDON	London Borough of Bromley. Central Library
136.	LONDON	London Borough of Hackney. C.L.R. James Library, Homerton Library
137.	LONDON	London Borough of Tower Hamlets. Limehouse Library
138.	LONDON	London Chamber of Commerce and Industry
139.	LONDON	The London Library

140.	LONDON	London School of Economics, University of London. British Library of Political and Economic Science
141.	LONDON	London School of Hygiene and Tropical Medicine, University of London
142.	LONDON	Marx Memorial Library
143.	LONDON	Maya: the Guatemalan Indian Centre
144.	LONDON	Mexicolore
145.	LONDON	Middlesex University. Tottenham Campus Library
146.	LONDON	Ministry of Defence (MOD). Admiralty Library
147.	LONDON	Ministry of Defence (MOD). Whitehall Library
148.	LONDON	National Art Library, Victoria and Albert Museum
149.	LONDON	National Maritime Museum. Caird Library
150.	LONDON	Natural History Museum
151.	LONDON	Office for National Statistics
152.	LONDON	Overseas Development Institute (ODI)
153.	LONDON	Panos Pictures
154.	LONDON	Peru Support Group
155.	LONDON	Philip Wolmuth
156.	LONDON	Queen Mary, University of London
157.	LONDON	Religious Society of Friends (Quakers)
158.	LONDON	Royal Anthropological Institute of Great Britain and Ireland. Photographic Library
159.	LONDON	Royal Geographical Society (with The Institute of British Geographers)
160.	LONDON	Royal Institute of British Architects. British Architectural Library
161.	LONDON	Royal Institute of International Affairs. Chatham House Library
162.	LONDON	Royal Society of Medicine
163.	LONDON	School of Oriental and African Studies, University of London
164.	LONDON	Thames Valley University
165.	LONDON	Tourism Concern
166.	LONDON	Trades Union Congress Library Collections
167.	LONDON	United Nations Information Centre
168.	LONDON	University College London, University of London
169.	LONDON	University of London Library

170.	LONDON	Venezuelan Embassy / Embajada de los Estados Unidos de Venezuela. Biblioteca Latinoamericana Andrés Bello
171.	LONDON	Wellcome Library for the History and Understanding of Medicine
172.	LONDON	Westminster City Libraries
173.	LONDON	Women's Art Library (MAKE Resource)
174.	LONDON	Worldaware
175.	LONDON	World Mission Association Ltd (WMA). Partnership House Mission Studies Library
176.	LONDON	Writers and Scholars Educational Trust (Index on Censorship)
177.	LONDON	Zoological Society of London
178.	MAIDSTONE	Horticulture Research International
179.	MANCHESTER	Latin America Information Centre
180.	MANCHESTER	University of Manchester. John Rylands University Library of Manchester
181.	NEWCASTLE-UPON-TYNE	University of Newcastle upon Tyne. Robinson Library
182.	NEWCASTLE-UPON-TYNE	University of Northumbria
183.	NORWICH	University of East Anglia
184.	NOTTINGHAM	University of Nottingham. Hallward Library
185.	OLDBURY	Millbrook House Picture Library (Railphotos)
186.	OXFORD	Bodleian Law Library, University of Oxford
187.	OXFORD	Bodleian Library, University of Oxford
188.	OXFORD	Department of Economics, University of Oxford
189.	OXFORD	Department of Plant Sciences and Oxford Forestry Institute, University of Oxford. Plant Sciences Library (Forestry Collection)
190.	OXFORD	International Development Centre, University of Oxford
191.	OXFORD	Modern Languages Faculty, University of Oxford
192.	OXFORD	Oxfam
193.	OXFORD	Radcliffe Science Library, Bodleian Library, University of Oxford
194.	OXFORD	Rhodes House, University of Oxford
195.	OXFORD	Saint Antony's College, University of Oxford. Latin American Centre

196.	OXFORD	School of Anthropology and Museum Ethnography, University of Oxford. Balfour Library, Pitt Rivers Museum
197.	OXFORD	School of Anthropology and Museum Ethnography, University of Oxford. Tylor Library, Institute of Social and Cultural Anthropology
198.	OXFORD	School of Geography, University of Oxford
199.	OXFORD	Taylor Institution, University of Oxford
200.	PORTSMOUTH	University of Portsmouth. Frewen Library
201.	READING	University of Reading. Main Library, Bulmershe Library
202.	RUGBY	Intermediate Technology
203.	SAINT ANDREWS	University of Saint Andrews
204.	SALFORD	University of Salford
205.	SHEFFIELD	University of Sheffield
206.	SOUTHAMPTON	Ordnance Survey, Overseas Surveys Directorate, Technical Information and Support Services. International Library
207.	SOUTHAMPTON	Ordnance Survey. Ordnance Survey Library
208.	SOUTHAMPTON	University of Southampton. Hartley Library
209.	STIRLING	University of Stirling
210.	STOKE-ON-TRENT	Staffordshire University. Thompson Library
211.	SWANSEA	University of Wales Swansea / Prifysgol Cymru Abertawe
212.	WELWYN	Cat Survival Trust
213.	WOLVERHAMPTON	University of Wolverhampton. Harrison Learning Centre
214.	WOODBRIDGE	South American Pictures
215.	YORK	University of York. J.B. Morrell Library

LIBRARIES INCLUDED IN EARLIER EDITIONS WHICH HAVE CLOSED, MERGED WITH OTHER LIBRARIES, OR WHICH NO LONGER HAVE SIGNIFICANT LATIN AMERICAN OR CARIBBEAN COLLECTIONS

The Agricultural Economics Unit Library and the Commonwealth Studies Library merged in 1989 to form the International Development Centre Library, Queen Elizabeth House, University of Oxford (no. 190).

The library of the Anglo-Chilean Society was donated to the Canning House Library (no. 110) during the early 1980s.

The Baptist Missionary Society Library no longer has significant holdings on the region.

Bedford College merged with Royal Holloway College at the Royal Holloway site in 1985 (no. 46).

The Brazilian Embassy Library closed in 1999.

British Broadcasting Corporation, BBC Hulton Picture Library. This became the Hulton–Deutsch Picture Library in 1988, the Hulton–Getty Picture Collection in 1996 and from 2000 is the Hulton|Archive (no. 112).

The British Medical Association, Nuffield Library, no longer has significant holdings on the region.

The British Numismatic Society library collections are held at the library of the Warburg Institute, School of Advanced Study, University of London, and include a small amount of material relating to the Caribbean.

Brunel University Library no longer has significant holdings on the region.

The CAB International Institute of Parasitology is now part of the CABI Bioscience UK Centre (no. 45).

The CAB International Mycological Institute is now part of the CABI Bioscience UK Centre (no. 45).

Carila no longer has an information centre on the region.

The Centre for New Religious Movements, Selly Oak Colleges, became the Research Unit for New Religions and Churches (RUNERC), in the Centre for Missiology and World Christianity, Department of Theology, University of Birmingham, Selly Oak (no. 7).

The Chartered Institute of Transport UK integrated with the Institute of Logistics in June 1999 to become the Institute of Logistics and Transport (no. 34).

The Church Missionary Society (CMS) Library was amalgamated with the post-1945 library of the United Society for the Propagation of the Gospel in 1987 on the CMS site to form the Partnership House Mission Studies Library (no. 175).

The College of Librarianship, Wales (now the Information and Library Studies Library of the University of Wales, Aberystwyth) no longer has significant holdings on the region.

The College of St Mark and St John formerly held the collection acquired by Devon Library and Information Services for the South West Regional Subject Specialisation Scheme. The material has now been returned to the Devon headquarters (no. 47).

The collections of the Commonwealth Bureau of Horticulture and Plantation Crops were transferred from the Institute of Horticultural Research, East Malling, to the CABI Bioscience UK Centre (no. 45).

The Commonwealth Institute, Scotland, Library closed in 1996. The collections were transferred to CUNIA (Centre for Commonwealth, United Nations and International Affairs). CUNIA closed in 1999.

The Department of Ethnology and Prehistory, University of Oxford, merged with the Institute of Social Anthropology in 1990 to form the Institute of Social and Cultural Anthropology (ISCA), University of Oxford. ISCA is part of the School of Anthropology and Museum Ethnography (nos 196, 197).

The Department of Trade and Industry Headquarters Library became the Victoria Street Information Centre and much of the stock was dispersed, including: (i) House of Lords and House of Commons papers from 1801; (ii) Overseas economic surveys, 1929–56; (iii) *Board of Trade Journal*, 1886–1969, and its successors, *Trade and Industry*, 1970–79, and *British Business*, 1979– ; (iv) *International Customs Journal*, 1891– .

The Department of Trade and Industry, Statistics and Market Intelligence Library became The Export Market Information Centre (EMIC). In May 1999 British Trade International was set up, with its subsidiary Trade Partners UK, and EMIC became Trade Partners UK Information Centre (no. 101).

The Directorate of Overseas Surveys, Technical Services Division, Overseas Development Administration, Foreign and Commonwealth Office merged with the Ordnance Survey in 1984 and the collections were transferred to the Ordnance Survey, Technical Information and Support Services, Overseas Surveys Directorate, at Southampton. The Library became the Ordnance Survey International Library in 1994 (no. 206).

University of Dundee Library no longer has significant holdings on the region.

Ealing Technical College (1st ed.) became Ealing College of Higher Education (2nd ed.) and then merged with other colleges to become the Polytechnic of West London in 1991 and Thames Valley University in 1992 (no. 164).

The Evangelical Union of South America's collections are no longer available for consultation.

The Foreign and Commonwealth Office (FCO), Overseas Development Administration (ODA) Library. The Overseas Development Administration became the Department for International Development (DFID) in 1997 and ceased to be part of the FCO. The main library is now at Abercrombie House, East Kilbride, Glasgow, and the London library acts as an enquiry point for that library (nos 50 and 100).

The library of the Geographical Association (known as the Fleure Collection) has been on permanent loan to the Main Library of the University of Sheffield (no. 205) since 1983.

The House of Commons Library no longer has significant holdings on the region.

The House of Lords Library no longer has significant holdings on the region.

The Institute of Agricultural Economics became the Agricultural Economics Unit and merged with the Institute of Commonwealth Studies in 1989 to form the International Development Centre, University of Oxford (no. 190).

The Institute of Horticultural Research, East Malling, became Horticulture Research International (no. 178).

The International Co-operative Alliance Library was transferred to the ICA headquarters in Geneva.

The library of the International Tin Council closed in the early 1990s.

The Land Resources Development Centre (formerly the Land Resources Division Library, Overseas Development Administration) became part of the Natural Resources Institute (NRI). The NRI became an institute of the University of Greenwich in 1996. Collections are held at the NRI (no. 32).

The library of the Latin America Bureau closed in 1998. A significant proportion of the periodicals and press cuttings were transferred to the library of the Institute of Latin American Studies, School of Advanced Study, University of London (no. 121).

Leicester Central Lending Library no longer has significant holdings on the region.

The Lloyds Bank plc, Economics Department Library no longer has significant holdings on the region. The Directors' Library, Bank of London and

South America Ltd (BOLSA), and additional books acquired by the directors of Lloyds, BOLSA International Bank Ltd and Lloyds Bank International Ltd, are held at the head office of Lloyds Bank plc and include Latin American travel books and histories from the nineteenth and twentieth centuries.

North Staffordshire Polytechnic became Staffordshire Polytechnic in 1988 and Staffordshire University in 1992 (no. 210).

Nottingham Central Library used to hold the store for history and travel literature relating to Latin America and the Caribbean for the East Midlands Regional Library System.

The library of the Oxford Forestry Institute became part of the Plant Sciences Library, University of Oxford, in 1996. It retains its identity as a service in collaboration with the successor to the Commonwealth Forestry Bureau, the Forestry Department of CAB International. The CABI–OFI Forestry Information Service is based on the Library's forestry collections (no. 189).

The library of Oxford Polytechnic (now Oxford Brookes University) no longer has significant holdings on the region.

The Regions Beyond Missionary Union collections are no longer available for consultation.

Reuters News Agency, Editorial Reference Unit is available to internal users and subscribers only.

The Rowett Research Institute, Reid Library, no longer has significant holdings on the region.

The Royal Commonwealth Society Library closed in 1992 and the collection was transferred to Cambridge University Library, where it remains on permanent deposit.

The Royal Geographical Society (RGS) merged with the Institute of British Geographers in 1995. The collections are held at the RGS (no. 159).

Royal Greenwich Observatory Library (Herstmonceux Castle) was transferred to Cambridge. The Library finally closed on 31 October 1998.

The Royal Scottish Geographical Society Library moved to Glasgow in 1983. The books and periodicals are kept in the Royal Scottish Geographical Library of the University of Strathclyde within the Andersonian Library (no. 52). The maps, photographs and archives are at the Society's headquarters (no. 54). Some antique maps are stored in the Map Library of the National Library of Scotland (no. 44).

Periodicals from the region held by the Royal Society of Edinburgh Library have been transferred to the Scottish Science Library (no. 44).

Southend-on-Sea Borough Libraries held responsibility for acquiring British publications on South American travel and history for the South Eastern Regional Library Bureau from 1955 to 1969, when the Bureau merged with the corresponding London cooperative organisation and the responsibility passed to the London Borough of Hackney (no. 136).

The Staff College Library, Ministry of Defence (Army), has become part of the library of the Joint Services Command and Staff College (JSCSC). The new library of the JSCSC at Shrivenham, opened in 2001, is one of the largest defence libraries in Europe.

Survival International's collections are no longer available for consultation.

The Trades Union Congress Library Collections were transferred to the Learning Centre, University of North London (no. 166).

The Tropical Development and Research Institute became part of the Natural Resources Institute (NRI). The NRI became an Institute of the University of Greenwich in 1996. Collections are held at the NRI (no. 32).

The Tropical Products Institute amalgamated with the Centre for Overseas Pest Research in 1983 to form the Tropical Development and Research Institute (see previous entry).

Westfield College, University of London, merged with Queen Mary College in 1989 at the Queen Mary College site to form Queen Mary and Westfield College. In 2000 the College was renamed Queen Mary (no. 156).

The West India Committee Library was deposited by the Crown Agents in the Library of the Institute of Commonwealth Studies, School of Advanced Study, University of London, in 1977 (no. 116).

Wye College, University of London, no longer has significant holdings on the region.

DESCRIPTIONS OF LIBRARIES AND COLLECTIONS

ABERDEEN

1 University of Aberdeen
Directorate of Information Systems and Services, Queen Mother Library, Meston Walk, Aberdeen AB24 3UE, Scotland

Tel.: 01224 272579. Holdings enquiries 01224 272579 (main collections), 01224 272598 (Special Libraries & Archives)
Fax: 01224 487048
E-mail: library@abdn.ac.uk
Telnet catalogue: library.abdn.ac.uk or 139.133.219.1
Web catalogue: http://www.abdn.ac.uk/diss/library/resources/webpac/
WWW: http://www.abdn.ac.uk/diss/library or /historic
Established: 1495

Director of Information Systems and Services: Graham Pryor, BA, DipLib, FRSA
Manager, Library Division: Carole Munro, MA, DipLib
Tel.: 01224 273321
E-mail: c.munro@abdn.ac.uk
Manager, Historic Collections: Alan G. Knox, BSc, PhD
Tel.: 01224 272599
E-mail: a.g.knox@abdn.ac.uk

Collections:

The Library's Latin American and Caribbean collections form a growing part of the overall stock. They include 4,500 books (with approximately 250 added each year) and 12 current periodicals, together with maps and videos. The main subject area is the twentieth-century literature of Spanish America and the Francophone Caribbean, with some history, politics and economics. The main collections are on open access. Collections of manuscripts include the George Robert Graham Conway Collection, which is held in the Directorate's Special Libraries & Archives on closed access.

Access to collections:

Opening hours: Term: Mon–Sat 0845–2200, Sun 1400–2200. Vacation: Mon–Fri 0900–2000, Sat 0900–1300, Sun closed. Closed 25–26 December, 1–2 January, Aberdeen July Holiday Monday.

Enquiries: By telephone, post, fax or e-mail.
Admission: Non-members are admitted for reference purposes. Prior arrangement is not required for main collections. Telephone in advance to enquire about admission to the Directorate's Special Libraries & Archives.
Lending: Yes (payment required).
Inter-library loans: Lends to other libraries.
Union record: BLDSC, BUCOP, SALSER, *Serials in the British Library*.
Catalogue: Dynix automated catalogue.
Classification: Dewey Decimal Classification (modified).

Electronic facilities for non-members:

Microcomputing facilities: No.
On-line search facilities: Yes (mediated searches only; payment required).
CD-ROM facilities: Yes.
Internet access: Yes (mediated searches only).
Portable computers: Use permitted; power points available.

Other facilities for non-members:

Photocopying: Yes (payment required).
Microform holdings: Yes.
Reader-printer facilities: Yes (payment required).

Publications

A.P. Thornton, 'The G.R.G. Conway Manuscript Collection in the Library of the University of Aberdeen', *Hispanic American Historical Review*, vol. 36, no. 3 (1956), pp. 345–7.

ABERYSTWYTH

2 National Library of Wales / Llyfrgell Genedlaethol Cymru
Aberystwyth, Ceredigion SY23 3BU, Wales

Tel.: 01970 632800
Fax: 01970 615709

E-mail: holi@llgc.org.uk
Web catalogue: http://geacweb.llgc.org.uk:8000/
WWW: http://www.llgc.org.uk
Established: 1907

Librarian: Andrew M.W. Green, MA, DipLib, ALA

Collections:

Since the Copyright Act of 1911 the Library has acquired all British publications. It now holds over 7,000 volumes on Latin America and about twenty-five per cent of purchases are of non-current material. The Library's collections are particularly strong in material on the genealogy, demography and history of the Welsh and Celtic peoples, and this includes material on Welsh emigration to Latin America and on the Welsh settlements in Patagonia. In addition to books and periodicals the Library collects manuscripts, maps, paintings, drawings, prints, photographs, films, videos, music, audio tapes and theses. The collections are on closed access.

Access to collections:

Opening hours: Mon–Fri 0930–1800, Sat 0930–1700. Closed on public holidays and for the first full week in October.

Enquiries: By telephone, post, fax or e-mail.
Admission: Non-members are admitted on presentation of a letter of introduction or proof of identity.
Lending: The Library is reference only.
Inter-library loans: Lends to other libraries (chiefly from duplicate stock).
Union record: BUCOP, CC–IW, *Serials in the British Library*, UNITY.
Catalogue: Geac Advance automated catalogue.
Classification: Library of Congress Classification.

Electronic facilities for non-members:

Microcomputing facilities: No.
On-line search facilities: In development.
CD-ROM facilities: Yes (payment required).
Internet access: No.
Portable computers: Use permitted; power points available.

Other facilities for non-members:

Photocopying: Yes (payment required).

Microform holdings: Include *Y Drafod* (Patagonian newspaper currently being filmed).
Reader-printer facilities: Yes (payment required).

Publications:
National Library of Wales Catalogue to 1970. (microfiche format).
W.L.C. Davies, *National Library of Wales: a Survey of its History, its Contents, and Activities* (Aberystwyth: National Library of Wales, 1937).

Trysorfa Cenedi: Hanes Llyfrgell Genedlaethol Cymru / A Nation's Treasury: the Story of the National Library of Wales (Aberystwyth: National Library of Wales, 1982).
Bibliotheca Celtica: a Register of Publications Relating to Wales and the Celtic Peoples and Languages (Aberystwyth: Llyfrgell Genedlaethol Cymru, 1910–90).
Cylchgrawn Llyfrgell Genedlaethol Cymru / The National Library of Wales Journal (Aberystwyth: Llyfrgell Genedlaethol Cymru, 1939–).

3 University of Wales Aberystwyth / Prifysgol Cymru Aberystwyth

Hugh Owen Library, Penglais, Aberystwyth, Ceredigion SY23 3DZ, Wales

Tel.: 01970 622399. Holdings enquiries 01970 622397
Fax: 01970 622404
E-mail: libinfo@aber.ac.uk
Web catalogue: http://voyager.aber.ac.uk
WWW: http://www.inf.aber.ac.uk/locations/libraries.asp
Established: 1872

Director of Information Services: Mike Hopkins, BA, PhD, ALA
Subject enquiries to: Elgan Davies, BA, DipLib, Librarian Old College
Specialist's tel.: 01970 622397/622788/622130
Specialist's e-mail address: epd@aber.ac.uk

Collections:

The Library has collected material on Spanish American history, politics and international relations since the 1930s, and on literature since the 1960s. The collection now contains 3,000 books and 6 current periodical titles; approximately 50 volumes are added each year. The material is on open access. A collection of maps is held in the E.G. Bowen Map Library, Institute of Geography and Earth Studies, Llandinam Building, Penglais (tel.: 01970 612603).

Access to collections:

Opening hours: Term: Mon–Fri 0900–2200, Sat 0900–1700, Sun 1100–1800. Vacation: Mon–Fri 0900–1730, Sat–Sun closed.

Enquiries: By telephone, post, fax or e-mail.
Admission: Non-members are admitted for reference purposes. Prior arrangement is required.
Lending: Non-members may be permitted to borrow to a limited extent, after consultation with Readers' Services (payment required).
Inter-library loans: Lends to other libraries.
Union record: BLDSC, BUCLA, WRLS.
Catalogue: Endeavor Voyager automated catalogue.
Classification: Library of Congress Classification.

Electronic facilities for non-members:

Microcomputing facilities: Yes (payment required).
On-line search facilities: Yes (payment required).
CD-ROM facilities: Yes.
Internet access: No.
Portable computers: Use permitted; power points available.

Other facilities for non-members:

Photocopying: Yes (payment required).
Microform holdings: Yes.
Reader-printer facilities: Yes (payment required).

BANGOR

4 University of Wales Bangor / Prifysgol Cymru Bangor
Main Library, Bangor, Gwynedd LL57 2DG, Wales

Tel.: 01248 382983. Holdings enquiries 01248 382981
Fax: 01248 382979
E-mail: library@bangor.ac.uk

Telnet catalogue: library.bangor.ac.uk
Web catalogue: http://library.bangor.ac.uk
WWW: http://www.bangor.ac.uk/is.html
Established: 1884

Deputy Director of Information Services and Head of Library Services: Nigel S. Soane, MA, DipLib
Subject enquiries to: Ellen P. Williams, Information Support Manager and Welsh Librarian
Specialist's tel.: 01248 382913
Specialist's e-mail address: ellen@bangor.ac.uk

Collections:

In the Welsh Library there is a small collection of books and 3 non-current periodical titles on the Welsh settlements in Patagonia. There is also a small amount of material on Latin America in the Main Library, mainly in the fields of history, politics and economics. The collections are on open access.

Access to collections:

Opening hours: Term: Mon–Thurs 0900–2200, Fri 0900–2000, Sat–Sun 1200–1700. Summer vacation: Mon–Fri 0900–1700, Sat–Sun closed.

Enquiries: By telephone, post, fax or e-mail.
Admission: Open to the general public for reference purposes.
Lending: Yes (payment required).
Inter-library loans: Lends to other libraries.
Union record: BLDSC, WRLS.
Catalogue: Innopac automated catalogue.
Classification: Own classification.

Electronic facilities for non-members:

Microcomputing facilities: No.
On-line search facilities: No.
CD-ROM facilities: No.
Internet access: No.
Portable computers: Use permitted in the Reading Room; power points available.

Other facilities for non-members:
Photocopying: Yes (payment required).
Microform holdings: Yes.
Reader-printer facilities: Yes (payment required).

BELFAST

5 *Queen's University*
Main Library, University Square, Belfast BT7 1LS, Northern Ireland

Tel.: 028 9024 5133. Holdings enquiries 028 9027 3613. Admissions 028 9033 5020
Fax: 028 9032 3340
E-mail: library@qub.ac.uk
Web catalogue: http://library.qub.ac.uk/qcat
WWW: http://www.qub.ac.uk/lib/
Established: 1845

Librarian: Norman J. Russell, BA, MPhil, DipLibStud, ALA
Subject enquiries to: Michael Smallman, Arts Librarian
Specialist's tel.: 028 9027 3604
Specialist's e-mail address: m.smallman@qub.ac.uk

Collections:

The Library began collecting material on Latin America and the Caribbean in the 1960s and now holds 9,000 books and 25 current periodicals. Some 200 volumes are added to the collection each year. The main subjects covered by the Library are anthropology and the humanities, particularly history, literature and linguistics. A collection of legal materials dating up to 1967, some of which were acquired from the Board of Trade in 1970, is held in the Law Library (tel.: 028 9027 3608).

Access to collections:

Opening hours: Term: Mon–Fri 0900–2200, Sat 0900–1230. Vacation: Mon–Fri 0900–1730, Sat 0900–1230. Sundays and public holidays closed.

Enquiries: By telephone, post, fax or e-mail.
Admission: Non-members are admitted for reference purposes. Prior arrangement is not required.
Lending: Yes (payment required).

Inter-library loans: Lends to other libraries.
Union record: BLCMP, BLDSC.
Catalogue: BLCMP Talis automated catalogue.
Classification: Library of Congress Classification.

Electronic facilities for non-members:
Microcomputing facilities: No.
On-line search facilities: No.
CD-ROM facilities: No.
Internet access: No.
Portable computers: Use permitted; power points available.

Other facilities for non-members:
Photocopying: Yes (payment required).
Microform holdings: Yes.
Reader-printer facilities: Yes (payment required).

BIRMINGHAM

6 Birmingham Department of Leisure and Community Services, Library and Learning Division
Birmingham Central Library, Chamberlain Square, Birmingham B3 3HQ

Tel.: 0121 303 4511
Fax: 0121 233 4458
E-mail: central.library@birmingham.gov.uk
Web catalogue: http://www.birmingham.gov.uk/libcat
WWW: http://www.birmingham.gov.uk/libraries
Established: 1861

Assistant Director: Libraries and Learning: Vivien M. Griffiths, BA, DipLib, ALA, MSocSci
Arts, languages and literature tel.: 0121 303 4227
E-mail: arts.library@birmingham.gov.uk; music.library@birmingham.gov.uk
Social sciences tel.: 0121 303 4545
E-mail: social.sciences.library@birmingham.gov.uk
Local studies and history (includes maps) tel.: 0121 303 4549/4220
E-mail: local.studies.library@birmingham.gov.uk

Collections:

The Library holds over 2,000 books and a few periodical titles on Latin America and the Caribbean. Maps, music, juvenilia, audio tapes, slides and microforms are also collected. The Shakespeare Research Collection includes editions, translations and works of criticism from Latin America. The collections are predominantly on closed access.

Access to collections:

Opening hours: Mon–Fri 0900–2000, Sat 0900–1700. Sundays and public holidays closed.

Enquiries: By telephone, post, fax or e-mail.
Admission: Open to the general public.
Lending: Most of the material is reference only.
Inter-library loans: Lends to other libraries.
Union record: BUCOP, COLALAS, WMRLS.
Catalogues: Card catalogue for accessions up to 1963. Galaxy automated catalogue for post-1964 accessions.
Classification: Dewey Decimal Classification.

Electronic facilities for non-members:

Microcomputing facilities: No.
On-line search facilities: Yes (payment required).
CD ROM facilities: Yes.
Internet access: Yes (users should book in advance). Payment required for printing.
Portable computers: Use permitted; circuit breakers provided free of charge.

Other facilities for non-members:

Photocopying: Yes (payment required).
Microform holdings: Yes.
Reader-printer facilities: Yes (payment required).

7 *Research Unit for New Religions and Churches (RUNERC), Centre for Missiology and World Christianity, Department of Theology, University of Birmingham, Selly Oak*
Harold Turner Collection, Orchard Learning Resources Centre, Information Services, University of Birmingham, Hamilton Drive, Weoley Park Road, Selly Oak, Birmingham, B29 6QW

Tel.: 0121 415 2255
Fax: 0121 415 2273
E-mail: olrc@bham.ac.uk
WWW: OLRC: http://www.olrc..bham.ac.uk/special/collection_turner.htm
    RUNERC: http://artsweb.bham.ac.uk/aanderson/Main/runerc.htm
Established: 1981

Deputy Director of the OLRC: Meline Nielsen
Administrator of the Harold Turner Collection: Fr Ralph Woodhall, SJ

Collections:

The Research Unit for New Religions and Churches became part of the University of Birmingham in August 1999. It had previously been known as The Centre for the Study of New Religious Movements (1996–99), INTERACT Research Centre (1991–95), The Centre for New Religious Movements (1984–91) and The Study Centre for New Religious Movements in Primal Societies (1981–84). Dr Harold Turner was its director from 1981 to 1986 and donated his collection of documents on and by new religious movements to the Central Library of the Selly Oak Colleges on his retirement. Since then the Collection has been continuously updated and expanded under the supervision of successive directors and of Fr Ralph Woodhall, SJ, its administrator. The main focus of the Collection is religious movements arising from the interaction between traditional cultures and Christianity. (To a lesser extent it covers the New Religious Movements which have emerged in the second half of the twentieth century, especially in Europe and North America.) Most of the Collection is arranged by continent and then by country, although there are also some subject boxes. There is a separate section on Latin America, which contains 1,500 pamphlets. Much of the material is also available on microfiche. It is hoped that eventually material will be made available on CD-ROM and the Internet. The Collection is on open access.

Access to collections:

Opening hours: Mon–Fri 0900–1700.

Enquiries: By telephone, post, fax or e-mail.
Admission: A letter of introduction from the reader's organisation or from a person of recognised position is required. Prior arrangement is recommended.
Lending: The Library is reference only.

Inter-library loans: Lends to other libraries.
Catalogues: Card index: author, title, country. RUNERC computer database: author, author/title, keyword (country, movement, etc). Index to material on microfiche.
Classification: Own classification.

Electronic facilities for non-members:

Microcomputing facilities: Yes.
On-line search facilities: No.
CD-ROM facilities: Yes (a deposit is required).
Internet access: No.
Portable computers: Battery-operated portable computers may be used, provided that they do not disturb other readers.

Other facilities for non-members:

Photocopying: All copies are made by staff and cannot be provided on demand (payment required). Some materials may not be copied.
Microform holdings: Yes.
Reader-printer facilities: No.

Publications:

Stan W. Nussbaum (ed.), *Turner Collection on Religious Movements, 1492–1992: Index to the Microfiche* (Birmingham: INTERACT, 1993).
Interactions [RUNERC electronic newsletter]. Available at http://artsweb.bham.ac.uk/aanderson/NRM/interactions.htm

8 South American Mission Society (*SAMS*)

Library, Allen Gardiner House, 12 Fox Hill, Selly Oak, Birmingham B29 6LQ

Tel.: 0121 472 2616
Fax: 0121 472 7977
E-mail: med@samsgb.org
WWW: http://ourworld.compuserve.com/homepages/SAMSGB
Established: 1844 (as Patagonian Missionary Society), 1864 (as SAMS)

Honorary Librarian: D. Newman

Collections:

The Library's collections include a large number of nineteenth-century works including general descriptions of the countries, travellers' accounts and missionaries' diaries. There is a small collection of works in Amerindian languages, mostly translations of parts of the New Testament and dictionaries in these languages compiled by missionaries. The geographical coverage reflects the areas in which the Society has been active: Argentina, Bolivia, Brazil, Chile, Peru and Uruguay. Most of the works concern mission and missionary activities, with some material on liberation theology, but other subjects covered include anthropology and social welfare, and there are some contemporary background works on the countries. The Library holds 1,200 books, 75 current and 30 non-current periodical titles, some manuscript material (letters and diaries) and audio tapes; much of the material has been acquired through donations; about 10 books are added each year. Periodicals include the *South American Missionary Magazine* (1867–) and several current church and missionary magazines, some of which are published in South America. There are 16 photograph albums and some 200 lantern slides containing scenes of church and village life in Southern Chile, Paraguay and Argentina, 1900–30. The collection is predominantly on open access.

Access to collections:

Opening hours: Tues, Fri 0930–1300. Public holidays closed.

Enquiries: By telephone, post, fax or e-mail.
Admission: Non-members are admitted for reference purposes (appointment required).
Lending: Yes.
Inter-library loans: No.
Union record: BUCLA.
Catalogue: Manuscript author and title catalogue.
Classification: Dewey Decimal Classification.

Electronic facilities for non-members:

Microcomputing facilities: No.
On-line search facilities: No.
CD-ROM facilities: No.
Internet access: No.
Portable computers: Use permitted.

Other facilities for non-members:
Photocopying: Yes (payment required).

9 University of Birmingham
Main Library, Information Services, The University of Birmingham, Edgbaston, Birmingham B15 2TT

Tel.: 0121 414 5817. Admissions 0121 414 3064
Fax: 0121 471 4691
E-mail: library@bham.ac.uk
Telnet catalogue: library.bham.ac.uk
Web catalogue: http://library.bham.ac.uk/
WWW: http://www.is.bham.ac.uk/
Established: 1900

Acting Director of Information Services: Michele Shoebridge, BA, MA, PGLibInfStud
Subject enquiries to: Karen Jackson, BA, MSc, Arts Liaison Librarian
Specialist's tel.: 0121 414 6511
Specialist's e-mail address: k.j.jackson@bham.ac.uk
Site Librarian, Language and Media Resource Centre: Lydia Priestley, BA, MA, ALA
E-mail: l.c.priestley@bham.ac.uk

Collections:

The Library has collected materials on Latin America since 1900 and now has more than 6,000 books, 1,000 pamphlets and 90 current periodical titles; 200 volumes are added each year. The main strengths of the collection are in literature, history and geography, and current acquisitions emphasise these subjects together with politics. The collection is on open access. A small number of video tapes of Latin American feature films are held in the Language and Media Resource Centre (tel.: 0121 414 5960/5962).

Access to collections:

Opening hours: Mon–Thurs 0900–2230, Fri 0900–1900. August: Mon–Fri 0900–1700. May holidays 0900–1700. Closed on other public holidays and in the third week of July.

Enquiries: By telephone, post, fax or e-mail.

Admission: Non-members are admitted for reference purposes. Occasional use is free; payment is required for regular use. A letter of introduction is required.
Lending: Yes (payment required).
Inter-library loans: Lends to other libraries.
Union record: BLCMP, BLDSC, BUCOP, COLALAS, CURL, *Serials in the British Library*, WMRLS.
Catalogues: Card catalogue (author and classified subject) for pre-1972 collections. BLCMP Talis automated catalogue for post-1972 collections.
Classification: Library of Congress Classification.

Electronic facilities for non-members:

Microcomputing facilities: No.
On-line search facilities: No.
CD-ROM facilities: No.
Internet access: No.
Portable computers: Use permitted (subject to inspection); power points available.

Other facilities for non-members:

Photocopying: Yes (payment required).
Microform holdings: Yes.
Reader-printer facilities: Yes (payment required).

BOSTON SPA

10 British Library Document Supply Centre
Boston Spa, Wetherby, West Yorkshire LS23 7BQ

Tel.: 01937 546060
Fax: 01937 546333
E-mail: dsc-customer-services@bl.uk
Web catalogue: http://blpc.bl.uk/
WWW: http://www.bl.uk/services/document/dsc.html
Established: 1959

Director, Public Services: Malcolm Smith, BA, FLA, DipM, MCI

Collections:

The National Lending Library was founded in 1959 in order to provide a fast and efficient inter-library loan service for scientific materials. Particular emphasis was given to the supply of photocopies of articles from scientific periodicals and the Library aimed to hold a large proportion of the periodicals cited in the standard abstracting and indexing tools. In 1967 the Library extended its services to the social sciences and in 1972 to the humanities. It now holds over 7,000,000 items, including 47,000 current and 170,000 non-current serial titles. In 1973, following the creation of the British Library, the book stock of the National Central Library (founded 1916), together with most of its activities, moved to Boston Spa. The BLDSC now holds 3,107,404 books, together with reports, conference proceedings and doctoral theses. Latin America holdings are estimated to be well in excess of 20,000 volumes, and more than 1,000 current and 500 non-current periodical titles, with music and microforms also held. It is the Library's policy to collect English-language material rather than publications in Spanish or Portuguese.

There is access to the inter-library loan service through academic, public and special libraries. Individuals can also order photocopies of journal articles and conference papers online through Articles Direct. There is an order form on the website at http://www.bl.uk/services/document/articles.html (tel.: 01937 546599; fax: 01937 546210; e-mail: articles-direct@bl.uk).

In addition, reference books, bibliographies and indexing publications are available on open access in the Reading Room at Boston Spa. All other materials are on closed access. Any item in the Document Supply Centre's collections may be consulted in the Reading Room, but advance notice request forms (available by post) should be used to ensure that the requested item is available. The completed forms should reach the Reading Room no fewer than five working days before the intended visit.

The Northern Listening Service provides free access to the collections of the British Library National Sound Archive (no. 83). Appointments should be booked by telephone one week in advance (tel.: 020 7412 7418).

Access to collections:

Opening hours: The Reading Room: Mon–Fri 0930–1630 (no admittance after 1600). Public holidays closed.

Enquiries: By telephone, post, fax or e-mail.
Admission: The Reading Room is open to all visitors over the age of 14.
Inter-library loans: Lends to other libraries.
Catalogue: The British Library Public Catalogue, in-house automated catalogue, can be accessed through the website.

Electronic facilities for non-members:

Microcomputing facilities: No.
On-line search facilities: Yes.
CD-ROM facilities: Yes.
Internet access: Yes.
Portable computers: Use permitted; power points available.

Other facilities for non-members:

Photocopying: Yes (payment required).
Microform holdings: Yes.
Reader-printer facilities: No.

Publications:

Books at Boston Spa (*BABS*) (Boston Spa: British Library Document Supply Centre, 1987–).
Current Serials Received (Boston Spa: British Library Document Supply Centre) Annual.
Index of Conference Proceedings (*ICP*) (Boston Spa: British Library Document Supply Centre, 1964–).
Keyword Index to Serial Titles (*KIST*) (Boston Spa: British Library Document Supply Centre, 1980–) Annual.

BRACKNELL

11 National Meteorological Library and Archive

The National Meteorological Library, London Road, Bracknell, Berkshire RG12 2SZ

The National Meteorological Archive, The Scott Building, Sterling Centre, Eastern Road, Bracknell, Berkshire RG12 2PW

Library tel.: 01344 854841
Archive tel.: 01344 855960/855962
Fax: 01344 854840

E-mail: metlib@metoffice.com
WWW: http://www.meto.gov.uk/corporate/library
Established: 1870
Librarian: Alan Heasman
Archive Manager: Ian MacGregor
Library Information Manager: Graham Bartlett

Collections:

The Library has collected Latin American and Caribbean material since the late nineteenth century. The materials form a minor part of the collection and include over 1,000 books, and 50 non-current, periodical titles, mainly on the subjects of meteorology and climatology, together with maps, slides, films and microforms. Periodical articles are catalogued on the MOLARS (Met. Office Library and Archive Reference Service) database, which contains all records from February 1972 onwards (earlier items being added gradually), with the last three months' accessions available on the Internet. Part of the collection is on closed access. Some relevant weather charts and marine records are held in the Archive.

Access to collections:

Opening hours: National Meteorological Library: Mon, Wed, Thurs 0830–1630, Tues 0915–1630, Fri 0830–1615. National Meteorological Archive: Mon, Wed, Thurs 0830–1300, 1400–1630, Tues 0915–1300, 1400–1630, Fri 0830–1300, 1400–1615.

Enquiries: By telephone, post, fax or e-mail (payment may be required).
Admission: Non-members are admitted. Advance notification of a visit (with a letter of introduction) is preferred.
Lending: Yes.
Inter-library loans: Lends to other libraries.
Union record: BLDSC.
Catalogue: Dynix automated catalogue.
Classification: Universal Decimal Classification and own classification.

Electronic facilities for non-members:

Microcomputing facilities: Yes.
On-line search facilities: No.
CD-ROM facilities: Yes.
Internet access: No.

Portable computers: Use permitted; power points available.

Other facilities for non-members:
Photocopying: Yes (payment required).
Microform holdings: Yes.
Reader-printer facilities: No.

Publications:
Monthly Accessions List, available in paper format; last three months in electronic format on the website.

BRADFORD

12 *Development and Project Planning Centre, University of Bradford*
DPPC Collection, J.B. Priestley Library, University of Bradford, Bradford, West Yorkshire BD7 1DP

Tel.: 01274 233984
Fax: 01274 233398
E-mail: s.pitts@bradford.ac.uk
Telnet catalogue: dynix.lib.brad.ac.uk (login and password: library)
Web catalogue: http://lib-webpac.lib.brad.ac.uk/webclient.html
WWW: http://www.brad.ac.uk/library/dppc/index.html
Established: 1969

Librarian: Susan Pitts

Collections:
The Collection was begun to support the staff and students of the Development and Project Planning Centre (originally the Project Planning Centre for Developing Countries). It is now located in the J.B. Priestley Library. The main subject area is development studies, particularly development planning. Latin American and Caribbean materials have been acquired since 1971, and, from a total collection of more than 20,000 volumes, these amount to more than 1,000 volumes and some current periodicals. Some government and international organisations' publications are held. The Collection is on open access.

Access to collections:

Opening hours: Mon–Fri 0845–2100, Sat–Sun 0845–1800.

Enquiries: By telephone, post, fax or e-mail.
Admission: Non-members are admitted for reference purposes (appointment must be made with the J.B. Priestley Library).
Lending: Non-members may borrow (payment required).
Inter-library loans: Lends to other libraries.
Union record: BLCMP.
Catalogue: Dynix automated catalogue.
Classification: Own classification.

Electronic facilities for non-members:

Microcomputing facilities: No.
On-line search facilities: No.
CD-ROM facilities: No.
Internet access: No.
Portable computers: Battery-operated portable computers may be used.

Other facilities for non-members:

Photocopying: Yes (payment required).
Microform holdings: Yes.
Reader-printer facilities: Yes (payment required).

Publications:

Guide to the DPPC Collection.
Journal Holdings List.

BRIGHTON

13 Brighton Public Library
Vantage Point, New England Street, Brighton BN1 2GW

Tel.: 01273 296957/296969
Fax: 01273 296965
E-mail: blibrary@hotmail.com
Web catalogue: http://www.brighton-hove.gov.uk/bhc/libraries/librarycat.html
WWW: http://www.libraries.brighton-hove.gov.uk
Established: 1873

Principal Librarian: Amanda Saville, MA, ALA
Rare Books Librarian: Lucy Dean, MA, DipILS

Collections:

The Library began acquiring Latin American materials in 1873 and the collection includes colonial handbooks and almanacs of the West Indies, and early travellers' accounts of Latin America and the Caribbean, including such rarities as John Constanse Davie, *Letters from Paraguay* (1806), Charles Stuart Cochrane, *Journal of a Residence and Travels in Colombia during 1823 and 1824* (1825), and Charles Waterton, *Wanderings in South America, the Northwest of the United States, and the Antilles in the Years 1812, 1816, 1820 & 1824* (1828). No significant rare material has been acquired since 1970. The collection is on closed access.

Access to collections:

Opening hours: Mon–Tues, Thurs–Fri 1000–1900, Sat 1000–1600. Public holidays closed.

Enquiries: By telephone, post, fax or e-mail.
Admission: Open to the general public. For items held in the Special Collections or published before 1850, membership of the Rare Books Scheme is required (contact Rare Books Librarian for details). Advance notice is required to consult certain items.
Lending: Rare materials are for reference only.
Inter-library loans: Lends to other libraries (except rare materials).
Union record: BLDSC, LASER.
Catalogues: Card catalogue for acquisitions to 1974. DS Galaxy automated catalogue for post-1974 stock.
Classification: Dewey Decimal Classification.

Electronic facilities for non-members:

Microcomputing facilities: Yes (payment required).
On-line search facilities: No.
CD-ROM facilities: Yes.
Internet access: Yes (payment required).
Portable computers: Battery-operated portable computers may be used.

Other facilities for non-members:

Photocopying: Yes (payment required).
Microform holdings: Yes.
Reader-printer facilities: Yes (payment required).

14 Institute of Development Studies, University of Sussex

British Library for Development Studies, Andrew Cohen Building, Falmer, Brighton BN1 9RE

Tel.: 01273 678263
Fax: 01273 621202
E-mail: blds@ids.ac.uk
Web catalogue: http://www.ids.ac.uk/blds/search.html
WWW: http://www.ids.ac.uk/blds/
Established: 1966

Head of Libraries and Information: Michael Bloom, BA, DipLib

Collections:

The British Library for Development Studies has collected material on Latin America and the Caribbean since the Institute's foundation in 1966 and now includes over 25,000 books and 400 current and 500 non-current periodical titles; approximately 500 volumes are acquired each year. The collection is strong in the social sciences, particularly economics, politics, social welfare and the environment. Government publications and journals from the region are well represented and there is a notable collection of material on regional organisations. There are also substantial holdings of microform material, including a significant number of national development plans. Much of the collection is on closed access.

Access to collections:

Opening hours: Mon–Fri 0930–1700.

Enquiries: By telephone, post, fax and e-mail.
Admission: Non-members are admitted for reference purposes. A letter of introduction is required. Notice of intention to use materials from closed access may be required a day in advance.
Lending: No.
Inter-library loans: Lends to other libraries.
Union record: BUCLA.
Catalogues: Earlier material is indexed in a card catalogue with author, alphabetical subject and country files. C2 automated catalogue for current acquisitions.
Classification: Own classification.

Electronic facilities for non-members:
Microcomputing facilities: No.
On-line search facilities: No.
CD-ROM facilities: Yes.
Internet access: Yes.
Portable computers: Use permitted in certain areas of the Reading Room where power points are available.

Other facilities for non-members:
Photocopying: Yes (payment required).
Microform holdings: Yes.
Reader-printer facilities: No.

15 University of Sussex
University of Sussex Library, Falmer, Brighton BN1 9QL

Tel.: 01273 678163
Fax: 01273 678441
E-mail: library@sussex.ac.uk
Web catalogue: http://catalogue.sussex.ac.uk/home
WWW: http://www.sussex.ac.uk/library
Established: 1961

Librarian: Deborah C. Shorley, BA, ALA

Collections:
The Library has acquired material on Latin America since its foundation and continues to expand its collection. The main strengths of the collection are in literature, history and the social sciences. The material is on open access.

Access to collections:
Opening hours: Term: Mon–Thurs 0900–2130, Fri 0900–1930, Sat–Sun 1230–1830. Vacation: Mon, Wed–Fri 0900–1730, Tues 0900–1930, Sat–Sun closed. May holidays 1230–1830. Christmas, New Year, Easter and August Bank Holiday closed.

Enquiries: By telephone, post, fax or e-mail.
Admission: Non-members are admitted for reference purposes.

Lending: Yes (payment required).
Inter-library loans: Lends to other libraries.
Union record: BLDSC, SUSPER.
Catalogues: Printed subject index for the arts and humanities. BLCMP Talis automated catalogue (author, title, keyword and classmark).
Classification: Library of Congress Classification and own classification.

Electronic facilities for non-members:

Microcomputing facilities: No.
On-line search facilities: No.
CD-ROM facilities: No.
Internet access: No.
Portable computers: Use permitted; power points available.

Other facilities for non-members:

Photocopying: Yes (payment required).
Microform holdings: Yes.
Reader-printer facilities: Yes (payment required).

BRISTOL

16 Bristol City Libraries
Bristol Reference Library, Central Library, College Green, Bristol BS1 5TL

Tel.: Central Library 0117 903 7200. Reference Library 0117 903 7202/7216
Fax: 0117 922 1081
Web catalogue: http://opac.bristol-city.gov.uk/www-bin/www_talis
WWW: http://www.bristol-city.gov.uk/libraries
Established: 1613 (collection)

Head of Libraries: Kate Davenport
Subject enquiries to: Jane Bradley, BLib, ALA, Local Studies Librarian
Specialist's tel.: 0117 903 7202/7216
Specialist's e-mail address: jane_bradley@bristol-city.gov.uk

Collections:

The Reference Library is the largest public reference library in the South West, with a collection of over 300,000 books. There is a large local history collection, which includes several hundred printed items and manuscripts relating to trade — and in particular the slave trade — with the Caribbean up to 1830. Some rare eighteenth-century Jamaican newspapers are held on microfilm. The collection is predominantly on closed access.

Access to collections:

Opening hours: Mon–Tues, Thurs 0930–1930, Wed, Fri–Sat 0930–1700, Sun 1300–1600. Public holidays closed.

Enquiries: By telephone, post, fax or e-mail (payment may be required from non-Bristol residents).

Admission: Open to the general public. Advance notice of at least two working days and proof of identity are required to view some rare or valuable works. During the year 2001 there will be restricted access to some materials and readers should enquire about availability in advance.

Lending: Most of the material is reference only.

Inter-library loans: Very occasionally lends to other libraries.

Union record: BLCMP, SWRLS.

Catalogues: Author and classified subject card catalogue supplement to *Bristol Bibliography*. Local history card catalogue is in the process of being transferred to the automated catalogue by digitisation (1999–2001). BLCMP Talis automated catalogue.

Classification: Dewey Decimal Classification.

Electronic facilities for non-members:

Microcomputing facilities: No.
On-line search facilities: Yes (payment required).
CD-ROM facilities: Yes (payment required).
Internet access: Yes; pilot scheme in place.
Portable computers: Use not permitted.

Other facilities for non-members:

Photocopying: Yes (payment required).
Microform holdings: Yes.
Reader-printer facilities: Yes (payment required).

Publications:

E.R.N. Mathews, *Early Printed Books and Manuscripts in the City Reference Library, Bristol* (Bristol: W.C. Hemmons, 1899).

E.R.N. Mathews (ed.), *Bristol Bibliography: City and County of Bristol*

Municipal Public Libraries: a Catalogue of the Books, Pamphlets, Collectanea, etc., Relating to Bristol, Contained in the Central Reference Library (Bristol: Printed by order of the Libraries Committee, 1916).

A Catalogue of Books in the Bristol Reference Library, which were Printed Abroad in Languages other than English during the Years 1473 to 1700 (Bristol: Corporation of Bristol, 1956).

A Catalogue of Books in the Bristol Reference Library, Printed in England and Ireland up to the Year 1640, and of English Books Printed Abroad, 1641–1700 (Bristol: Corporation of Bristol, 1958).

17 University of Bristol

University of Bristol Library, Tyndall Avenue, Bristol BS8 1TJ

Tel.: 0117 928 9000
Fax: 0117 925 5334
E-mail: library@bristol.ac.uk
Web catalogue: http://www.lib.bris.ac.uk/ALEPH
WWW: http://www.bris.ac.uk/is/
Established: 1876 (as University College Bristol), 1909 (as University of Bristol)

University Librarian: Geoffrey Ford, MSc, ALA
Subject enquiries to: Emer Stubbs, BA, DipLib, Hispanic Studies Subject Librarian
Specialist's tel.: 0117 928 9063
Specialist's e-mail address: emer.stubbs@bristol.ac.uk

Collections:

The Library has collected Latin American materials since the 1950s and now has about 6,000 books and 20 current periodical titles; 200 volumes are added each year, 10–15 per cent of which are of non-current material. The main subject areas are history and literature, but particularly well-represented are nineteenth- and twentieth-century Brazilian literature, nineteenth- and twentieth-century Cuban literature and history, nineteenth- and twentieth-century Mexican history, and modern Latin American literature. There is a significant amount of Argentine material and the social sciences, especially sociology, are also collected. Although the Latin American collections form a minor part of the overall stock, some of the material is of research quality. The collections are predominantly on open access.

Access to collections:

Opening hours: Term: Mon–Wed 0845–2300, Thurs 0945–2300, Fri–Sat 0845–1800, Sun 1400–2200. Christmas and Easter Vacations: Mon–Wed 0845–1900, Thurs 0945–1900, Fri 0845–1645, Sat 0845–1300, Sun closed. Summer Vacation: Mon–Wed 0845–1900, Thurs 0945–1900, Fri 0845–1645, Sat 0845–1300, Sun closed. May Day Bank Holiday 0900–1700, Spring Bank Holiday 0900–2100. Christmas, New Year, Easter and August Bank Holiday closed.

Enquiries: By telephone, post, fax or e-mail.
Admission: Non-members are admitted for reference purposes at Librarian's discretion (payment may be required). Permission should be sought in advance of a visit.

Lending: Non-members may be permitted to borrow at Librarian's discretion (payment may be required).
Inter-library loans: Lends to other libraries.
Union record: BLDSC, BUCLA, COLALAS, SWRLS.
Catalogue: Ex Libris Aleph 500 automated catalogue.
Classification: Library of Congress Classification.

Electronic facilities for non-members:

Microcomputing facilities: No.
On-line search facilities: No.
CD-ROM facilities: Yes.
Internet access: Yes.
Portable computers: Use permitted after a safety test; power points available.

Other facilities for non-members:

Photocopying: Yes (payment required).
Microform holdings: Yes.
Reader-printer facilities: Yes (payment required).

18 University of the West of England (UWE)
Bolland Library, Coldharbour Lane, Frenchay, Bristol BS16 1QY

Tel.: 0117 344 2277. Admissions 0117 344 2408
Fax: 0117 344 2407

Web catalogue: http://www.uwe.ac.uk/library/catalogue/
WWW: http://www.uwe.ac.uk/library/
Established: 1969

Head of Library Services: Ali Taylor
Subject enquiries to: Jill Kempshall, BA, ALA, Languages and European Studies Librarian
Specialist's tel.: 0117 344 3685
Specialist's e-mail address: Jill.Kempshall@uwe.ac.uk

Collections:

The Library started collecting on Latin America in 1993. The material forms a minor part (about three per cent) of the collection and consists of 10 current periodicals and about 600 books. Approximately 150 books (current material only) are added each year. Within an overall coverage of Latin America there is an emphasis on Peru, Colombia and Nicaragua. Subject fields are in the social sciences: economics, political science and sociology. The material is predominantly on open access.

Access to collections:

Opening hours: Term: Mon–Thurs 0900–2100, Fri 0900–1900, Sat–Sun 1000–1600. Easter Vacation: Mon–Thurs 0900–1700, Fri 0900–1630, Sat–Sun 1000–1600. Christmas and Summer Vacations: Mon–Thurs 0900–1700, Fri 0900–1630, Sat 1000–1300, Sun closed. Easter weekend Fri–Tues and public holidays closed.

Enquiries: By telephone, post, fax or e-mail.
Admission: Non-members are admitted for reference purposes.
Lending: Yes (payment required, unless members of United Kingdom Libraries Plus scheme).
Inter-library loans: Lends to other libraries.
Union record: SWRLS (English language material only).
Catalogue: SIRSI Unicorn automated catalogue.
Classification: Dewey Decimal Classification.

Electronic facilities for non-members:

Microcomputing facilities: Yes.
On-line search facilities: No.
CD-ROM facilities: No.
Internet access: No.
Portable computers: Use permitted; power points available.

Other facilities for non-members:
Photocopying: Yes (payment required).
Microform holdings: Yes.
Reader-printer facilities: Yes (payment required).

CAMBRIDGE

19 BirdLife International
Library, Wellbrook Court, Girton Road, Cambridge CB3 0NA

Tel.: 01223 277318
Fax: 01223 277200
E-mail: birdlife@birdlife.org.uk
WWW: http://www.birdlife.net
Established: 1993 (1922 as International Council for Bird Preservation)

Librarian: Jeremy Speck, BA, MA, DipLib
Librarian's e-mail address: jeremy.speck@birdlife.org.uk

Collections:
BirdLife is an international charity dedicated to saving the world's bird species and their habitats and, through this, to work for the world's biological diversity and the sustainability of human use of natural resources. It works closely with the World Conservation Monitoring Centre and International Union for the Conservation of Nature and Natural Resources in compiling Red Data lists on bird species and in other projects. BirdLife has a large number of key field and research projects underway worldwide (including a Brazilian Atlantic Forest project), and supports the formation of conservation organisations in developing countries. Its Americas Regional Office is based in Quito, Ecuador. The Library began collecting material on the birdlife and environment of Latin America and the Caribbean in the 1980s, and these holdings now constitute a special part of the total collection: 600 books and reprints and 90 current periodicals on the region; these are kept separate from the rest of the collection and are predominantly on open access. A special photo library containing slides of birds and bird conservation worldwide is also available.

Access to collections:

Opening hours: Mon–Fri 0930–1700. Easter, Christmas and public holidays closed.

Enquiries: By telephone, post, fax or e-mail.
Admission: Open to the general public.
Lending: No.
Inter-library loans: No.
Catalogues: Papyrus automated catalogue; Dbase (for periodicals).
Classification: Own classification.

Electronic facilities for non-members:

Microcomputing facilities: By appointment and for bona fide research purposes.
On-line search facilities: No.
CD-ROM facilities: No.
Internet access: No.
Portable computers: Use permitted.

Other facilities for non-members:

Photocopying: Yes (payment required).

Publications:

Guide to the Species Files.
Journals Catalogue.
Library Guide / Resource Book.

20 Cambridge University Library
West Road, Cambridge CB3 9DR

Tel.: 01223 333000. Holdings enquiries 01223 333016. Admissions 01223 333084
Fax: 01223 333160
E-mail: library@ula.cam.ac.uk
Telnet catalogue: ul.cam.ac.uk
Web catalogue: http://www.lib.cam.ac.uk/Catalogues/OPAC/
WWW: http://www.lib.cam.ac.uk
Established: Beginning of the fifteenth century

Librarian: P.K. Fox, MA, AKC, ALA
Subject enquiries to: Sonia Morcillo García
Specialist's tel.: 01223 333092
Specialist's e-mail address: smg@ula.cam.ac.uk

Subject enquiries for the Royal Commonwealth Society Collections to:
  Rachel Rowe
Specialist's tel.: 01223 333198
Specialist's e-mail address: rmr@cam.ac.uk

Collections:

The Library has enjoyed the privilege of copyright deposit since the Act of Queen Anne in 1709 (and before that benefited from the Licensing Acts during the periods 1662–79 and 1685–95), and, since it is a library from which books can be borrowed, it has one of the largest lending collections in England of material in English on Latin America. Although deposit was only partially effective before about 1812, it now embraces not only Irish publications (nominally since 1801) but also (from about the early 1960s) an increasing amount of material from North American publishers who maintain branch offices in London. Regular extensive buying from Latin America started in 1966. Earlier acquisitions of Latin American material included the library of Lord Acton, which has various items on the region, books from the library of F.A. Kirkpatrick, which was strong on the River Plate countries, and the Conway Collection. Conway was a businessman long resident in Mexico and his library includes many microfilmed documents from the Archivo General de la Nación, particularly documents relating to the treatment by the Inquisition of Jews and captured Elizabethan seamen. Cambridge University Library also possesses some microfilms of United States National Archives holdings relating to Latin America and the Latin American Documents microfilm series, and has made extensive purchases of nineteenth-century official publications. The Library's holdings are strongest in literature and history; Brazil, Mexico, Argentina and Uruguay are the best represented countries. There is also an extensive map collection. The University Library's collections of Latin American and Caribbean materials include more than 100,000 books, 196 current and 264 non-current periodical titles, manuscripts, microforms and photographs in the Royal Commonwealth Society's collection. The collections are on open access.

The Royal Commonwealth Society's collection was placed on permanent deposit in the University Library following the closure of the Society's Library in 1992. The scope of the collection is the Commonwealth and its members, past and present, and for those areas a wide range of subjects, including history, geography, politics, economics, literature, education, art and natural history, is covered. The main arrangement of the catalogue (available in the Official Publications Room) is geographical, and there is a very substantial section on the Caribbean, including printed material from the eighteenth century onwards and many official publications. A large collection of pamphlets on slavery contains much West Indian material. There is also material on the Falkland Islands and a small collection on non-Commonwealth countries of Central and South America. There are significant holdings of early almanacs, and the photographic collection includes West Indian material. The collections are on closed access.

Access to collections:

Opening hours: Mon–Fri 0900–1915, Sat 0900–1300. Christmas, New Year, Easter and August Bank Holiday closed.
Official Publications Room: Mon–Fri 0930–1845, Sat 0930–1245. Christmas, New Year, Easter and August Bank Holiday closed.

Enquiries: By telephone, post, fax or e-mail.
Admission: On proof of identity with academic letter of introduction.
Lending: No.
Inter-library loans: Lends to other libraries.
Union record: BLDSC, BUCLA, BUCOP, Cambridge University Union List of Serials, COLALAS, CURL, *Keyword Index to Serial Titles (KIST)*, *Serials in the British Library.*
Catalogues: Author, title and alphabetical manual catalogue for earlier material. In-house automated system developed by Cambridge University Library (to be replaced in 2001) for current acquisitions. Author and classified subject catalogue for the Royal Commonwealth Society Collection is available in the Official Publications Reading Room.
Classification: Own classifications for Cambridge University Library, and for the Royal Commonwealth Society's collection.

Electronic facilities for non-members:

Microcomputing facilities: No.
On-line search facilities: No.
CD-ROM facilities: No.
Internet access: Yes.
Portable computers: Use is permitted, provided that they are silent and do not disturb other readers. Power points are available. New readers must have their machines checked by a member of the Library's technical staff.

Other facilities for non-members:
Photocopying: Yes (payment required).
Microform holdings: Yes.
Reader-printer facilities: No.

Publications:

Current Serials Available in the University Library and in Other Libraries Connected with the University (Cambridge: Cambridge University Press, 1980), 2 vols.
Subject Catalogue of the Library of the Royal Empire Society (London: Royal Empire Society, 1931–37), 4 vols.
Subject Catalogue of the Royal Commonwealth Society, London (Boston, Mass.: G.K. Hall, 1971), 7 vols.
Royal Commonwealth Society, London: Photograph Collection (Zug: IDC, 1987), 774 microfiches.

21 Centre of Latin American Studies, University of Cambridge

Library, Mill Lane Library, Third Floor, Mill Lane Lecture Block, 8 Mill Lane, Cambridge, CB2 1RX

Tel.: 01223 335398
Fax: 01223 335397
E-mail: jac46@cam.ac.uk
Telnet catalogue: ul.cam.ac.uk
Web catalogue: http://www.lib.cam.ac.uk/Catalogues/OPAC/union.shtml
WWW: http://www.latin-american.cam.ac.uk/library/index.html
Established: 1967

Librarian: Julie Coimbra
Tel.: 01223 335398

Collections:

The Library was founded in 1967 and now has a collection of 10,430 books and 25 current periodical titles. It is housed within the Mill Lane Library. The collection is strong in materials on the Andean region, Brazil and Mexico. The main subject areas are history, politics and sociology. The material is on open access.

Access to collections:

Opening hours: Mon–Fri 0900–1700.

Enquiries: By telephone, post, fax or e-mail.
Admission: Non-members are admitted for reference purposes.
Lending: No.
Inter-library loans: Lends to other libraries.
Union record: Cambridge University Union Catalogue of Departmental and College Libraries, Cambridge University Union List of Serials, *Serials in the British Library*.
Catalogue: In-house automated system developed by Cambridge University Library (to be replaced in 2001).
Classification: None.

Electronic facilities for non-members:

Microcomputing facilities: No.
On-line search facilities: No.
CD-ROM facilities: No.
Internet access: No.
Portable computers: Use permitted; power points available.

Other facilities for non-members:

Photocopying: Yes (payment required).

22 *Faculty of Archaeology and Anthropology, University of Cambridge*

Haddon Library, Downing Street, Cambridge CB2 3DZ

Tel.: 01223 333505
Fax: 01223 333503
E-mail: haddon-library@lists.cam.ac.uk
Telnet catalogue: ul.cam.ac.uk
Web catalogue: http://www.lib.cam.ac.uk/Catalogues/OPAC/union.shtml
WWW: http://www.archanth.cam.ac.uk/library/
Established: 1884

Librarian: Aidan Baker, MA, ALA

Collections:

Latin American materials form a minor part (about three per cent) of the collection. The Library began collecting material on archaeology and anthropology in the region in 1904 and now has approximately 1,000 books, and 15 current and 20 non-current periodical titles; 20–30 volumes are acquired annually and about five per cent of acquisitions are of non-current material. The collection is predominantly on open access.

Access to collections:

Opening hours: Term: Mon–Fri 0845–1715, Sat 0900–1700. Vacation: Mon–Fri 0900–1700, Sat closed. 23 December to 2 January, Easter and August Bank Holiday closed.

Enquiries: By telephone, post or e-mail.
Admission: Non-members are admitted for reference purposes (written application is required).
Lending: Non-members may be permitted to borrow.
Inter-library loans: Lends to other libraries.
Union record: BUCLA, BUCOP, Cambridge University Union Catalogue of Departmental and College Libraries, Cambridge University Union List of Serials.
Catalogues: Card catalogue for material received before 1991 (author, alphabetical subject and classified subject). In-house automated system developed by Cambridge University Library (to be replaced in 2001).
Classification: Bliss Bibliographic Classification.

Electronic facilities for non-members:

Microcomputing facilities: No.
On-line search facilities: Yes.
CD-ROM facilities: Yes.
Internet access: Yes.
Portable computers: Use permitted; power points available.

Other facilities for non-members:

Photocopying: Yes (payment required).
Microform holdings: Yes.
Reader-printer facilities: No.

23 Faculty of Economics and Politics, University of Cambridge

Marshall Library of Economics, University of Cambridge, Sidgwick Avenue, Cambridge CB3 9DB

Tel.: 01223 335217
Fax: 01223 335475
E-mail: marshlib@econ.cam.ac.uk
Telnet catalogue: ul.cam.ac.uk
Web catalogue: http://www.lib.cam.ac.uk/Catalogues/OPAC/union.shtml
WWW: http://www.econ.cam.ac.uk/marshlib
Established: 1925

Librarian: H.R. Thomas, BA, ALA

Collections:

The Library has one of the finest economics collections in the country, with over 70,000 monographs and working papers and 30,000 journal volumes. About 1,000 monographs are added each year; there are 350 current periodical titles and 200 working paper series. Latin American materials form a minor part of this collection (in excess of 500 volumes). Most acquisitions are of English-language materials from the United Kingdom and the USA. The collection is on open access.

Access to collections:

Opening hours: Term: Mon–Fri 0830–2100, Sat 0900–1300. Vacation: Mon–Fri 0900–1700, Sat closed. Public holidays closed.

Enquiries: By telephone, post, fax or e-mail.
Admission: Non-members are admitted for reference purposes at the Librarian's discretion (prior appointment required).
Lending: No.
Inter-library loans: Lends some materials to other libraries.
Union record: BLDSC (periodicals), Cambridge University Union Catalogue of Departmental and College Libraries, Cambridge University Union List of Serials, COLALAS.
Catalogue: In-house automated system developed by Cambridge University Library (to be replaced in 2001).
Classification: Own classification.

Electronic facilities for non-members:

Microcomputing facilities: No.

On-line search facilities: No.
CD-ROM facilities: No.
Internet access: No.
Portable computers: Use permitted; power points available.

Other facilities for non-members:
Photocopying: Yes (payment required).
Microform holdings: Yes.
Reader-printer facilities: No.

24 Faculty of History, University of Cambridge

Seeley Historical Library, University of Cambridge, Faculty of History, West Road, Cambridge CB3 9EF

Tel.: 01223 335335
Fax: 01223 335968
E-mail: seeley@hist.cam.ac.uk
Telnet catalogue: ul.cam.ac.uk
Web catalogue: http://www.lib.cam.ac.uk/Catalogues/OPAC/union.shtml
WWW: http://www.hist.cam.ac.uk/resources/library/
Established: 1807 (1897 name changed to Seeley Historical Library)

Librarian: D. Linda Washington, PhD

Collections:

Latin American history materials form a minor part of the Library's overall stock; book holdings are in excess of 600 volumes. Half the Library's annual acquisitions are of non-current material. The collection is held on open access.

Access to collections:

Opening hours: Term: Mon–Fri 0900–1915, Sat 0900–1800. Vacation: Mon–Fri 0900–1300, 1415–1700, Sat closed. Closed for two weeks at Christmas, ten days at Easter and three weeks in September.

Enquiries: By telephone, post, fax or e-mail.
Admission: Non-members are admitted for reference purposes (letter of introduction required).
Lending: No.
Inter-library loans: No.

Union record: Cambridge University Union Catalogue of Departmental and College Libraries, Cambridge University Union List of Serials.
Catalogues: Card catalogue (author, classified and alphabetical subject). The author catalogue is being maintained as a back-up to the automated catalogue. In-house automated system developed by Cambridge University Library (to be replaced in 2001).
Classification: Library of Congress Classification.

Electronic facilities for non-members:

Microcomputing facilities: No.
On-line search facilities: No.
CD-ROM facilities: No.
Internet access: No.
Portable computers: Use permitted; power points available. Equipment must be checked and certified by University Library technicians.

Other facilities for non-members:

Photocopying: Yes (payment required).
Microform holdings: Yes.
Reader-printer facilities: Yes (payment required)

25 Faculty of Modern and Medieval Languages, University of Cambridge

Modern and Medieval Languages Library, Raised Faculty Building, Sidgwick Avenue, Cambridge CB3 9DA

Tel.: 01223 335041
Fax: 01223 335062
Telnet catalogue: ul.cam.ac.uk
Web catalogue: http://www.lib.cam.ac.uk/Catalogues/OPAC/union.shtml
WWW: http://www.mml.cam.ac.uk/library/

Librarian: Anne E. Cobby, MA, PhD, DipLib
Subject enquiries to: Kathleen Manson, Senior Assistant, Romance Languages
Specialist's e-mail address: kam44@cam.ac.uk

Collections:

The Library is concerned primarily with literature and secondly with language, and has a total holding of 111,000 volumes. The Latin American section is a minor part of the collection (2.5 per cent) and was created in 1970 from books already in the Spanish section (which dates from 1918) and from new accessions. It now holds 2 current periodicals and some 2,050 books, approximately 50 new items being added annually (chiefly current material). A small amount on Brazil is included in the Portuguese section. A small but significant collection of nineteenth-century travel works on Latin America is also held. The collection is on open access.

Access to collections:

Opening hours: Term: Mon–Fri 0900–1900, Sat 0900–1600. Vacation: Mon–Fri 0900–1700, Sat closed. Public holidays in vacation closed.

Enquiries: In person, by post and telephone.
Admission: Non-members admitted for reference purposes. Letter of introduction required.
Lending: No.
Inter-library loans: Exceptionally, as back-up to Cambridge University Library.
Union record: BUCLA, Cambridge University Union Catalogue of Departmental and College Libraries, Cambridge University Union List of Serials.
Catalogues: Manual shelflist. In-house automated system developed by Cambridge University Library (to be replaced in 2001).
Classification: Own classification. Latin American material separate (primary division of the material is geographical).

Electronic facilities for non-members:

Microcomputing facilities: No.
On-line search facilities: No.
CD-ROM facilities: No.
Internet access: No.
Portable computers: Use permitted; power points available.

Other facilities for non-members:

Photocopying: Yes (payment required).
Microform holdings: Yes.
Reader-printer facilities: No.

26 *Institute of Criminology, University of Cambridge*

Radzinowicz Library of Criminology, 7 West Road, Cambridge CB3 9DT
Tel.: 01223 335386
Fax: 01223 335356
E-mail: crimlib@hermes.cam.ac.uk
Telnet catalogue: ul.cam.ac.uk
Web catalogue: http://www.lib.cam.ac.uk/Catalogues/OPAC/union.shtml
WWW: http://www.law.cam.ac.uk/crim/libhpg.htm
Established: 1960

Librarian: Helen Krarup, BA, MSc

Collections:

The Library is the most comprehensive criminological collection in the country, with 35,000 books, 15,000 pamphlets and 250 current periodicals. Latin American material, which forms a minor part of the collection, has been acquired since 1962. The main subject areas are penology, treatment of juveniles and criminal law. The collection is on open access.

Access to collections:

Opening hours: Term: Mon–Fri 0900–1915, Sat 0900–1300. Vacation: Mon–Fri 0900–1300, 1400–1700, Sat closed. Closed public holidays and for a period in August.

Enquiries: By post, fax or e-mail.
Admission: Non-members are admitted for reference purposes. Written application to the Librarian required.
Lending: No.
Inter-library loans: Lends to other libraries.
Union record: Cambridge University Union Catalogue of Departmental and College Libraries, Cambridge University Union List of Serials, CURL.
Catalogues: Classified card catalogue. In-house automated system developed by Cambridge University Library (to be replaced in 2001).
Classification: Bliss Bibliographic Classification.

Electronic facilities for non-members:

Microcomputing facilities: No.
On-line search facilities: No.
CD-ROM facilities: No.

Internet access: Yes.
Portable computers: Use permitted; power points available.

Other facilities for non-members:
Photocopying: Yes (payment required).
Microform holdings: Yes.
Reader-printer facilities: No.

Publications:
The Library Catalogue of the Radzinowicz Library, Institute of Criminology, University of Cambridge (Boston, Mass.: G.K. Hall, 1979), 6 vols.
Rosina Perry, 'The Radzinowicz Library of Criminology', *Law Librarian*, vol. 7, no. 1 (1976), pp. 3–6.

27 Scientific Periodicals Library, Cambridge University Library
Bene't Street, Cambridge CB2 3PY

Tel.: 01223 334742. Admissions 01223 334744
Fax: 01223 334748
E-mail: mlw1003@cus.cam.ac.uk
Telnet catalogue: ul.cam.ac.uk
Web catalogue: http://www.lib.cam.ac.uk/Catalogues/OPAC.shtml
WWW: http://www.lib.cam.ac.uk/SPL
Established: 1819

Librarian: Michael L. Wilson, MA

Collections:
The Library was founded as the Cambridge Philosophical Library in 1819 and has occupied its present building since 1935. It has been collecting Latin American periodicals since 1880 and now holds 45 current and 60 non-current titles. Subject fields include geology, geography, anthropology, archaeology, mathematics and biology. The last ten years of current journals are on open access. Older volumes and items from the Old Book Collection are on closed access.

Access to collections:
Opening hours: Term: Mon–Fri 0900–2000, Sat 0900–1300. Vacation: Mon–Fri 0900–1800, Sat 0900–1300. Closed Christmas, New Year,

Easter, August Bank Holiday and one week in September.

Enquiries: By telephone, post, fax or e-mail.
Admission: Non-members are admitted for reference purposes. Written application to the Librarian required. Undergraduates are normally only admitted during vacations. Individuals outside formal education may be given access (written application and payment required).
Lending: No.
Inter-library loans: Lends to other libraries.
Union record: BLDSC, BUCOP, Cambridge University Library Union List of Serials, COLALAS, WLSP.
Catalogue: In-house automated system developed by Cambridge University Library (to be replaced in 2001).
Classification: Own classification.

Electronic facilities for non-members:

Microcomputing facilities: No.
On-line search facilities: Yes (nominal fee for extensive mediated searches to cover costs).
CD-ROM facilities: Yes.
Internet access: Yes.
Portable computers: Use permitted if not disturbing other readers; power points available. Equipment must be checked and certified by University Library technicians.

Other facilities for non-members:

Photocopying: Yes (payment required).
Microform holdings: Yes.
Reader-printer facilities: Yes (payment required).

28 Scott Polar Research Institute, University of Cambridge
Library, Lensfield Road, Cambridge CB2 1ER

Tel.: 01223 336552. Holdings enquiries 01223 336565
Fax: 01223 336549
E-mail: wjm13@cus.cam.ac.uk
Telnet catalogue: ul.cam.ac.uk
WWW: http://www.spri.cam.ac.uk/#lib/
Established: 1920

Librarian: William J. Mills, MA, ALA
Subject enquiries to: Hilary Shibata, BA, Antarctic Bibliographer
Specialist's tel.: 01223 336565
Specialist's e-mail address: jhs1001@cus.cam.ac.uk

Collections:

Within the world's most comprehensive information centre on the Polar regions, the Library holds what is probably the most extensive collection on Latin American aspects of the Antarctic region in Britain, covering Patagonia, Tierra del Fuego, Chilean and Argentine claims to Antarctic territories, the British Antarctic Territory and the Falkland Islands and Dependencies. Materials include books, manuscripts, maps, pamphlets, periodicals, photographs, pictures, slides, films, video tapes, sound recordings, press cuttings and microforms. The Library (together with the World Data Centre for Glaciology, Cambridge) produces *SPRILIB: a Polar and Glaciological Bibliographic Database* and has made subsets of the database, *SPRILIB Antarctica* and *SPRILIB Ice and Snow*, available on the website. The entire *SPRILIB* database is available on the *Arctic & Antarctic Regions* CD-ROM produced by NISC. The printed *Polar and Glaciological Abstracts* is published by Cambridge University Press, and the Library develops and maintains the *Universal Decimal Classification for Use in Polar Libraries*. Total holdings relating to Latin America amount to about 500 books, 2,000 pamphlets and 20 current and 20 non-current periodical titles. There are 5 metres of manuscript material and relevant maps and charts of southern South America. The collection is on open access.

Access to collections:

Opening hours: Mon–Fri 0900–1300, 1400–1730. Public holidays closed.

Enquiries: By telephone, post, fax or e-mail.
Admission: Non-members are admitted for reference purposes.
Lending: No.
Inter-library loans: Lends to other libraries.
Union record: BUCOP, COLALAS, Cambridge University Union Catalogue of Departmental and College Libraries, Cambridge University Union List of Serials.
Catalogues: In-house automated system developed by Cambridge University Library (to be replaced in 2001). *SPRILIB* (see above).
Classification: Universal Decimal Classification.

Electronic facilities for non-members:

Microcomputing facilities: Yes, by arrangement.
On-line search facilities: No.
CD-ROM facilities: Yes.
Internet access: Yes.
Portable computers: Use permitted; power points available.

Other facilities for non-members:

Photocopying: Yes (payment required).
Microform holdings: Yes.
Reader-printer facilities: Yes (payment required).

Publications:

The Library Catalogue of the Scott Polar Research Institute, Cambridge, England (Boston, Mass.: G.K. Hall, 1976), 19 vols. *Supplement* (1981), 5 vols.

Clive Holland (ed.), *Manuscripts in the Scott Polar Research Institute, Cambridge, England: a Catalogue* (New York: Garland, 1982).

CANTERBURY

29 University of Kent at Canterbury
Templeman Library, University of Kent, Canterbury, Kent CT2 7NU

Tel.: 01227 764000
Fax: 01227 823984
E-mail: library-enquiry@ukc.ac.uk
Web catalogue: http://opac.ukc.ac.uk/
WWW: http://library.ukc.ac.uk/library/
Established: 1964

Librarian: Margaret Coutts, MA, MA, ALA
French and Spanish Literature enquiries to: John Ion, BA, DipLib
Specialist's tel.: 01227 823109
Specialist's e-mail address: J.A.Ion@ukc.ac.uk
History enquiries to: Anna Miller, BA
Specialist's tel.: 01227 827113
Specialist's e-mail address: V.A.Miller@ukc.ac.uk
English and American literature enquiries to: Sue Crabtree, BA, DipLib,

Specialist's tel.: 01227 827609
Specialist's e-mail address: S.A.Crabtree@ukc.ac.uk

Collections:

Since 1964 the Library has built up a modest collection of over 1,000 volumes on the region, together with a small range of current and non-current periodicals, to serve the teaching needs of the University or as background material to courses where the focus is elsewhere (e.g. slavery or colonialism). The main strength is in West Indies and Caribbean material, especially English and French literature, and history. The collection is on open access.

Access to collections:

Opening hours: Term: Mon–Fri 0900–2200, Sat–Sun 1200–1900. Vacation: Mon–Fri 0900–1900, Sat 1200–1700, Sun closed. Public holidays closed.

Enquiries: By telephone, post, fax or e-mail.
Admission: Non-members may be admitted for reference purposes on application to the Librarian. Payment may be required.
Lending: No.
Inter-library loans: Lends to other libraries.
Union record: BLDSC (to 1972), BUCOP.
Catalogue: Endeavor Voyager automated catalogue.
Classification: Library of Congress Classification (modified).

Electronic facilities for non-members:

Microcomputing facilities: No.
On-line search facilities: Yes (on application).
CD-ROM facilities: Yes.
Internet access: Yes (on application).
Portable computers: Use permitted; power points available.

Other facilities for non-members:

Photocopying: Yes (payment required).
Microform holdings: Yes.
Reader-printer facilities: Yes (payment required).

CARDIFF

30 Cardiff University / Prifysgol Caerdydd
Arts & Social Studies Resource Centre, Colum Drive, Cardiff, South Glamorgan CF10 3XT, Wales

Address for correspondence: Arts & Social Studies Resource Centre, P.O. Box 430, Cardiff, South Glamorgan CF10 3XT, Wales
Tel.: 029 2087 4818
Fax: 029 2037 1921
E-mail: asslliby@cardiff.ac.uk
Web catalogue: http://library.cf.ac.uk/
WWW: http://www.cf.ac.uk/infos/
Established: 1883

Librarian: John Kenyon Roberts, MSc, ALA
Subject enquiries to: Tom Dawkes, BA, MA, Senior Assistant Librarian
Specialist's e-mail address: dawkest@cardiff.ac.uk

Collections:

The Library has collected material on Latin America in the humanities and social sciences since the 1960s. It forms a minor part of the overall stock; the main strengths are in literature, linguistics, education and law, with smaller collections on demography, economics and environment. There is a general geographical coverage of the region with particular emphasis on Mexico and Brazil. The material is held on open access.

Access to collections:

Opening hours: Term: Mon–Fri 0845–2130, Sat 1000–1730, Sun 1200–1700. Vacation: Mon–Fri 0845–1700, Sat–Sun closed. Public holidays closed except holidays in May.

Enquiries: By telephone, post, fax or e-mail.
Admission: Non-members are admitted for reference purposes (written application to the Librarian required).
Lending: Yes (payment required).
Inter-library loans: Lends to other libraries.
Union record: BLDSC, *Serials in the British Library*, WRLS.
Catalogue: Endeavor Voyager automated catalogue.
Classification: Dewey Decimal Classification and Library of Congress Classification.

Electronic facilities for non-members:
Microcomputing facilities: No.
On-line search facilities: Yes (payment required).
CD-ROM facilities: No.
Internet access: No.
Portable computers: Use permitted; power points available.

Other facilities for non-members:
Photocopying: Yes (payment required).
Microform holdings: Yes.
Reader-printer facilities: Yes (payment required).

31 International Bee Research Association
The Eva Crane IBRA Library, 18 North Road, Cardiff, South Glamorgan CF1 3DY, Wales

Tel.: 029 2037 2409
Fax: 029 2066 5522
E-mail: ibra@cardiff.ac.uk
WWW: http://www.cf.ac.uk/ibra/library2.shtml
Established: 1949

Librarian: Pamela Munn, PhD

Collections:
The Library began collecting in 1949 and in 1959 acquired the library of the Apis Club. The Institute and its library moved to Cardiff in 1986. Relevant material is acquired from all parts of the world and the collection is continually growing: more than 1,000 items and issues of 200 journals are added each year. It includes books, journals, reprints, theses, research papers, reports, colour slides and video tapes. The Latin American and Caribbean holdings are in excess of 500 volumes, with a few current and non-current periodicals, and represent a small part of the Library's collection. The collection is on open access.

Access to collections:
Opening hours: Mon–Fri 0900–1600.

Enquiries: By telephone, post, fax or e-mail.

Admission: Members only (membership information on the website). The Librarian will conduct information searches for non-members and supply photocopies.
Lending: Members only.
Inter-library loans: Lends to other libraries.
Union record: BLDSC, *Serials in the British Library*.
Catalogues: Author and classified subject card catalogues. Records from issues of *Apicultural Abstracts* (1973–) are stored on the Library computer and staff can execute subject searches or locate specific items.
Classification: Universal Decimal Classification.

Electronic facilities:

Microcomputing facilities: No.
On-line search facilities: No.
CD-ROM facilities: Yes.
Internet access: No.
Portable computers: Battery-operated portable computers may be used.

Other facilities:

Photocopying: Yes.
Microform holdings: Yes.
Reader-printer facilities: Yes.
Abstracting: Services are provided.

Publications:

Apicultural Abstracts.

CHATHAM

32 *Natural Resources Institute, Medway Campus, University of Greenwich*
Natural Resources Library, Nelson Building, Central Avenue, Chatham Maritime, Kent ME4 4AW

Tel.: 020 8331 9617
Fax: 020 8331 9837
E-mail: enquiries.library@nri.org
Web catalogue: http://lib.gre.ac.uk:8080/www-bin/www_talis

WWW: http://www.gre.ac.uk/directory/library/sites/mw/mw-site.htm
Established: 1894

Librarian: Tim Cullen, MSc, ALA, MIBiol, MIInfSci
Librarian's e-mail address: Tim.Cullen@nri.org or T.Cullen@gre.ac.uk

Collections:

The Natural Resources Institute includes within its library the collections of the Land Resources Development Centre and the Tropical Development and Research Institute. Latin American and, to a greater extent, Caribbean materials form a minor part of the overall stock. Subjects covered include economics, environment and the life sciences, especially agriculture, including plant and animal products, agricultural pests and land resource assessment. The collections are predominantly on open access.

Access to collections:

Opening hours: Term: Mon–Thurs 0900–2100, Fri 0900–1800, Sat 1000–1400. Vacation: Mon–Fri 0900–1700, Sat closed. Public holidays closed.

Enquiries: By telephone, post, fax or e-mail.
Admission: Non-members are admitted for reference purposes (advance application to the Librarian required; payment may be required).
Lending: No.
Inter-library loans: Lends to other libraries.
Union record: BLCMP.
Catalogue: BLCMP Talis automated catalogue.
Classification: Dewey Decimal Classification.

Electronic facilities for non-members:

Microcomputing facilities: No.
On-line search facilities: Yes (payment required).
CD-ROM facilities: Yes (payment required).
Internet access: No.
Portable computers: Use permitted; power points available.

Other facilities for non-members:

Photocopying: Yes (payment required).

Microform holdings: Yes.
Reader-printer facilities: Yes.

COLCHESTER

33 University of Essex
Albert Sloman Library, Wivenhoe Park, Colchester

Address for correspondence: PO Box 24, Colchester CO4 3UA
Tel.: 01206 873181. Holdings 01206 873181. Admissions 01206 873477
Fax: 01206 872289
E-mail: libcomment@essex.ac.uk
Telnet catalogue: serlib0.essex.ac.uk (login: library)
Web catalogue: http://serlib0.essex.ac.uk
WWW: http://libwww.essex.ac.uk/
Established: 1964

Librarian: Robert Butler, BSc, MSc, ALA
Subject enquiries to: Chris Anderton, MA
Specialist's tel.: 01206 873181
Specialist's e-mail address: chrisa@essex.ac.uk

Collections:

Since its inception in 1964, the Albert Sloman Library has built up one of the most important Latin American collections in the United Kingdom. The Latin American collection, which represents about ten per cent of Library holdings, totals over 70,000 books and pamphlets and over 1,400 periodicals, of which some 120 are current. It is growing at an average rate of about 1,800 items a year. Some ten per cent of acquisitions are of non-current material. The major subject strengths of the collection, reflecting the Latin American teaching and research strengths of the University, are in most fields in the humanities and social sciences: art history, economic and social history, history, language, literature and politics. Mention should also be made of the outstanding collection of reference materials: bibliographies, encyclopaedias, dictionaries and atlases. Minor specialities which have been cultivated include Latin American cinema, Brazilian chapbooks (*literatura de cordel*) and an extensive collection of Mexican codices in facsimile. All countries of Latin America and the Caribbean are well represented, with the largest collections being those pertaining to Argentina, Brazil and Mexico. Uruguayan and Chilean holdings are among the most extensive in the country. In addition, publications in the field of Latin American studies are acquired selectively from all over the world, with a special interest being taken in Russian works on the region. A substantial amount of material is held in microform. The Latin American collection is not housed separately but is integrated into the main stock of the Library and dispersed throughout it by subject. The materials are predominantly on open access.

Access to collections:

Opening hours: Term: Mon–Fri 0900–2200, Sat 0900–1800, Sun 1400–1900. Vacation: Mon–Fri 0900–1730, Sat–Sun closed. The last week of the Easter Vacation has term-time opening hours and the last week of the Summer Term has vacation opening hours.

Enquiries: By telephone, post, fax or e-mail.
Admission: Non-members are admitted for reference purposes (letter of introduction required).
Lending: No.
Inter-library loans: Lends to other libraries.
Union record: BLDSC, BUCLA, BUCOP, COLALAS, Essex Union List of Serials, OCLC.
Catalogue: Innopac automated catalogue.
Classification: Library of Congress Classification.

Electronic facilities for non-members:

Microcomputing facilities: No.
On-line search facilities: No.
CD-ROM facilities: No.
Internet access: Yes.
Portable computers: Use permitted.

Other facilities for non-members:

Photocopying: Yes (payment required).
Microform holdings: Yes.
Reader-printer facilities: Yes (payment required for printing).

Publications:
Guide to the Albert Sloman Library.

Guide to the Latin American Collection.
Microforms: a Guide to Materials in the Library.

CORBY

34 Institute of Logistics and Transport
Library, Earlstrees Court, Earlstrees Road, Corby, Northamptonshire NN17 4AX
Tel.: 01536 740112
Fax: 01536 740102
E-mail: enquiry@iolt.org.uk
WWW: http://www.iolt.org.uk/
Established: 1919

Librarian: Peter Huggins, BA, MA
Librarian's e-mail address: phuggins@iolt.org.uk

Collections:

Founded in 1919 as the Institute of Transport and granted the Royal Charter in 1926, the Chartered Institute of Transport was restructured in 1994 as ten National Councils with the Institute acting as a co-ordinating body. In June 1999 the United Kingdom National Council (Chartered Institute of Transport in the United Kingdom) was integrated with the Institute of Logistics to form the Institute of Logistics and Transport. The offices of the Institute are located in two sites, Corby and London. Most of the stock of the London library has been transferred to the library in Corby, which holds material on all three areas of the Institute's research and activities: logistics, supply-chain management and transport. The Library's collections in the field of transport — 7,000 books and reports, official publications and Acts of Parliament, 100 current periodicals and files of articles from the press — focus on the economic, commercial and administrative, rather than the engineering aspects of air, sea, road and rail transport. Latin American and Caribbean material forms a minor part of the overall stock. The collections are on open access.

Access to collections:

Opening hours: Mon–Fri 0930–1645. Public holidays closed.

Enquiries: By telephone, post or e-mail (payment required, written enquiries preferred).
Admission: Non-members are admitted for reference purposes (appointment required). Full-time students are admitted free of charge; there is a fee for other non-members.
Lending: No.
Inter-library loans: No.
Catalogue: Alice automated catalogue.
Classification: Own classification.

Electronic facilities for non-members:

Microcomputing facilities: No.
On-line search facilities: Yes.
CD-ROM facilities: Yes.
Internet access: No.
Portable computers: Use permitted; power points available.

Other facilities for non-members:

Photocopying: Yes (payment required).

CORK

35 University College Cork
Boole Library, College Road, Cork, Ireland

Tel.: +353 21 4902281
Fax: +353 21 2734208
E-mail: library@ucc.ie
Web catalogue: http://library.ucc.ie/
WWW: http://booleweb.ucc.ie/
Established: 1849

Librarian: John A. Fitzgerald, BA, MPhil, DLIS

Collections:

The Library has a total collection of 600,000 books and 4,000 periodicals. Latin American and Caribbean materials form a minor part of the overall stock. The Library has collected material on the history and politics of the region since 1984 and now holds approximately 2,500 books. The collection is on open access.

Access to collections:

Opening hours: 1st Term: Mon–Thurs 0830–2145, Fri 0830–2045, Sat 1000–1245, Sun closed. 2nd and 3rd terms: Mon–Thurs 0830–2215, Fri 0830–2115, Sat 1000–1745 (2nd term) 1000–2145 (3rd term), Sun 1000–1745 (March–May). Summer Vacation: Mon–Fri 0830–1615, Sat 1000–1245, Sun closed. Public holidays closed.

Enquiries: By telephone, post, fax or e-mail (payment required for extensive searching).
Admission: Non-members may be admitted for reference purposes (application in writing to the Librarian required).
Lending: Yes (payment required).
Inter-library loans: Lends to other libraries.
Union record: BLDSC.
Catalogue: Innopac automated catalogue.
Classification: Dewey Decimal Classification.

Electronic facilities for non-members:

Microcomputing facilities: No.
On-line search facilities: Yes (payment required).
CD-ROM facilities: Yes.
Internet access: Yes.
Portable computers: Use permitted; power points available.

Other facilities for non-members:

Photocopying: Yes (payment required).
Microform holdings: Yes.
Reader-printer facilities: Yes (payment required).

COVENTRY

36 University of Warwick
University of Warwick Library, Gibbet Hill Road, Coventry CV4 7AL

Tel.: 024 7652 4103. Holdings enquiries 024 7652 8133. Admissions 024 7652 2877
Fax: 024 7652 4211
E-mail: library@warwick.ac.uk
Telnet catalogue: opac.warwick.ac.uk

Web catalogue: http://opac.warwick.ac.uk
WWW: http://www.warwick.ac.uk/services/library/
Established: 1964

Librarian: John A. Henshall, PhD
Subject enquiries to: W.R. Pine-Coffin, MA, Acquisitions Librarian and Subject Specialist for Latin American and Caribbean History
Specialist's tel.: 024 7652 8133
Specialist's fax: 024 7652 8958
Specialist's e-mail address: william.pine-coffin@warwick.ac.uk

Collections:

The Library began collecting material on Latin America and the Caribbean in 1964 and now has over 12,500 books and 45 current periodical titles; approximately 250 volumes are added each year. Subject strengths are in Latin American and Caribbean history and literature and related subjects; most material is in English. All geographical areas are represented, but Mexico, Argentina, Colombia, Venezuela and the English-, Spanish- and French-speaking Caribbean are given greater coverage. A collection of economic reports and statistical material has been developed in support of the Department of Economics and the Business School, based originally on duplicates from the Department of Trade and Industry's Statistics and Market Intelligence Library and publications received from Argentina, Brazil, Chile, Costa Rica, Ecuador, Haiti, Jamaica, Mexico, St Lucia and St Vincent. A Black Media Archive is held within the Resources Centre of the Centre for Research in Ethnic Relations (tel.: 024 7652 3605, e-mail: crer@warwick.ac.uk). which moved to Warwick from Aston University in 1984. This includes newspaper cuttings, video tapes and ephemera. The collections are predominantly on open access.

Access to collections:

Opening hours: Term: Mon–Fri 0830–2400, Sat 1000–2000, Sun 1300–2100. Vacation: Mon–Fri 0900–1930, Sat–Sun 1400–1800. Christmas, Easter and August Bank Holiday closed.

Enquiries: By telephone, post, fax or e-mail.
Admission: Academic and related staff, and research students, are admitted throughout the year for reference purposes (proof of identity required). Taught students are admitted during Warwick vacations and three times in term-time in one academic year (proof of identity required). Members

Descriptions of Libraries and Collections 55

of the public are admitted three times in one academic year (proof of identity required). Further use may be permitted on written application to the Librarian. Corporate Membership is also available.
Lending: Yes, within limited conditions (payment required).
Inter-library loans: Yes.
Union record: BLCMP, BLDSC, BUCLA, BUCOP, COLALAS, CURL, WMRLS.
Catalogue: BLCMP Talis automated catalogue.
Classification: Library of Congress Classification.

Electronic facilities for non-members:

Microcomputing facilities: No.
On-line search facilities: No.
CD-ROM facilities: No.
Internet access: No.
Portable computers: Use permitted, and may be connected to power points in the Reading Room; elsewhere in the Library may only be used with a power-breaker (available from Library staff).

Other facilities for non-members:

Photocopying: Yes (payment required).
Microform holdings: Yes.
Reader-printer facilities: Yes (payment required).

DENBIGH

37 ASTIC Research Associates
Talwrn Glas, Fron Gelyn, Llandurnog, Denbigh LL16 4LY, Wales

Tel./Fax: 01824 790100
Established: 1947

Director of Research and Documentation: H.G.A. Hughes, MA, DPhil, CSc, FLA

Collections:

ASTIC is a cooperative, not-for-profit research and documentation agency, working exclusively to subscribing clients' commissions. The

Library holds 4,750 volumes and 28 current periodical titles (60 non-current), 1,000 manuscripts, 6,000 microforms and theses. The Library collects in a wide range of topics in the social sciences and humanities (particularly anthropology, education, geography, history, linguistics, politics, sociology and social welfare), covering all of Latin America and the Caribbean (special emphasis on Cuba and Mexico), plus Hispanics in the United States. About 100 items are added per year, and approximately sixty per cent of acquisitions are of non-current material. The Latin American and Caribbean material forms a separate collection; mostly open access.

Access to collections:

Opening hours: Mon–Sun 0800–1600.

Enquiries: By telephone, post or e-mail.
Admission: Normally no public access or services (subscribing clients only); bona fide researchers may be admitted (on application).
Lending: No.
Inter-library loans: No.
Catalogues: Author and subject catalogues; internal use only.
Classification: Universal Decimal Classification.

Electronic facilities for non-members:

Microcomputing facilities: No.
On-line search facilities: No.
CD-ROM facilities: Yes.
Internet access: No.
Portable computers: Use of battery-operated portable computers permitted.

Other facilities for non-members:

Photocopying: Yes.
Microform holdings: Yes.
Reader-printer facilities: No.

DUBLIN

38 Dublin City University
Library, Dublin City University, Dublin 9, Ireland
Tel.: +353 1 7045212

Fax: +353 1 7045602
E-mail: infodesk@dcu.ie
Telnet catalogue: library.dcu.ie
Web catalogue: http://library.dcu.ie
WWW: http://www.dcu.ie/~library/
Established: 1980 (1989 as Dublin City University)

Librarian: Paul Sheehan, BA, LLB

Collections:

Latin American materials form a minor part of the overall stock. There are about 500 volumes, mainly on politics and economics, and some video tapes. The material is on open access.

Access to collections:

Opening hours: Term and Easter Vacation: Mon–Thurs 0830–2200, Fri 0830–2100, Sat 0930–1700. Summer Vacation: Mon–Thurs 0830–2100, Fri 0830–1645, Sat closed.

Enquiries: By telephone, post, fax or e-mail.
Admission: Non-members are admitted as external members (payment required).
Lending: Yes.
Inter-library loans: Lends to other libraries.
Union record: ALCID.
Catalogue: BLCMP Talis automated catalogue.
Classification: Dewey Decimal Classification.

Electronic facilities for non-members:

Microcomputing facilities: Yes.
On-line search facilities: Yes.
CD-ROM facilities: Yes.
Internet access: Yes.
Portable computers: Use permitted; power points available.

Other facilities for non-members:

Photocopying: Yes (payment required).

39 Trinity College Dublin Library
College Street, Dublin 2, Ireland

Tel.: General +353 1 677 2941. Holdings enquiries +353 1 608 1668. Admissions +353 1 608 1657
Fax: +353 1 671 9003
E-mail: emcglade@tcd.ie (Admissions)
Telnet catalogue: library.tcd.ie (login: opacg) or 134.226.1.100
Web catalogue: http://www.tcd.ie/Library/online.htm
WWW: http://www.tcd.ie/Library
Established: 1591

Librarian: William G. Simpson, BA, ALA
Subject enquiries to: Sue M.G. Tucker, BBS, MA, DipLib, DipInfStud, ALA, Assistant Librarian
Specialist's tel.: +353 1 608 1151
Specialist's e-mail address: sue.tucker@tcd.ie

Collections:

The Library has received material published in the United Kingdom and Ireland through legal deposit since 1801 and therefore has a comprehensive collection of British publications on Latin America and the Caribbean. It is the largest research library in Ireland. In addition it has developed a small collection of material on Latin America in support of teaching in the Department of Spanish and Portuguese. Some material is on open access.

Access to collections:

Opening hours: Term and Easter Vacation: Mon–Fri 0930–2200, Sat 0930–1300. Christmas and Summer Vacations: Mon–Fri 0930–1700, Sat 0930–1300. Last two weeks of July and public holidays closed.

Enquiries: By telephone, post or e-mail.
Admission: Non-members are admitted for reference purposes (written application to the Librarian required).
Lending: No.
Inter-library loans: Lends to other libraries.
Union record: BLDSC, CURL, IRIS, Irish Central Library for Students.
Catalogue: Geac Advance automated catalogue.
Classification: Dewey Decimal Classification.

Electronic facilities for non-members:

Microcomputing facilities: No.
On-line search facilities: No.
CD-ROM facilities: Yes.
Internet access: Yes.
Portable computers: Use permitted, provided it does not disturb the other readers; power points in certain areas of the Library.
Information service: A fee-based information service is provided by the staff, using the Library's stock and access to electronic databases. Tel.: +353 1 608 1673 or 677 2125; fax: +353 1 671 9003; e-mail: infoserv @tcd.ie

Other facilities for non-members:

Photocopying: Yes (payment required).
Microform holdings: Yes.
Reader-printer facilities: Yes (payment required).

Publications:

Catalogus Librorum Impressorum qui in Bibliotheca Collegii Sacrosanctae et Individuae Trinitatis, Reginae Elizabethae, juxta Dublin, Adservantur (Dublin: E Typographeo Academico, 1864–87).

40 Trócaire
Library, 169 Booterstown Avenue, Blackrock, Co. Dublin, Ireland

Tel.: +353 01 288 5385
Fax: +353 01 288 3577
E-mail: library@trocaire.ie
WWW: http://www.trocaire.org or http://www.trocaire.ie
Established: 1973

Librarian / Information Officer: Anne Kinsella
Librarian's e-mail address: anne@trocaire.ie

Collections:

Trócaire is the Irish Catholic Development agency established in 1973 by the Irish Catholic Bishops. It works overseas, through local partners, on a number of wide-ranging development programmes, including food security programmes, the promotion of human rights and democracy, healthcare, leadership and skills training and education. In this way, more than

5,000 programmes have been developed in 60 countries in Asia, Africa and Latin America. Trócaire also responds to emergencies worldwide using a network of local partners and Catholic relief organisations. The Library has about 900 books and reports on Latin America out of a total collection of approximately 9,000. There are also 13 English-language periodicals and newsletters on the region (other periodical titles in Spanish and Portuguese are available in the Overseas Department), videos, a collection of photographs and press cuttings. In addition, Trócaire has Resource Centres in Dublin, Cork and Belfast, which will provide schools with information packs on development issues in Latin America and the Caribbean.

Access to collections:

Opening hours: Mon–Fri 0930–1300, 1400–1730.

Enquiries: By telephone, post, fax or e-mail.
Admission: Open to the general public. It is advisable to telephone before an intended visit.
Lending: By arrangement (books only).
Catalogue: Dataease automated catalogue; searches from database made on request.
Classification: Universal Decimal Classification.

Electronic facilities for non-members:

Microcomputing facilities: No.
On-line search facilities: No.
CD-ROM facilities: No.
Internet access: No.
Portable computers: Use permitted; power points available.

Other facilities for non-members:

Photocopying: Yes (payment required).

41 *University College Dublin*

Main Library, University College Dublin, Belfield, Dublin 4, Ireland

Tel.: +353 1 716 7512
Fax: +353 1 716 1148
E-mail: library@ucd.ie
Telnet catalogue: library.ucd.ie

Web catalogue: http://udtal.ucd.ie/
WWW: http://www.ucd.ie/~library/
Established: 1908
Librarian: Sean Phillips, BA, ALA, ALAI

Collections:

The Library has a collection of 975,000 books and 5,000 periodicals. Latin American materials, which have been acquired from the foundation of the Library, form a minor part of the overall stock. There is a general collection of over 2,500 books and a small number of periodical titles. The collection is on open access.

Access to collections:

Opening hours: Term: Mon–Fri 0830–2200, Sat 0900–1700. Summer Vacation: Mon–Fri 0830–1730, Sat closed. Public holidays closed.

Enquiries: By telephone, post, fax or e-mail.
Admission: Non-members are admitted for reference purposes.
Lending: Yes (payment required).
Inter-library loans: Lends to other libraries.
Union record: ALCID, BLDSC, IRIS, *Serials holdings in Irish libraries*, Irish Central Library for Students.
Catalogue: BLCMP Talis automated catalogue.
Classification: Dewey Decimal Classification.

Electronic facilities for non-members:

Microcomputing facilities: No.
On-line search facilities: No.
CD-ROM facilities: Yes (payment may be required, depending on licensing agreement).
Internet access: Yes.
Portable computers: Use permitted; power points available.

Other facilities for non-members:

Photocopying: Yes (payment required).
Microform holdings: Yes.
Reader-printer facilities: Yes (payment required).

DURHAM

42 Durham University
Durham University Library, Stockton Road, Durham DH1 3LY

Tel.: 0191 374 3018
Fax: 0191 374 7481
E-mail: main.library@durham.ac.uk
Web catalogue: http://library.dur.ac.uk/
WWW: http://www.dur.ac.uk/library/
Established: 1833

Librarian: John T.D. Hall, MA, PhD
Subject enquiries to:
Anthropology: David Sowerbutts, Liaison Librarian for Anthropology
Specialist's tel.: 0191 374 3011
Specialist's e-mail address: d.l.sowerbutts@durham.ac.uk
Geography: John Lumsden, BSc, ALA, Liaison Librarian for Geography
Specialist's tel.: 0191 374 3020
Specialist's e-mail address: j.c.lumsden@durham.ac.uk
Literature: John Lumsden, BSc, ALA, Liaison Librarian for Modern European Languages
Specialist's tel.: 0191 374 3036
Specialist's e-mail address: j.c.lumsden@durham.ac.uk

Collections:

The Library began collecting Latin American material in the early 1970s in support of teaching in the geography and anthropology departments. Latin American literature is now also collected in support of courses in the Spanish department. The material constitutes a minor part of the Library's total holdings of over one million books and 3,200 current periodical titles. The Latin American collection is held on open access.

Access to collections:

Opening hours: Michaelmas and Epiphany Terms: Mon–Thurs 0845–2200, Fri 0845–1900, Sat 1000–1700, Sun 1400–2200. Easter Term: Mon–Fri 0845–2200, Sat 0900–2200, Sun 1400–2200. Vacation: Mon–Thurs 0900–1900 (1700 August), Fri 0900–1700, Sat 1000–1300 (closed August), Sun closed.

Enquiries: By telephone, post, fax or e-mail.
Admission: Non-members may apply to register as readers for reference purposes. Undergraduates may use the Library during Durham vacations.
Lending: Yes (payment required).
Inter-library loans: Lends to other libraries.
Union record: CURL, NRLS.
Catalogue: Innopac automated catalogue.
Classification: Dewey Decimal Classification and Universal Decimal Classification.

Electronic facilities for non-members:

Microcomputing facilities: No.
On-line search facilities: No.
CD-ROM facilities: No.
Internet access: No.
Portable computers: Use permitted; power points available in certain areas of the Library.

Other facilities for non-members:

Photocopying: Yes (payment required).
Microform holdings: Yes.
Reader-printer facilities: Yes (payment required).

EDINBURGH

43 Edinburgh University
Library, George Square, Edinburgh EH8 9LJ, Scotland

Tel.: General 0131 650 3409/3384. Holdings enquiries 0131 650 3374. Admissions 0131 650 3409/3384
Fax: 0131 667 9780
E-mail: Library@ed.ac.uk
Web catalogue: http://catalogue.lib.ed.ac.uk/
WWW: http://www.lib.ed.ac.uk/
Established: 1580

Librarian: Ian R.M. Mowat, MA, BPhil, FLA, FRSA

Collections:

The Library has collected material on Latin America and the Caribbean since the eighteenth century. While it forms a minor part of the overall stock, there are substantial holdings, mainly in the humanities and social sciences and covering most countries in the region with some emphasis on former British colonies. Modern collections support teaching in Latin American and Caribbean literature, economics, geography and history, and in tropical animal production, veterinary medicine and medical science. There is also material on anthropology, demography and political science. The Statistical Reference Collection includes economic, trade and production statistics series for the Latin American countries. There is material relating to the Caribbean in the manuscript collections and in theses by early medical graduates who came from the Caribbean. Edinburgh University Library operates on 23 sites and some relevant collections will be found on sites other than the Main Library. In addition some may be held in departmental and class libraries (access by prior arrangement with the department). Twentieth- and twenty-first-century materials are mainly on open access. Eighteenth- and nineteenth-century materials are on closed access.

Access to collections:

Opening hours: Term: Mon–Thurs 0900–2200, Fri–Sat 0900–1700, Sun 1200–1700. Christmas Vacation: Mon–Fri 0900–1700, Sat–Sun closed. Easter and Summer Vacations: Mon–Tues, Thurs–Fri 0900–1700, Wed 0900–2100, Sat–Sun closed. Public holidays: see website. Second full week of August closed.

Enquiries: By telephone, post, fax or e-mail.
Admission: Non-members are admitted for reference purposes (letter of introduction required for undergraduates). Corporate members are charged.
Lending: Yes (payment required).
Inter-library loans: Lends to other libraries.
Union record: BLDSC, BUCLA, BUCOP, CURL, ELF, SALSER, SCOLCAP.
Catalogues: Guard-Book Catalogue 1580–1984 available on microfiche. Geac Advance automated catalogue includes all books acquired subsequently.
Classification: Dewey Decimal Classification (modified) in the Main Library, other classification systems in faculty libraries.

Electronic facilities for non-members:

Microcomputing facilities: No.
On-line search facilities: Yes (payment required) subject to licences.
CD-ROM facilities: Yes (subject to licences).
Internet access: No.
Portable computers: Use permitted; power points available in certain areas of the Library.

Other facilities for non-members:

Photocopying: Yes (payment required).
Microform holdings: Yes.
Reader-printer facilities: Yes (payment required).

Publications:

Catalogue of the Printed Books in the Library of the University of Edinburgh (Edinburgh: Constable, 1918–23).
Index to Manuscripts: Edinburgh University Library (Boston, Mass.: G.K. Hall, 1964).
Index to Manuscripts: Edinburgh University Library. 1st Supplement (Boston, Mass.: G.K. Hall, 1981).

44 National Library of Scotland
George IV Bridge, Edinburgh EH1 1EW, Scotland

Tel.: 0131 226 4531
Fax: 0131 622 4803
E-mail: enquiries@nls.uk
Web catalogue: http://www.nls.uk/catalogues/index.html
WWW: http://www.nls.uk
Established: 1925 (1689 as Advocates' Library, 1925 as National Library of Scotland)

Librarian: Ian D. McGowan, BA
Subject enquiries to: Chris Taylor, MA, BA, ALA, Curator, French and Italian Collections
Specialist's tel.: 0131 226 4531 ext. 2216
Specialist's fax: 0131 622 4803
Specialist's e-mail address: c.taylor@nls.uk

Collections:

The Library was founded as the Library of the Faculty of Advocates. Since the Copyright Act of 1710 it has had the right to receive a copy of every book published in Great Britain and, as a result, has a large collection of English-language material on Latin America and the Caribbean. The collections, with the exception of legal material, were presented to the nation in 1925. Acquisitions of foreign-language materials on the region increased after 1945. Special collections include the Hume Collection of books and pamphlets on South America, which was presented to the Library in 1924 and contains 114 items printed between 1863 and 1920 on history, folklore, language, costume and the anthropology of Chile and Patagonia. The Astorga Collection (formerly part of the Library of the Marqueses de Astorga) of pre-1800 imprints was acquired in 1826 and includes 21 items from Latin America. Current acquisitions emphasise the humanities and social sciences and there is selective purchasing of music and juvenilia. Some 1,000 volumes are added each year and over 100 current periodical titles are held. There is a collection of maps (1:1,000,000 scale), thematic maps and national atlases held in the Map Library (tel.: 0131 466 3813, fax: 0131 466 3812, e-mail: maps@nls.uk). Scientific collections and business information are held in the Scottish Science Library (tel.: Science: 0131 466 3811; Business: 0131 667 9554; e-mail: ssl-enquiries@nls.uk). Since 1995 no monographs published in Latin America and Spain have been purchased, owing to budget restrictions; Latin American and Spanish journal subscriptions and standing orders are still maintained. Material on Latin America and Spain published in the United Kingdom and Ireland continues to be received through legal deposit. The material is on closed access.

Access to collections:

Opening hours: General Reading Room and North Reading Room: Mon–Tues, Thurs–Fri 0930–2030, Wed 1000–2030, Sat 0930–1300.

Microform Reading Room: Mon–Tues, Thurs–Fri 0930–2000, Wed 1000–2000, Sat 0930–1230.

Map Library: Mon–Tues, Thurs–Fri 0930–1700, Wed 1000–1700, Sat 0930–1300.

Scottish Science Library: Mon–Tues, Thurs–Fri 0930–1700, Wed 1000–2030, Sat closed.

Closed 25 and 26 December, 1 and 2 January, Good Friday, two Mondays in May and the Annual Closed Week in September/October.

Enquiries: By telephone, post, fax or e-mail.
Admission: The National Library of Scotland is a library of last resort. If material is not available elsewhere, an application form should be completed at the Library and proof of identity is required. For a General Reader's Ticket (not available to undergraduates and school students) two colour, passport-type photographs should be supplied. A short-term Reader's Ticket is available to undergraduates if approved by their universities.
Lending: No.
Inter-library loans: Lends to other libraries.
Union record: BUCLA, BUCOP, NLSLS, SCOLCAP.
Catalogues: Manual. Manuscripts: Catalogue of Manuscripts acquired since 1925 (continuation of published catalogue, see below); Inventories of Accessions and Deposits (summarise the content of larger collections which have not yet been catalogued); Index to Accessions. Maps: Map Card Catalogue; Slip Indexes; Graphic Indexes; Shelf List. Music: Main Music Catalogue (card catalogue containing records for about 100,000 printed scores). Online. Main Catalogue: Endeavor Voyager automated catalogue; Manuscripts Catalogue; Collections and Named Manuscripts Index; Special and Named Printed Collections in the National Library of Scotland; Principal Additions to the Collections.

Electronic facilities for non-members:

Microcomputing facilities: No.
On-line search facilities: No.
CD-ROM facilities: Yes.
Internet access: Yes.
Portable computers: Use is permitted (users must sign an undertaking accepting certain restrictions). There are mains electricity facilities for only four PCs at any one time.

Other facilities for non-members:

Photocopying: Photocopies and other reproductions are made by staff (payment required).
Microform holdings: Yes.
Reader-printer facilities: Controlled access will be introduced shortly.

Publications:

A Short-title Catalogue of Foreign Books Printed up to 1600: Books Printed or *Published Outside the British Isles Now in the National Library of Scotland and the Library of the Faculty of Advocates, Edinburgh* (Edinburgh: H.M.S.O., 1970).

Catalogue of Manuscripts Acquired since 1925 (Edinburgh: H.M.S.O., 1938–92).

Summary Catalogue of the Advocates' Manuscripts (Edinburgh: H.M.S.O., 1971).

General Catalogue of Printed Books (Edinburgh: National Library of Scotland, 1988) Microfiche.

EGHAM

45 CABI Bioscience UK Centre
Library, Bakeham Lane, Egham, Surrey TW20 9TY

Tel.: 01784 470111
Fax: 01491 829100
E-mail: bioscience@cabi.org
WWW: http://www.cabi.org/
Established: 1913 (1985 as CAB International)

Senior Librarian: Elizabeth Wheater, BA

Collections:

CAB International (formerly Imperial Agricultural Bureaux 1929–48, and Commonwealth Agricultural Bureaux, 1948–85) had its origins in a service established in 1913 to support agricultural scientists by identifying insects and providing scientific information and technical assistance. Bureaux studying other organisms were added in later years. In 1985 CAB changed from a Commonwealth to a completely international organisation with membership open to any country. The Library at Egham contains material on pure and applied mycology: fungal taxonomy and systematics, nematode taxonomy and plant nematology, plant pathology, medical and veterinary mycology, biodegradation, biodeterioration, and related aspects of fungal biotechnology and industrial mycology, on biodiversity and on all branches of parasitology. The collection includes annual reports, serials, books and conference proceedings, and 140,000 reprints and photocopies. The Library at Silwood Park (Buckhurst Road, Ascot, Berks SL5 7TA) contains annual reports, serials, books and conference proceedings on medical and veterinary entomology, biological control, pesticides, and on horticulture and plantation crops. The material is on open access.

Access to collections:

Opening hours: Mon–Thurs 0930–1430.

Enquiries: By telephone, post, fax or e-mail.
Admission: Open to researchers (appointment required).
Lending: No.
Inter-library loans: No.
Classification: Barnard Classification (for parasitology). Universal Decimal Classification (modified).

Electronic facilities for non-members:

Microcomputing facilities: No.
On-line search facilities: No.
CD-ROM facilities: Yes.
Internet access: No.
Portable computers: Use permitted; power points available.

Other facilities for non-members:

Photocopying: Yes (payment required).

46 Royal Holloway, University of London
Library, Royal Holloway, Egham Hill, Egham, Surrey TW20 0EX

Tel.: 01784 443823
Fax: 01784 477670
E-mail: library@rhul.ac.uk
Web catalogue: http://library.rhul.ac.uk
WWW: http://www.rhul.ac.uk/information-services/library
Established: Merged college 1984

Librarian: Sarah E. Gerrard, BA, DipLib, ALA
Subject enquiries to: Roger Shrigley, BA, ALA, MIInfSc, MiMgt, Liaison Librarian for Management, Economics, European Studies and Geography
Specialist's tel.: 01784 443333
Specialist's e-mail address: r.shrigley@rhul.ac.uk

Collections:

Royal Holloway was formed from the merger in 1984 of Royal Holloway College (founded 1883) and Bedford College (founded 1849). Royal Holloway College began collecting material on the history of Latin America and the Caribbean in 1964; approximately 600 volumes are held currently. Bedford College specialised in the geography of Latin America (particularly the physical and ecological geography of the tropical areas and the human geography of the Caribbean), and from a starting point in 1965 built a collection which now numbers approximately 1,200 volumes. The Library's overall holdings on the region now total some 3,000 volumes. The collections are on open access.

Access to collections:

Opening hours: Term: Mon–Thurs 0900–2100, Fri 0800–1900, Sat 1100–1700, Sun 1300–1800. Vacation: Mon–Fri 0900–1700, Sat 1100–1700, Sun 1300–1800. Christmas, Easter and August Bank Holiday closed.

Enquiries: By telephone, post, fax or e-mail.
Admission: Non-members are admitted for reference purposes.
Lending: Yes (payment required).
Inter-library loans: Lends to other libraries.
Union record: BUCLA (to 1980), BUCOP, COLALAS, University of London Union List of Serials.
Catalogue: Libertas automated catalogue.
Classification: Dewey Decimal Classification.

Electronic facilities for non-members:

Microcomputing facilities: No.
On-line search facilities: No.
CD-ROM facilities: No.
Internet access: No.
Portable computers: Facilities are under review; power points are being installed.

Other facilities for non-members:

Photocopying: Yes (payment required).
Microform holdings: Yes.
Reader-printer facilities: Yes.

EXETER

47 Devon County Council
Devon Library and Information Services, Barley House, Isleworth Road, Exeter EX4 1RQ

Tel.: 01392 384315
Fax: 01392 384316
E-mail: devlibs@devon.gov.uk
Web catalogue: http://www.devon.gov.uk/library/catalogue
WWW: http://www.devon.gov.uk/library
Established: 1959 (collection)

Collections:

The collection, acquired by Devon Library and Information Services for the South West Regional Subject Specialisation Scheme, is available through inter-library loan only. The collection covers the topography and history of Mexico, Central America, Cuba and the Caribbean. Over 1,000 books are held.

Access to collections:

Inter-library loans: The material can be accessed only through inter-library loan.
Union record: BLDSC, SWRLS.
Catalogue: Galaxy automated catalogue.
Classification: Dewey Decimal Classification.

48 University of Exeter
Library, Stocker Road, Exeter EX4 4PT

Tel.: 01392 263867. Holdings enquiries 01392 264051
Fax: 01392 263871
E-mail: library@exeter.ac.uk
Telnet catalogue: library.ex.ac.uk (login: library)
Web catalogue: http://www.lib.ex.ac.uk/
WWW: http://www.ex.ac.uk/library/
Established: The University received its charter in 1955, having previously awarded University of London degrees. The Main Library opened in 1983

Librarian: Alasdair T. Paterson, MA, ALAI
Subject enquiries to: J. Paul C. Auchterlonie, MA, DipLib, Subject Librarian for Spanish Studies
Specialist's address: Old Library, Prince of Wales Road, Exeter EX4 4PX
Specialist's tel.: 01392 264051
Specialist's e-mail address: j.p.c.auchterlonie@exeter.ac.uk

Collections:

The Library has been collecting material on Latin America and the Caribbean since the 1960s. The collection is mainly in the humanities — particularly literature — with some history. There is basic coverage of most countries in the region, but the current emphasis is on Argentina, especially Argentine literature. There are now 3,000 volumes and 10 current periodical titles; about 100 volumes are added each year. There is also a small collection of recordings of Caribbean music. The collection is on open access.

Access to collections:

Opening hours: Term: Mon–Fri 0900–2200, Sat 0900–1700, Sun 1400–2000 (Spring and Summer terms only). Vacation: Mon–Fri 0900–1730, Sat–Sun closed. Christmas, Easter and August Bank Holiday closed.

Enquiries: By telephone, post, fax or e-mail.
Admission: Non-members are admitted for reference purposes (letter of introduction preferred).
Lending: Yes (written application to the Librarian required).
Inter-library loans: Lends to other libraries.
Union record: BLDSC, BUCLA, BUCOP, COLALAS, SWRLS.
Catalogue: Innopac automated catalogue.
Classification: Dewey Decimal Classification.

Electronic facilities for non-members:

Microcomputing facilities: No.
On-line search facilities: No, unless mediated by a member of the library staff.
CD-ROM facilities: No, unless mediated by a member of the library staff.
Internet access: No.
Portable computers: Permission must be sought in advance.

Other facilities for non-members:

Photocopying: Yes (payment required).
Microform holdings: Yes.
Reader-printer facilities: Yes (payment required); limited hours of availability.

GALWAY

49 *National University of Ireland, Galway*
James Hardiman Library, University Road, Galway, Ireland

Tel.: +353 91 524411
Fax: +353 91 522394
E-mail: library@nuigalway.ie
Telnet catalogue: library.nuigalway.ie
Web catalogue: http://opac.nuigalway.ie/ALEPH
WWW: http://www.library.ucg.ie/
Established: 1849

Librarian: Marie Reddan, DipLIS, DipSA, ALA, FLAI

Collections:

The Library has a collection of 400,000 books and 1,937 periodicals. Latin American materials form a minor part of the total stock; there are over 1,000 books on a range of subjects, mainly in the social sciences. The collection is on open access.

Access to collections:

Opening hours: Term: Mon–Fri 0900–2200, Sat 0900–1300. Summer Vacation: Mon–Fri 0900–1730, Sat closed.

Enquiries: By telephone, post, fax or e-mail.
Admission: Non-members are admitted for reference purposes (appointment required).
Lending: No.
Inter-library loans: Lends to other libraries.
Union record: BLDSC, IMLC, IRIS.
Catalogue: Dynix automated catalogue.
Classification: Dewey Decimal Classification.

Electronic facilities for non-members:

Microcomputing facilities: No.
On-line search facilities: No.
CD-ROM facilities: During vacation only.
Internet access: During vacation only.
Portable computers: Use permitted; power points available.

Other facilities for non-members:

Photocopying: Yes (payment required).
Microform holdings: Yes.
Reader-printer facilities: Yes (payment required).

GLASGOW

50 Department for International Development (DFID)
Library, Abercrombie House, Eaglesham Road, East Kilbride, Glasgow G75 8EA, Scotland

Tel.: 08405 300 4100
Fax: 01355 84 3632
E-mail: enquiry@dfid.gov.uk
WWW: http://www.dfid.gov.uk/
Established: 1997 (1964 as Ministry of Overseas Development Library, 1970 as Overseas Development Administration Library)

Librarian: M. Anne Fraser, MA, ALA, MLib

Collections:

The Library (of the then Ministry of Overseas Development) began collecting material on the region in 1963. The total stock of the Library is 80,000 books and 850 periodical titles; of this, Latin American and Caribbean material forms a minor part. The main subjects covered are development assistance, economic and geographic descriptions of developing countries, aid-giving bodies, and aid aspects of scientific and technical disciplines such as agriculture and medicine. The Library has a range of electronic sources and collects statistical publications from national and international bodies. The collection is on open access.

Access to collections:

Opening hours: Mon–Fri 0900–1700. Public holidays closed.

Enquiries: By telephone, post, fax or e-mail.
Admission: Non-members are admitted for reference purposes (appointment required).
Lending: No.
Inter-library loans: Lends to other libraries.
Union record: BLDSC.
Catalogue: SIRSI Unicorn automated catalogue.
Classification: Library of Congress Classification.

Electronic facilities for non-members:

Microcomputing facilities: No.
On-line search facilities: No.
CD-ROM facilities: No.
Internet access: No.
Portable computers: Use not permitted.

Other facilities for non-members:

Photocopying: Yes (payment required).
Microform holdings: Yes.
Reader-printer facilities: No.

51 Glasgow City Libraries and Archives

The Mitchell Library, North Street, Glasgow G3 7DN, Scotland

Tel.: 0141 287 2999
Fax: 0141 287 2815
E-mail: R_S_M@gcl.glasgow.gov.uk
WWW: http://www.mitchelllibrary.org/
Established: 1877

Director: Andrew Miller, MA, FLA

Collections:

The Mitchell Library, founded in 1877, is one of the largest public reference libraries in Europe. It has been collecting Latin American and

Caribbean material since its foundation, and is strongest in English-language, and more particularly British, imprints. The collection is predominantly on closed access.

Access to collections:

Opening hours: Mon–Thurs 0900–2000, Fri–Sat 0900–1700. Public holidays closed.

Enquiries: By telephone, post, fax or e-mail.
Admission: Open to the general public.
Lending: No.
Inter-library loans: No.
Union record: BLCMP, BUCOP, SALSER, SCOLCAP.
Catalogue: BLCMP Talis automated catalogue.
Classification: Dewey Decimal Classification.

Electronic facilities for non-members:

Microcomputing facilities: Yes (payment required).
On-line search facilities: Yes (payment required).
CD-ROM facilities: Yes (payment required).
Internet access: Yes (payment required for printing).
Portable computers: Use permitted in the Business Information Section, where power points are available.

Other facilities for non-members:

Photocopying: Yes (payment required).
Microform holdings: Yes.
Reader-printer facilities: Yes (payment required).

Publications:

Catalogue of Additions, 1915–1949 (Glasgow: Printed for the Committee on Libraries by the Corporation of Glasgow Printing and Stationery Department, 1959–60).
The Mitchell Library, Glasgow, 1877–1977 (Glasgow: Glasgow District Libraries, 1977).

52 Royal Scottish Geographical Society
Graham Hills Building, 40 George Street, Glasgow G1 1QE, Scotland

Tel.: 0141 552 3330
Fax: 0141 552 3331
E-mail: R.S.G.S@strath.ac.uk
Web catalogue: http://zen.lib.strath.ac.uk (books and periodicals)
WWW: http://www.geo.ed.ac.uk/home/scotland/rsgs/
Established: 1884

Map and Photography Curator: Kerr Jamieson, MA
E-mail: Kerr.Jamieson@strath.ac.uk
Book and Periodical enquiries to: Gill Morris, MA, Sub-Librarian
Address: Royal Scottish Geographical Library of the University of Strathclyde, Andersonian Library, Curran Building, 101 St James' Road, Glasgow G4 0NS, Scotland
Tel.: 0141 548 4607/4591
E-mail: G.Morris@strath.ac.uk

Collections:

The Society was founded in 1884 and moved to Glasgow in 1993. In 1994 the books and periodicals were deposited in the Andersonian Library of the University of Strathclyde. They are kept in a separate reading room close to the University's geographical collections and named The Royal Scottish Geographical Library of the University of Strathclyde. The Society's collections of maps, photographs and archives are kept at the Graham Hills Headquarters. The collections include works on geography, travel, mountaineering and polar exploration. There are 15,000 books, 3,000 volumes of journals, 180 foreign-language serials, 15,000 maps, 20,000 35mm colour slides, over 6,000 lantern slides and a smaller collection of prints and negatives. Some antique maps are at present stored in the Map Library of the National Library of Scotland. Material on Latin America and the Caribbean forms a minor part of the collection. The collections are predominantly on open access.

Access to collections (maps, photographs, archives):
Enquiries: By telephone, post, fax or e-mail. If subject searches extend beyond ten minutes, a charge of £20 per hour is made.
Admission: On application to the Curator.
Lending: In exceptional circumstances, at the discretion of the Director.

Inter-library loans: No.
Catalogue: Cataloguing in process. Microcomputer gives access to the catalogue records.
Classification: Own classification.

Electronic facilities for non-members:

Microcomputing facilities: No.
On-line search facilities: No.
CD-ROM facilities: Yes.
Internet access: No.
Portable computers: Use permitted; power points available.

Other facilities for non-members:

Photocopying: Yes (payment required).

Access to collections (books and periodicals):

Opening hours: (books and periodicals) Term: Mon–Fri 0850–2200, Sat 0900–1200. Christmas and Summer Vacations: Mon–Fri 0900–1700, Sat 0900–1200. Easter Vacation: Mon–Fri 0850–2100, Sat 0900–1200. Christmas, New Year, Easter and Glasgow local holidays closed.

Enquiries: By telephone, post, fax or e-mail.
Admission: Non-members are admitted for reference purposes (payment required). Written application to the University Librarian is required.
Lending: No.
Inter-library loans: Lends to other libraries.
Catalogue: Endeavor Voyager automated catalogue.
Classification: Dewey Decimal Classification.

Electronic facilities for non-members:

Microcomputing facilities: No.
On-line search facilities: No.
CD-ROM facilities: No.
Internet access: No.
Portable computers: Use permitted; power points available.

Other facilities for non-members:

Photocopying: Yes (payment required).

53 University of Glasgow

Glasgow University Library, Hillhead Street, Glasgow G12 8QE, Scotland

Tel.: 0141 330 6704
Fax: 0141 330 4952
E-mail: library@gla.ac.uk
Web catalogue: http://eleanor.lib.gla.ac.uk/search/
WWW: http://www.lib.gla.ac.uk
Established: 1451

University Librarian and Keeper of the Hunterian Books and MSS: Andrew Wale, BA, ALA
Subject enquiries to: John N. Moore, MA, MLitt, ALA, FSA(Scot), Senior Assistant Librarian
Specialist's tel.: 0141 330 6749
Specialist's e-mail address: j.n.moore@lib.gla.ac.uk

Collections:

The Library began collecting Latin American and Caribbean material in 1957 and acquisitions increased after the foundation of the Institute of Latin American Studies in 1965. The bulk of the Institute's collections was transferred to the University Library in 1986. The collection now includes 15,000 books, and 35 current and 60 non-current periodical titles. Acquisitions have decreased substantially since the closure of the Institute in 1997. Within a general collection in the humanities and social sciences, the collection is particularly strong in history and in the economics, politics and sociology of Brazil, Cuba and Mexico. Anthropology, demography, environment and geography are also collected. The material is predominantly on open access.

Access to collections:

Opening hours: Term: Mon–Fri 0900–2125, Sat 0900–1925, Sun 0930–2125. Vacation: Mon–Fri 0900–1700, Sat 0900–1230, Sun closed. Open public holidays, except Christmas, New Year, Glasgow Fair (Monday of 3rd week of July), late September holiday.

Enquiries: By telephone, post, fax or e-mail.
Admission: Non-members are admitted for reference purposes (payment required). Written application to the Librarian is required.
Lending: No.

Inter-library loans: Lends to other libraries.
Union record: BLDSC, BUCLA, BUCOP, COLALAS, NLSLS, SCOL-CAP, *Serials in the British Library*.
Catalogue: Innopac automated catalogue.
Classification: Own classification, based on Library of Congress Classification.

Electronic facilities for non-members:

Microcomputing facilities: No.
On-line search facilities: Yes (payment required).
CD-ROM facilities: Yes.
Internet access: No.
Portable computers: Use permitted; power points available.

Other facilities for non-members:

Photocopying: Yes (payment required).
Microform holdings: Yes.
Reader-printer facilities: Yes (payment required).

54 University of Strathclyde
Andersonian Library, Curran Building, 101 St James' Road, Glasgow G4 0NS, Scotland

Tel.: 0141 548 4620
Fax: 0141 552 3304
E-mail: library@strath.ac.uk
Web catalogue: http://zen.lib.strath.ac.uk
WWW: http://www.lib.strath.ac.uk/
Established: 1964

University Librarian and Director of Information Resources: Derek Law, MA, DipLib
Subject enquiries to: Janette Davidson, MA, ALA, Sub-Librarian
Specialist's tel.: 0141 548 4607/4591
Specialist's e-mail address: j.davidson@strath.ac.uk

Collections:
The Library began collecting on Latin America and the Caribbean in 1964 and now has about 6,500 volumes and 15 current periodical titles.

The main subject strengths are in literature, linguistics, history and political science, and the countries best represented are Argentina, Brazil, Chile, Mexico and Peru. The books and periodicals library of the Royal Scottish Geographical Society was deposited in the Andersonian Library in 1994 and forms The Royal Scottish Geographical Library of the University of Strathclyde (no. 52).

Access to collections:

Opening hours: Term: Mon–Fri 0850–2200, Sat 0900–1200. Christmas and Summer Vacations: Mon–Fri 0900–1700, Sat 0900–1200. Easter Vacation: Mon–Fri 0850–2100, Sat 0900–1200. Christmas, New Year, Easter and Glasgow local holidays closed.

Enquiries: By telephone, post, fax or e-mail.
Admission: Non-members are admitted for reference purposes (payment required). Written application to the University Librarian is required.
Lending: No.
Inter-library loans: Lends to other libraries.
Union record: BLDSC, BUCLA, SCOLCAP.
Catalogue: Dynix Horizon automated catalogue.
Classification: Dewey Decimal Classification and Universal Decimal Classification.

Electronic facilities for non-members:

Microcomputing facilities: No.
On-line search facilities: No.
CD-ROM facilities: No.
Internet access: No.
Portable computers: Use permitted; power points available.

Other facilities for non-members:

Photocopying: Yes (payment required).
Microform holdings: Yes.
Reader-printer facilities: No.

GODALMING

55 World-Wide Fund for Nature–UK (*WWF–UK*)
Library, Panda House, Weyside Park, Catteshall Lane, Godalming, Surrey GU7 1XR

Tel.: 01483 426444
Fax: 01483 426409
E-mail: jrivers@wwf.org.uk
WWW: http://www.wwf-uk.org
Established: 1961

Librarian: Jan Rivers

Collections:
WWF's mission is to conserve threatened wildlife species and their natural habitats internationally, working closely with local and indigenous people. The Library holds nearly 200 books on Latin America — the best represented subjects are plants and wildlife species, habitats, rainforests, conservation and sustainable development, indigenous people and Amazonia — and over 70 current periodical titles, most of which are of relevance to the region. Latin American material is also included in the collection of WWF reports on specific areas, and of quarterly reports on approved WWF projects within specific regions.

Access to collections
Opening hours: Mon–Fri 0900–1700.

Enquiries: By telephone, post, fax or e-mail.
Admission: Non-members are admitted for reference purposes (appointment required).
Lending: In exceptional circumstances, by arrangement.
Inter-library loans: No.
Catalogue: Alice automated system.

Electronic facilities for non-members:
Microcomputing facilities: Yes.
On-line search facilities: No.
CD-ROM facilities: No.
Internet access: No.

Portable computers: Use not permitted.

Other facilities for non-members:
Photocopying: Yes (payment required).

GUILDFORD

56 University of Surrey
The George Edwards Library, University of Surrey, Guildford, Surrey GU2 5XH

Tel.: 01483 683325. Evenings and weekends 01483 689287
Fax: 01483 689500
E-mail: library-enquiries@surrey.ac.uk
Telnet catalogue: opac.lib.surrey.ac.uk
Web catalogue: http://opac.lib.surrey.ac.uk/
WWW: http://www.surrey.ac.uk/Library/
Established: 1894

University Librarian and Dean of Information Services: T.J.A. Crawshaw, BEng, DipLIS
Linguistics and International Studies subject enquiries to: Mark Ashworth, BSc, MA, ALA, Liaison Librarian, Linguistics and International Studies
Specialist's tel.: 01483 683363
Specialist's e-mail address: m.ashworth@surrey.ac.uk
Dance subject enquiries to: Coffey Holland, BA, MA, ALA, Liaison Librarian, Dance
Specialist's tel.: 01483 683202
Specialist's e-mail address: m.holland@surrey.ac.uk

Collections:

The Library began collecting material on Latin America and the Caribbean in 1970. It now has a small collection of material acquired for the study of international relations, material on the Francophone Caribbean and on Creole as a linguistic form, and some material on dance. The collections are on open access.

Access to collections:

Opening hours: Term: Mon 1000–2200, Tues–Fri 0900–2200, Sat 1300–1800, Sun 1400–1800. Spring Part 2: Mon–Fri 0900–2200, Sat 0900–1800, Sun 1400–1800. Christmas Vacation: Mon–Fri 0900–1700, Sat–Sun closed. Easter Vacation: Mon–Fri 0900–2200, Sat 0900–1800, Sun closed. Summer Vacation: Mon–Fri 0900–2200, Sat 1300–1800, Sun closed. Christmas, New Year, Easter and August Bank Holiday closed.

Enquiries: By telephone, post, fax or e-mail.
Admission: Non-members are admitted for reference use (undergraduates during Surrey vacations only).
Lending: Yes (payment required).
Inter-library loans: Lends to other libraries.
Union record: BLCMP.
Catalogue: BLCMP Talis automated catalogue.
Classification: Universal Decimal Classification.

Electronic facilities for non-members:

Microcomputing facilities: No.
On-line search facilities: Yes, mediated by a member of staff (payment required).
CD-ROM facilities: No.
Internet access: No.
Portable computers: Use permitted (on application to library staff).

Other facilities for non-members:

Photocopying: Yes (payment required).
Microform holdings: Yes.
Reader-printer facilities: Yes (payment required).

HARPENDEN

57 *Institute of Arable Crops Research–Rothamsted*
Harpenden, Hertfordshire AL5 2JQ

Address for correspondence: Library, IACR–Rothamsted, Harpenden, Hertfordshire AL5 2JQ
Tel.: 01582 763133 ext. 2659

Fax: 01582 760981
E-mail: liz.allsopp@bbsrc.ac.uk
Web catalogue: http://www.iacr.bbsrc.ac.uk/res/depts/library/tcatalogue.html
WWW: http://www.iacr.bbsrc.ac.uk/res/depts/library/tlibindex.html
Established: 1843

Librarian: S.E. Allsopp, BA, ALA, DipLib, MInfSc

Collections:

The IACR–Rothamsted Library is one of the oldest agricultural libraries in the country. The collections are particularly strong in soil science, plant sciences, agronomy, entomology (including apiculture), nematology, pesticide science, plant diseases, mycology and biomathematics. The Latin American materials are a minor part of the collection. Collections in the Main Library are on open access.

Access to collections:

Opening hours: Mon–Thurs 0900–1730, Fri 0900–1700. Public holidays closed.

Enquiries: By telephone, post, fax or e-mail.
Admission: Non-members are admitted for reference purposes (written application to the Librarian required).
Lending: No.
Inter-library loans: Lends to other libraries.
Union record: BUCOP, Periodicals held in Hertfordshire libraries, WLSP.
Catalogues: Card catalogue (author, alphabetical subject and classified subject) for books up to 1984. Automated catalogue for books and conferences 1985 to date, all plant pathology books, historical books and journals.
Classification: Universal Decimal Classification.

Electronic facilities for non-members:

Microcomputing facilities: Yes (subject to availability).
On-line search facilities: Most services are not available to external users, but occasionally searches can be undertaken; contact the Librarian for availability and costs.
CD-ROM facilities: Yes.
Internet access: Yes (subject to availability).

Portable computers: Battery-operated portable computers may be used.

Other facilities for non-members:

Photocopying: Yes (payment required).
Microform holdings: Yes.
Reader-printer facilities: Yes (payment required).

KEW

58 Royal Botanic Gardens, Kew
Library & Archives, Royal Botanic Gardens, Kew, Richmond, Surrey TW9 3AE

Tel.: 020 8332 5414
Fax: 020 8332 5430
E-mail: library@rbgkew.org.uk
WWW: http://www.rbgkew.org.uk/collections/library.html
Established: 1852

Acting Head of Library and Archives: John Flanagan, ALA

Collections:

The Library holds one of the largest collections of works relating to botany in the world. Special strengths are taxonomy, conservation, horticulture, biochemistry, anatomy, genetics and economic botany. The historic collections include such works as Hipólito Ruiz's *Florae Peruvianae et Chilensis* (Madrid: Imprenta de Sancha, 1794). The collections have been expanded by purchase (including valuable works bought for the Library by the Bentham-Moxon Trust), donation and exchange (currently with 302 institutions). The Library collects all formats: books, serials, microforms, maps, prints and drawings, CD-ROMs and other electronic media, video tapes and audio tapes. Material is held on all countries of the region and in a variety of formats including botanical illustrations (e.g. the work of Margaret Mee). The Archives (tel.: 020 8332 5417; fax: 020 8332 5430; e-mail: archives@rbgkew.org.uk) hold the private papers of botanists including Charles Darwin, Richard Spruce and Alfred Russel Wallace. The Library collections are predominantly on open access.

Access to collections:

Opening hours: Mon–Fri 0900–1700. Public holidays closed.

Enquiries: By telephone, post, fax or e-mail.
Admission: Bona fide researchers are admitted for reference purposes (written application to the Librarian and appointment required).
Lending: No.
Inter-library loans: No.
Catalogues: SIRSI Unicorn automated catalogue. Kew Record of Taxonomic Literature (bibliographical database). Index Kewensis.
Classification: Dewey Decimal Classification (horticulture), Universal Decimal Classification, Bentham-Hooker Classification of Plants.

Electronic facilities for non-members:

Microcomputing facilities: Yes.
On-line search facilities: No.
CD-ROM facilities: Yes.
Internet access: Contact Library for availability.
Portable computers: Use permitted; power points available.

Other facilities for non-members:

Photocopying: Yes, by Library staff (payment required).
Microform holdings: Yes.
Reader-printer facilities: Yes (payment required).

Publications:

Author Catalogue of the Royal Botanic Gardens Library, Kew, England (Boston, Mass.: G.K. Hall, 1974), 5 vols.

Classified Catalogue of the Royal Botanic Gardens Library, Kew, England, (Boston, Mass.: G.K. Hall, 1974), 4 vols.

Index Kewensis on CD-ROM (Oxford: Oxford University Press). Print and microfiche editions of some volumes also available. Also incorporated in the International Plant Names Index and available on the Internet (http://www.ipni.org).

Kew Record of Taxonomic Literature Relating to Vascular Plants (London: H.M.S.O., 1971–). To be made available on the Internet in 2001.

KEYWORTH

59 British Geological Survey
Library and Information Service, Kingsley Dunham Centre, Keyworth, Nottingham NG12 5GG

Tel.: 0115 936 3205
Fax: 0115 936 3200
E-mail: libuser@bgs.ac.uk
Web catalogue: http://geolib.bgs.ac.uk/
WWW: http://www.bgs.ac.uk/contacts/library.html
Established: 1835

Chief Librarian and Archivist: Graham McKenna, MA, ALA, MIInfSc

Collections:

The Library holds one of the world's largest earth science collections. Material is acquired by purchase and exchange and by the incorporation of other collections (e.g. the former Overseas Geological Surveys in 1965). The collection includes 500,000 books and pamphlets, 3,000 current and 14,000 non-current serial titles, 75,000 photographs and 200,000 maps. Material on Latin America and the Caribbean has been collected since the nineteenth century and forms a minor, although sizeable, part of the overall coverage, including books, periodicals, maps and archives. The recent book collections are on open access; other materials are held in closed-access areas, but can be retrieved on request.

Access to collections:

Opening hours: Mon–Thurs 0900–1700, Fri 0900–1630. Public holidays closed.

Enquiries: By telephone, post, fax or e-mail.
Admission: Non-members are admitted for reference purposes (appointment recommended; payment required for commercial users).
Lending: No.
Inter-library loans: Lends to other libraries only in exceptional circumstances.
Catalogues: Author and classified subject card catalogue. BGS Library World Maps Register Index. GEOLIB WebView.
Classification: Universal Decimal Classification.

Electronic facilities for non-members:
Microcomputing facilities: Yes (payment required).
On-line search facilities: Yes (payment required).
CD-ROM facilities: Yes (payment required).
Internet access: No.
Portable computers: Use permitted with special adapter plug supplied by the Library.

Other facilities for non-members:
Photocopying: Yes (payment required).
Microform holdings: Yes.
Reader-printer facilities: Yes (microfiche only).

KINGSTON-UPON-HULL

60 Hull City Council
Hull Local Studies Library, Central Library, Albion Street, Hull HU1 3TF

Tel.: 01482 210077
Fax: 01482 616858
E-mail: Local.Studies@hullcc.gov.uk
Telnet catalogue: library.hull.ac.uk or 150.237.200.220
Web catalogue: http://library.hull.ac.uk:81/
WWW: http://www.hullcc.gov.uk/libraries/
Established: 1901

Information Services Librarian: Jo Edge
Local Studies Librarian: David Smith, BA, MSc, Cert. Regional and Local History

Collections:
The Local Studies Library contains the Wilberforce Collection on Slavery: over 1,500 volumes on William Wilberforce, the abolition of slavery and all aspects of slavery, ancient and modern. A small proportion of the material relates to Latin America and the Caribbean. The bulk of the collection is modern printed material, with reprints of older items. The collection is on closed access.

Access to collections:

Opening hours: Mon–Thurs 0930–2000, Fri 0930–1730, Sat 0900–1630.

Enquiries: By telephone, post, fax or e-mail.
Admission: Open to the general public.
Lending: No.
Inter-library loans: Lends to other libraries.
Union record: East Yorkshire Bibliography.
Catalogues: Author and title card catalogue. East Yorkshire Bibliography (automated catalogue, hosted at the University of Hull, on the Innopac system, containing records of the local history collections of Hull Local Studies Library, Beverly Library, the University of Hull and the University of Lincolnshire and Humberside).
Classification: Own classification.

Electronic facilities for non-members:

Microcomputing facilities: No.
On-line search facilities: No.
CD-ROM facilities: No.
Internet access: In Arts and Humanities section only.
Portable computers: Battery-operated portable computers may be used.

Other facilities for non-members:

Photocopying: Yes (payment required).
Microform holdings: Yes.
Reader-printer facilities: Yes (payment required).

61 *University of Hull*

Brynmor Jones Library, Cottingham Road, Hull HU6 7RX

Tel.: 01482 466581. Holdings enquiries 01482 465250. Admissions 01482 465440
Fax: 01482 466205
E-mail: library@acs.hull.ac.uk or libhelp@acs.hull.ac.uk
Telnet catalogue: library.hull.ac.uk or 150.237.200.220
Web catalogue: http://library.hull.ac.uk/
WWW: http://www.hull.ac.uk/lib/
Established: 1928

Director of Academic Services and Librarian: R.G. Heseltine, BA, DPhil, DipLib, ALA

Collections:

The Library has been collecting Latin American and Caribbean materials since the 1930s. They form a minor part of the overall stock: 5,000 books, 20 current and 30 non-current periodical titles, a few manuscripts and a few microforms; about 75 volumes are added each year. The main subject strengths of the collection are literature, history and economic and social history. The areas with the greatest coverage are Argentina, Brazil, Chile, Mexico and the Caribbean. The Library also holds archive material from the Chile Committee for Human Rights, the Chile Solidarity Campaign, the El Salvador Solidarity Campaign, Sir Charles Chichester (relating to his experiences in the Caribbean and Venezuela) and the Scarlett family (relating to the management of sugar plantations in Jamaica and Peru). The collection (with the exception of the archives) is predominantly on open access.

Access to collections:

Opening hours: Term and Christmas and Easter Vacations: Mon–Thurs 0900–2200, Fri 0900–1730, Sat 0900–2100, Sun 1300–2100. Summer Vacation: Mon–Tues, Thurs–Fri 0900–1730, Wed 0900–1900 (except August), Sat 0900–1300 (except August), Sun closed. Christmas, New Year, Easter and August Bank Holiday closed.

Enquiries: By telephone, post, fax or e-mail.
Admission: Non-members may apply for Associate Readership (payment required).
Lending: Associate Readers may borrow (payment required).
Inter-library loans: Lends to other libraries.
Union record: Association of Yorkshire and Humberside Library Services (to 1990), BLDSC (to 1990), BUCLA, BUCOP, COLALAS.
Catalogue: Innopac automated catalogue.
Classification: Library of Congress Classification.

Electronic facilities for non-members:

Microcomputing facilities: Yes (for Associate Readers; separate registration required).
On-line search facilities: No.

CD-ROM facilities: Yes (for Associate Readers; separate registration required).
Internet access: Yes (for Associate Readers; separate registration required).
Portable computers: Use permitted; power points available.

Other facilities for non-members:
Photocopying: Yes (for Associate Readers; payment required).
Microform holdings: A few items.
Reader-printer facilities: Yes (for Associate Readers; payment required).

KINGSTON-UPON-THAMES

62 Kingston University
Kingston University Library, Penrhyn Road, Kingston Upon Thames, Surrey KT1 2EE

Tel.: 020 8547 7101
Fax: 020 8547 7111
E-mail: library@kingston.ac.uk
Telnet catalogue: opac.kingston.ac.uk
Web catalogue: http://opac.kingston.ac.uk:8001/
WWW: http://www.kingston.ac.uk/library_media/
Established: 1970

Head of Library and Media Services: Nicholas Pollard, BA, ALA
Subject enquiries to: Jerome Farrell, BA, MA, ALA, Information Librarian: Languages, Politics
Specialist's tel.: 020 8547 7095

Collections:

The Library has a small collection (under 1,000 volumes) on the history, geography and politics of the region. Mexico, Brazil, Peru and the Caribbean are best represented. The collections are on open access.

Access to collections:

Opening hours: Term: Mon–Thurs 0845–2100, Fri 1000–1730, Sat–Sun 1015–1545. Vacation: Mon–Fri 0900–1730, Sat closed, Sun 1015–1545. Public holidays closed.

Enquiries: By telephone or e-mail.
Admission: Non-members are admitted for reference purposes.
Lending: Yes (payment required).
Inter-library loans: Lends to other libraries.
Union record: BLCMP.
Catalogue: BLCMP Talis automated catalogue.
Classification: Dewey Decimal Classification.

Electronic facilities for non-members:

Microcomputing facilities: No.
On-line search facilities: Yes (payment required).
CD-ROM facilities: No.
Internet access: No.
Portable computers: Use permitted; power points available.

Other facilities for non-members:

Photocopying: Yes (payment required).
Microform holdings: Yes.
Reader-printer facilities: Yes (payment required).

63 Sue Cunningham Photographic
56 Chatham Road, Kingston upon Thames, Surrey KT1 3AA

Tel.: 020 8541 3024
Fax: 020 8541 5388
E-mail: pictures@scphotographic.com
WWW: http://www.scphotographic.com/
Established: 1989

Subject enquiries to: Researcher.

Collections:

A commercial picture library supplying text and photograph features, with a stock of specialist images on Eastern and Western Europe, Africa and Latin America, from 1985 to the present. Over 150,000 images on file. The Latin American collection covers Argentina, Bolivia, Brazil, Chile, Guatemala and Peru, with Brazil most strongly represented. The library includes the most comprehensive collection of images of Brazil in Europe, covering all aspects of the country, including agriculture, commerce, culture, education, environment, flora and fauna, health, indigenous people, industry, people, poverty, religion, tourism and transport.

Access to collections:

Opening hours: Mon–Fri 0900–1800, by appointment.

Enquiries: By telephone, post, fax or e-mail.
Admission: By appointment.
Search/service fee: £20–£40. Commissions undertaken.
Lending: Photographs are loaned for the period necessary for selection and reproduction.
Catalogues: Promotional colour leaflets with sample images.
Classification: Pictures are stored using a proprietary classification system.

Electronic facilities for non-members:

Online search of images: No.
Online delivery of images: Yes.
CD-ROM facilities: To be available shortly.
Portable computers: Use permitted.

Other facilities for non-members:

Copying: Only by agreement for specified purposes.

Publications:

Promotional leaflets with sample images and stock list.

LEEDS

64 Leeds Library Service
Central Library, The Headrow, Leeds LS1 3AB

Tel.: 0113 247 8274
Fax: 0113 247 8271
E-mail: peter.kelly@leeds.gov.uk
WWW: http://www.leeds.gov.uk/library/library.html
Established: 1870

Head of Library Services: Catherine Blanshard, BA, ALA

Collections:

The Library was founded in 1870 and has a number of general works on the region. Directories and other commercial information sources on Latin American and Caribbean countries are held in Information for Business (tel.: 0113 247 8265/6; fax: 0113 247 8268; e-mail: information.for.business@leeds.gov.uk). The Research and Study Library (tel.: 0113 247 8282/3; fax: 0113 247 8426; e-mail: research.and.study@leeds.gov.uk) is strongest in the fields of history and travel. Some relevant material is held in the Gascoigne Collection of books, pamphlets and periodicals relating to military history, which was given to the Library in 1968 (closed access).

Access to collections:

Opening hours: Mon, Wed 0900–2000, Tues, Fri 0900–1730, Thurs 0930–1730, Sat 1000–1700. Public holidays closed.

Enquiries: By telephone, post, fax or e-mail.
Admission: Open to the general public.
Lending: No.
Inter-library loans: Lends to other libraries.
Union record: BLCMP, BLDSC, YHJLS.
Catalogue: BLCMP Talis automated catalogue.
Classification: Dewey Decimal Classification.

Electronic facilities for non-members:

Microcomputing facilities: No.
On-line search facilities: Information for Business will make on-line searches (payment required).
CD-ROM facilities: Yes.
Internet access: Yes (advance booking necessary).
Portable computers: Use permitted; power points available.

Other facilities for non-members:

Photocopying: Yes (payment required).
Microform holdings: Yes.
Reader-printer facilities: Yes (payment required).

65 Trinity and All Saints College, University of Leeds
Library, Brownberrie Lane, Horsforth, Leeds LS18 5HD

Tel.: 0113 283 7100. Holdings enquiries 0113 283 7246
Fax: 0113 283 7200
Web catalogue: http://geoweb.tasc.ac.uk:8000/
WWW: http://www.tasc.ac.uk/iss/lib/newindex.html
Established: 1967

Director of Information Support Service: John Matthews, BA, MSc, ALA
Subject enquiries to: Jessica Laughton, BA, DipInfoStudies, Assistant Librarian, Liaison: School of Modern Languages
Specialist's e-mail address: j.laughton@tasc.ac.uk

Collections:

The Library collects Latin American and Caribbean materials in support of the College's undergraduate teaching in sociology and Spanish. It has approximately 4,000 books and 10 current periodicals, and some audio tapes, slides and video tapes, in the social sciences (chiefly anthropology and sociology), history and literature, with a country focus on Argentina, Bolivia, Brazil, Chile, Colombia, Peru and Venezuela. About 100 volumes are added annually to the collection. The materials are on open access.

Access to collections:

Opening hours: Term: Mon–Thurs 0850–2100, Fri 0850–1800, Sat 1300–1700, Sun 1400–2100. Vacation: Mon–Fri 0910–1645, Sat–Sun closed.

Enquiries: By telephone or e-mail.
Admission: Non-members may apply for reference use of the Library; limited loan facilities are available.
Lending: Yes.
Inter-library loans: Lends to other libraries.
Catalogue: Urica automated catalogue.
Classification: Dewey Decimal Classification.

Electronic facilities for non-members:

Microcomputing facilities: Yes.
On-line search facilities: No.
CD-ROM facilities: No.

Internet access: Yes.
Portable computers: Use permitted; power points available.

Other facilities for non-members:
Photocopying: Yes (payment required).
Microform holdings: Yes.
Reader-printer facilities: Yes (payment required).

Publications:
Guide to Modern Languages Resources.

66 University of Leeds
Brotherton Library, University of Leeds, Leeds LS2 9JT

Tel.: 0113 233 5513
Fax: 0113 233 5561
E-mail: library@library.leeds.ac.uk
Telnet catalogue: lib.leeds.ac.uk
Web catalogue: http://lib.leeds.ac.uk/
WWW: http://www.leeds.ac.uk/library/
Established: 1936

University Librarian and Keeper of the Brotherton Collection: Jan Wilkinson, BA, DipLib, DMS, CNAA, FLA, FRSA
Subject enquiries to: John M. Porter, BA, MA, Senior Assistant Librarian
Specialist's tel.: 0113 233 4985
Specialist's e-mail address: j.m.porter@leeds.ac.uk

Collections:

The Library has collected material on the region since its foundation and now has a substantial collection of mainly twentieth-century Spanish American and Brazilian literature. It also collects literature of the Anglophone Caribbean, and on the history, politics, economics, geography and sociology of the region. About 210 volumes are added each year and five per cent of this is non-current material. The collection is on open access.

Access to collections:

Opening hours: Term: Mon–Thurs 0900–2400, Fri 0930–2100 (opens 0900 in third term before examinations), Sat 1000–1700, Sun 1200–1900. Christmas and Easter Vacations: Mon–Thurs 0900–2100, Fri 0930–2100, Sat 1000–1700, Sun 1200–1900. Summer Vacation: Mon–Thurs 0900–1900, Fri 0930–1700, Sat–Sun closed. Christmas, New Year, Easter and August Bank Holiday closed. Opening hours are under review and it is advisable to consult the website before making a visit.

Enquiries: By telephone, post, fax or e-mail.
Admission: Non-members may be granted access for reference purposes. They should apply in advance to the Head of Reader Services, Pippa Jones (tel.: 0113 233 5573; fax: 0113 233 5539; e-mail: p.f.jones@leeds.ac.uk). Payment may be required.
Lending: Yes (payment required).
Inter-library loans: Lends to other libraries.
Union record: BLDSC, BUCLA, BUCOP, COLALAS, CURL, *Serials in the British Library*, YHJLS.
Catalogues: Manual catalogue (author, classified subject, and alphabetical subject index) for some pre-1991 accessions. Innopac automated catalogue for accessions 1991– .
Classification: Own classification with Library of Congress Subject Headings.

Electronic facilities for non-members:

Microcomputing facilities: No.
On-line search facilities: No.
CD-ROM facilities: Yes.
Internet access: Yes.
Portable computers: Use permitted (after safety inspection); power points available.

Other facilities for non-members:

Photocopying: Yes (payment required).
Microform holdings: Yes.
Reader-printer facilities: Yes.

LEICESTER

67 University of Leicester

Leicester University Library, P.O. Box 248, University Road, Leicester LE1 9QD

Tel.: 0116 252 2042
Fax: 0116 252 2066
E-mail: libdesk@le.ac.uk
Web catalogue: http://library.le.ac.uk/
WWW: http://www.le.ac.uk/library/
Established: 1921

University Librarian: Timothy Hobbs, MA, PhD, DipLib, ALA

Collections:

The Library has a small collection of approximately 2,000 volumes on Latin America and the Caribbean, which is strongest in holdings on Mexico and Brazil. The main subject areas are economics, geography, politics and history. The collection is on open access.

Access to collections:

Opening hours: Term: Mon–Fri 0900–2200, Sat 0900–1800, Sun 1500–2100. Summer Vacation: Mon, Thurs–Fri 0900–1730, Tues–Wed 0900–1900, Sat 0900–1800, Sun closed.

Enquiries: By telephone, post, fax or e-mail.
Admission: Non-members are admitted for reference purposes (written application required).
Lending: Yes.
Inter-library loans: Lends to other libraries.
Union record: BLDSC, BUCLA, BUCOP, COLALAS, EMRLS.
Catalogue: SIRSI Unicorn automated catalogue.
Classification: Dewey Decimal Classification.

Electronic facilities for non-members:

Microcomputing facilities: No.
On-line search facilities: No.
CD-ROM facilities: No.
Internet access: No.

Portable computers: Use permitted; power points available.

Other facilities for non-members:
Photocopying: Yes (payment required).
Microform holdings: Yes.
Reader-printer facilities: Yes.

LIMERICK

68 University of Limerick
Library and Information Services, Limerick, Ireland

Tel.: +353 61 202166
Fax: +353 61 213090
E-mail: libinfo@ul.ie
Web catalogue: http://catalogue.ul.ie:8001/www-bin/www_talis32?www_welcome.tgml
WWW: http://www.ul.ie/~library/
Established: 1970 (1989 as University of Limerick)

Manager, Library Services: Lindsay Mitchell, MA, DipLib, DipComp

Collections:
The Library has a collection of 160,000 books and 2,165 periodicals. Latin American materials form a minor part of the overall stock; there are about 700 books, mainly on economics, history, literature and politics. The collection is on open access.

Access to collections:
Opening hours: Term: Mon–Fri 0830–2100, Sat 0900–1245. Vacation: Mon–Fri 0900–1700, Sat closed.

Enquiries: By telephone, post, fax or e-mail.
Admission: Non-members are admitted for reference purposes (appointment required).
Lending: No.
Inter-library loans: Lends to other libraries.
Catalogue: BLCMP Talis automated catalogue.
Classification: Dewey Decimal Classification.

Electronic facilities for non-members:

Microcomputing facilities: No.
On-line search facilities: No. A fee-based commercial information service is available.
CD-ROM facilities: No.
Internet access: No.
Portable computers: Use permitted; power points available.

Other facilities for non-members:

Photocopying: Yes (payment required).
Microform holdings: Yes.
Reader-printer facilities: Yes (payment required).

LIVERPOOL

69 The Athenaeum
Library, Church Alley, Liverpool L1 3DD

Tel.: 0151 709 7770
Fax: 0151 709 0418
E-mail: library@athena.force9.net
WWW: http://www.athena.force9.co.uk/lib.htm
Established: 1797

Librarian: E.H. Seagroatt, FLA

Collections:

A private academic library with a collection of 70,000 books, 5,000 pamphlets, 40 current periodicals and 500 maps. Special areas covered include Liverpool and Merseyside, early law, and classical literature and fine art. The Latin America and Caribbean material forms a minor part of the overall collection: approximately 200 volumes including some local imprints on the region and grammars of Amerindian languages, and around 100 titles belonging to José Blanco White bequested to the Rev. J.H. Thom. The collections are mainly on open access.

Access to collections:

Opening hours: Members: Mon–Fri 0930–1600. Visitors: Tues, Wed, Thurs 1300–1600 (appointment required).

Enquiries: By post and telephone.
Admission: Non-members should apply in writing.
Lending: No.
Inter-library loans: None.
Catalogues: Sheaf and card catalogues, by author and subject.
Classification: Dewey Decimal Classification.

Electronic facilities for non-members:

Microcomputing facilities: No.
On-line search facilities: No.
CD-ROM facilities: No.
Internet access: No.

Other facilities for non-members:

Photocopying: Yes (payment required).

Publications:

Catalogue of the Library of the Athenaeum, Liverpool (Liverpool: Proprietors of the Athenaeum, 1864).
Neville Carrick and Edward L. Ashton, *The Athenaeum, Liverpool, 1797–1997* (Liverpool: Athenaeum Liverpool, 1997).

70 Liverpool Libraries and Information Services
Central Library, William Brown Street, Liverpool, L3 8EW

Tel.: 0151 233 5829
Fax: 0151 233 5886
WWW: http://www.liverpool.gov.uk/quicklinks/Libraries/lib_index.htm
Established: 1852

Head of Library Services: Paul Catcheside, BA, MIMgmt, ALA
Subject enquiries for archives and local history to: David Stoker, BA, MArAd, Manager, Liverpool Record Office, Local Studies and Family History Services
Archives, local studies and family history tel.: 0151 233 5817
E-mail address: recoffice.central.library@liverpool.gov.uk

Collections:

Liverpool's commercial and cultural relations with Latin America and the Caribbean are reflected in the holdings of the Central Library. There is a strong English-language collection of history, geography, language and literature, a small collection of literature in Spanish and Portuguese, some relevant material in the commercial, technical and art departments and some archival material (e.g. the papers of the Booth Steamship Company) in the Liverpool Record Office and Local Studies Department. The material is predominantly on open access.

Access to collections:

Opening hours: Central Library: Mon–Thurs 0900–1930, Fri 0900–1700, Sat 1000–1600. Public holidays closed.
Archives, local studies and family history: Mon–Thurs 0900–1930, Fri 0900–1700, Sat 0900–1600. Public holidays closed.

Enquiries: By telephone, post, fax or e-mail.
Admission: Open to the general public.
Lending: No.
Inter-library loans: Lends to other libraries.
Union record: BLCMP, BLDSC, BUCOP, COLALAS, LADSIRLAC, NWRLS.
Catalogue: BLCMP Talis automated catalogue.
Classification: Dewey Decimal Classification.

Electronic facilities for non-members:

Microcomputing facilities: Yes, through Connect (payment required).
On-line search facilities: No.
CD-ROM facilities: No.
Internet access: Yes, through Connect (payment required).
Portable computers: Use permitted; power points available in the Reference Library.

Other facilities for non-members:

Photocopying: Yes (payment required).
Microform holdings: Yes.
Reader-printer facilities: Yes (payment required).

71 University of Liverpool

Sydney Jones Library, Chatham Street, Liverpool, L69 3DA

Address for correspondence: Sydney Jones Library, P.O. Box 123, Liverpool, L69 3DA
Tel.: 0151 794 2679
Fax: 0151 794 2681
E-mail: library@liv.ac.uk
Telnet catalogue: lib.liv.ac.uk
Web catalogue: http://library.liv.ac.uk/
WWW: http://www.liv.ac.uk/Library/libhomep.html
Established: 1881

University Librarian: Frances M. Thomson, MA, BLitt
Subject enquiries to: Colin Morgan, BA, Arts Librarian
Specialist's tel.: 0151 794 2684
Specialist's e-mail address: C.Morgan@liverpool.ac.uk

Collections:

The Library began collecting material on Latin America and the Caribbean in the early twentieth century, but greatly increased its acquisitions following the foundation of the Centre for (now Institute of) Latin American Studies in 1966. The collection now includes 37,000 volumes and 66 current and around 250 non-current periodical titles. A few scientific publications are held in the Harold Cohen Library (tel.: 0151 794 5411; fax: 0151 794 5417) but most of the Latin American material is in the Sydney Jones Library. Since 1966 the Library has built up research collections on Peru, Brazil and the Anglophone Caribbean in history, literature and the social sciences, in addition to less intensive acquisitions of mainly English-language material on other countries in the region. Official statistical data are also acquired. In the past ten years special attention has been paid to establishing the basis for research collections in the areas of cinema, the drugs trade, environmental and ecological problems, NGOs and religious movements (especially the growth of Protestantism). Following staff changes there will be more emphasis on Mexico, and on social anthropology and linguistics. A collection of nineteenth-century English-language travel books on Latin America may be consulted in the Special Collections and Archives Reading Room (tel.: 0151 794 2696; fax: 0151 794 2681; e-mail: k.hooper@liverpool.ac.uk). The collections are predominantly on open access.

Access to collections:

Opening hours: Term: Mon–Fri 0900–2130, Sat 0900–1700, Sun 1200–1700. Vacation: Mon–Fri 0900–1700, Sat 0900–1300, Sun closed.

Enquiries: By telephone, post, fax or e-mail.
Admission: Non-members are admitted for reference purposes (application forms available at the enquiry desk).
Lending: Yes (payment required). Written application should be made to Ian Jackson, Head of User Services, Sydney Jones Library, tel.: 0151 794 2687; e-mail: qljacksn@liv.ac.uk.
Inter-library loans: Lends to other libraries.
Union record: BLDSC, BUCLA, CURL, RLG.
Catalogue: Innopac automated catalogue.
Classification: Library of Congress Classification.

Electronic facilities for non-members:

Microcomputing facilities: No.
On-line search facilities: No.
CD-ROM facilities: Yes.
Internet access: No.
Portable computers: Use permitted; power points available, but apply to the enquiry desk.

Other facilities for non-members:

Photocopying: Yes (payment required).
Microform holdings: Yes.
Reader-printer facilities: Yes (payment required).

LONDON

72 ActionAid
Resource Centre, Hamlyn House, Macdonald Road, Archway, London N19 5PG

Tel.: 020 7561 7561
Fax: 020 7281 0899/7263 7599
E-mail: mail@actionaid.org.uk
WWW: http://www.actionaid.org/
Established: 1972

Knowledge Officer: Ami Liggett / Amy Barber
E-mail address: aliggett@actionaid.org.uk

Collections:

ActionAid began as Action in Distress (AID) in 1972, originally set up to help individual children in India and Kenya to receive an education. Today, ActionAid works with over five million of the world's children in more than 30 countries across Latin America, the Caribbean, Asia and Africa; the regional office for Latin America and the Caribbean is based in Guatemala City and works with local partners in Haiti, the Dominican Republic and Brazil. The Resource Centre began acquiring material on Latin America and the Caribbean in 1994; this constitutes a minor part (10–15 per cent) of the collection and numbers 200 books, a large number of internal reports and under 10 current periodicals. Some 60 new titles are acquired annually, about one-tenth of which is non-current material. The collection emphasises geography and the environment, politics, education, anthropology, demography and social welfare, with a country focus on Bolivia, Brazil, Colombia, the Dominican Republic, Guatemala, Haiti, Nicaragua and Peru.

Access to collections:

Opening hours: Tues–Thurs 1000–1700. Closed between Christmas and New Year.

Enquiries: By telephone, post, fax or e-mail.
Admission: By appointment, at least 24 hours in advance. A charge is made.
Lending: No.
Inter-library loans: No.
Catalogue: DB/TextWorks automated catalogue.
Classification: Own classification.

Electronic facilities for non-members:

Microcomputing facilities: No.
On-line search facilities: No.
CD-ROM facilities: No.
Internet access: No.
Portable computers: Use not permitted.

Other facilities for non-members:
Photocopying: Yes (payment required).

Publications:
Current Awareness Bulletin (monthly).

73 Amnesty International, International Secretariat
Amnesty International Library, 1 Easton Street, London WC1X 8DJ

Tel.: 020 7413 5500
Fax: 020 7956 1157
E-mail: amnestyis@amnesty.org
WWW: http://www.amnesty.org/
Established: 1961

Director of Information Resources: G. Bennett, MA
Subject enquiries to: Elizabeth Reiner, BA, DipLIS, ALA, Americas Information Officer

Collections:

The Library began collecting Latin American and Caribbean material in 1977, and covers all aspects of human rights in the region. It now holds 1,500 books and 160 current periodical titles (two years only are kept). Approximately 100 volumes are added each year (all current material). There is a special collection of Organization of American States material. Videos are also held. The Latin America collection is a major part of overall holdings, accounting for twenty per cent of the total collection. It is predominantly on closed access, dispersed within the Research Department. Archival material, including microfiche material, has been transferred to the International Institute for Social History (IISH), Amsterdam (tel.: +31 20668 5866; http://www.iisg.nl).

Access to collections:

Opening hours: Mon–Fri 0930–1730.

Enquiries: By telephone, post, fax or e-mail.
Admission: Visitors are admitted for reference use by appointment only. Please apply in writing to the Americas Information Officer.
Lending: No.

Inter-library loans: No.
Catalogue: Heritage automated catalogue.
Classification: Own classification.

Electronic facilities for non-members:

Microcomputing facilities: No.
On-line search facilities: No.
CD-ROM facilities: No.
Internet access: No.
Portable computers: Use permitted; power points available.

Other facilities for non-members:

Photocopying: Yes, to a limited extent.

74 Andes Press Agency
26 Padbury Court, London E2 7EH

Tel.: 020 7613 5417
Fax: 020 7739 3159
E-mail: library@andespressagency.com
WWW: http://www.andespressagency.com
Established: 1983

Subject enquiries to: Val Baker

Collections:

A commercial picture library updated with regular contributions from photographers around the world. The black-and-white and colour photographs cover twentieth-century social, religious, political, economic and environmental issues worldwide. There is a specialist collection of images on Latin America and the Caribbean, covering social documentary issues and travel subjects. There are large collections from the following countries: Bolivia, Brazil, Chile, Mexico, Panama and Peru. Historical black-and-white photographs of Panama dating from 1976–79 include the signing of the Torrijos—Carter Panama Canal Treaty.

Access to collections:

Opening hours: Mon–Fri 0900–1800.

Enquiries: By telephone, post or e-mail.
Admission: By appointment.
Search/service fee: Negotiable. Commissions undertaken.
Lending: Pictures are supplied for publication purposes only.
Catalogue: Subject list available.

Electronic facilities for non-members:

Microcomputing facilities: No.
On-line search facilities: No.
CD-ROM facilities: No.
Internet access: No.
Portable computers: Use not permitted.

Other facilities for non-members:

Copying: None permitted.

Publications:

Brochure.

75 *Anti-Slavery International*

Library, Thomas Clarkson House, The Stableyard, Broomgrove Road, London SW9 9TL

Tel.: 020 7501 8939
Fax: 020 7738 4110
WWW: http://www.antislavery.org/
Established: 1839

Librarian: Jeff Howarth, BA, DipInfStud
Librarian's e-mail address: j.howarth@antislavery.org

Collections:

Anti-Slavery International is a research and campaigning organisation in the areas of bonded labour, child and migrant labour, other forms of modern slavery, prostitution, and indigenous peoples. Since its inception in 1839, the Reference Library has accumulated 3,000 books, a large number of periodicals (including *Anti-Slavery Reporter* 1825– and *Aborigines' Friend* 1839–1909), a unique collection of over 600 tracts and pamphlets covering both abolitionist and pro-slavery arguments worldwide 1760s–1860s, reports on ASI's research and campaigns 1892–1971, photographs and video recordings, and press cuttings. Relevant documents of the United Nations and the International Labour Office are held, as well as Anti-Slavery reports and submissions to the United Nations. There is also an archive of personal papers. The Latin American and Caribbean material — which is not kept separate from the rest of the collection and is predominantly on open access — forms a minor part of the collection and consists of some 50 books and 10 current periodicals, a few videos and microforms, and a small amount of manuscript material. The subjects covered are missionary and other expeditions in Latin America, slavery, street children and child labour. There is a geographical focus on Brazil, Haiti and the Dominican Republic.

Access to collections:

Opening hours: Mon–Fri 1000–1700.

Enquiries: By telephone, post, fax or e-mail.
Admission: It is advisable to telephone before a visit.
Lending: No.
Inter-library loans: No.
Union record: BLDSC, LASER, NWRLS.
Catalogue: CDS/Isis automated catalogue.
Classification: HURIDOCS; local classification.

Electronic facilities for non-members:

Microcomputing facilities: No.
On-line search facilities: No.
CD-ROM facilities: No.
Internet access: Yes.
Portable computers: Battery-powered portable computers may be used.

Other facilities for non-members:

Photocopying: Yes (payment required).
Microform holdings: Yes.
Reader-printer facilities: No.

76 Association of Commonwealth Universities (ACU)
Reference Library, 36 Gordon Square, London WC1H 0PF

Tel.: 020 7380 6729
Fax: 020 7387 2655
E-mail: info@acu.ac.uk
WWW: http://www.acu.ac.uk/
Established: 1913

Librarian: Nick Mulhern, MA, DipLib

Collections:

The Library has an estimated total stock of 18,500 books and pamphlets in addition to numerous periodical titles. It collects materials relating to higher education: university calendars, prospectuses, annual and research reports, newsletters and gazettes, as well as relevant government publications, higher education reports and statistics. A small part of the collection relates to higher education in the Commonwealth Caribbean (mainly Barbados, Jamaica and Trinidad) and Guyana. Much of the material is acquired by exchange. The collection is predominantly on closed access.

Access to collections:

Opening hours: Mon–Fri 1000–1300, 1400–1730.

Enquiries: By telephone, post, fax or e-mail.
Admission: Open to the general public for reference purposes (appointment recommended to ensure availability of material).
Lending: No.
Inter-library loans: No.
Catalogue: CAIRS–TMS automated catalogue.
Classification: Universal Decimal Classification (modified).

Electronic facilities for non-members:

Microcomputing facilities: No.
On-line search facilities: No.
CD-ROM facilities: No.
Internet access: No.
Portable computers: Use permitted.

Other facilities for non-members:
Photocopying: Yes (payment required).

77 Bank of England
The Information Centre, Threadneedle Street, London EC2R 8AH

Tel.: 020 7601 4846/4715
Fax: 020 7601 4356
E-mail: infocentre@bankofengland.co.uk
WWW: http://www.bankofengland.co.uk/
Established: 1931

Librarian: P.A. Hope, MA, MSc, DipLib, ALA

Collections:
The Library collects material on banking, economics, finance and business. Material on Latin America and the Caribbean forms a minor part of the collection: 4,800 volumes on Latin America, 2,400 on the Caribbean; 20–30 volumes are added each year. There are 16 current periodical titles. The collection is strong in central bank annual reports. Some statistical and trade material is held. The collection is predominantly on open access.

Access to collections:
Opening hours: Mon–Fri 0930–1730.

Enquiries: By telephone, post, fax or e-mail.
Admission: Non-members are admitted for reference purposes (written application required).
Lending: No.
Inter-library loans: Lends to other libraries.
Catalogues: Pre-1985 material on microfiche catalogue. Current material on Soutron automated catalogue.
Classification: Dewey Decimal Classification (modified and extended).

Electronic facilities for non-members:
Microcomputing facilities: No.
On-line search facilities: No.

CD-ROM facilities: Yes.
Internet access: No.
Portable computers: Use permitted; power points available.

Other facilities for non-members:

Photocopying: Yes (payment required).
Microform holdings: Yes.
Reader-printer facilities: Yes (payment required).

78 Birkbeck College, University of London

Birkbeck College Library, Malet Street, London WC1E 7HX

Tel.: 020 7631 6239. Holdings enquiries 020 7631 6062
Fax: 020 7631 6066
E-mail: library-help@bbk.ac.uk
Web catalogue: http://webpac.lib.bbk.ac.uk/webpac/
WWW: http://www.bbk.ac.uk/lib/
Established: 1823
Librarian: Philippa Dolphin, MA, DipLib, ALA
Subject enquiries to: Ken Mackley, BA, CertEd, DipLib, Subject Librarian, Languages, Literature and Philosophy
Specialist's tel.: 020 7631 6062
Specialist's e-mail address: k.mackley@bbk.ac.uk

Collections:

Latin American and Caribbean materials form a minor part of the collections. Approximately 3,000 books and 20 current periodical titles are held. The Malet Street Library covers all subjects except economics, geography, and business and management, which are held in the Gresse Street Library (7–15 Gresse Street, London W1P 2LL; tel.: 020 7631 6492). There is a special emphasis on the literature of exploration, notably the *Crónicas de América* series. The material is predominantly on open access.

Access to collections:

Opening hours: Term: Mon–Thurs 1000–2230 (Gresse St 2130), Fri 1100–2230 (Gresse St 2130), Sat 1000–2000 (Gresse St 1700), Sun 1000–2000 (Gresse St closed). Christmas and Summer Vacations: Mon–Thurs 1000–2000, Fri 1100–2000, Sat 1200–1700 (Gresse St closed), Sun closed. Easter Vacation: Mon–Thurs 1000–2100 (Gresse St 2000), Fri 1100–2100 (Gresse St 2000), Sat 1000–2000 (Gresse St 1700), Sun 1000–2000 (Gresse St closed).

Enquiries: By telephone.
Admission: Non-members are admitted for reference purposes (payment required). Members of United Kingdom higher education institutions are admitted during vacations free of charge.
Lending: Yes (payment required).
Inter-library loans: No.
Union record: BLDSC, BUCLA, University of London Union List of Serials.
Catalogue: Dynix Horizon automated catalogue.
Classification: Bliss Bibliographic Classification (for material acquired before July 1996), Dewey Decimal Classification (from July 1996).

Electronic facilities for non-members:

Microcomputing facilities: No.
On-line search facilities: No.
CD-ROM facilities: No.
Internet access: Yes.
Portable computers: Use permitted; power points available.

Other facilities for non-members:

Photocopying: Yes (payment required).
Microform holdings: Yes.
Reader-printer facilities: Yes (payment required).

79 *British Broadcasting Corporation (BBC)*

BBC Information and Archives Research Services, Music, Room G001, Broadcasting House, London W1A 1AA

Tel.: 020 7765 2195
Fax: 020 7765 2741
E-mail: jane.plaster@bbc.co.uk
Established: 1922

Operational coordinator, Research Centre: Jane Plaster

Collections:

The Library's holdings include 1,200,000 commercial music recordings and 4,500,000 items of sheet music. There are musical scores of works by major Latin American classical composers, a small number of books (including *Composers of the Americas*, published by the Organization of American States), and the journal *Revista de Música Latinoamericana*, 1980–95 (on microfiche). Latin American and Caribbean popular titles form a small proportion of titles in the sheet music collection and there is a small collection of reference sources on popular music. The collections are predominantly on closed access.

Access to collections:

Opening hours: Mon–Fri 0930–1930, Sat 0930–1730. Public holidays closed.

Enquiries: By telephone, post, fax or e-mail (payment required).
Admission: Non-members are admitted for reference purposes (appointment and payment required).
Lending: Yes (at Librarian's discretion).
Inter-library loans: Lends to other libraries (at Librarian's discretion).
Union record: BLCMP.
Catalogues: CAIRS automated catalogue (sound recordings), PANDORA automated catalogue (sheet music), BLCMP Talis automated catalogue (books).
Classification: Dewey Decimal Classification.

Electronic facilities for non-members:

Microcomputing facilities: No.
On-line search facilities: Yes (payment required).
CD-ROM facilities: Yes (payment required).
Internet access: No.
Portable computers: Use not permitted.

Other facilities for non-members:

Photocopying: Yes (payment required).
Microform holdings: Yes.
Reader-printer facilities: Yes (payment required).

Publications:

Song Catalogue (London: British Broadcasting Corporation, 1966), 4 vols (BBC Music Library catalogues).

Choral and Opera Catalogue (London: British Broadcasting Corporation, 1967), 2 vols (BBC Music Library catalogues).

Orchestral Catalogue (London: British Broadcasting Corporation, 1982), 4 vols (BBC Music Library catalogues).

BBC Popular Music Index (London: BBC Data, 1985), 2051 microfiches.

80 British Film Institute (*BFI*)

BFI National Library, 21 Stephen Street, London W1P 2LN

Tel.: 020 7255 1444
Fax: 020 7436 2338
E-mail: library@bfi.org.uk
Web catalogue: http://www.bfi.org.uk/nationallibrary/olib/index.html
WWW: http://www.bfi.org.uk/nationallibrary/
Established: 1933

Head of Library Services: Ray Templeton, BA, DipLib, ALA, FRSA

Collections:

The Library has collected material on Latin American and Caribbean film and television since the 1940s. The acquisitions policy limits purchases to publications which cover the national output, excluding those which mainly cover international film and television. The Library now holds 200 books, and 10 current and 30–50 non-current periodical titles; approximately 15 volumes are added each year. Newspaper clippings and publicity material for all Latin American films released in the United Kingdom, or shown in major festivals, are also held. Periodicals are indexed by film and television programme title, personality and subject, giving a good overall coverage of Latin American and Caribbean output. The collections are on closed access.

Access to collections:

Opening hours: Mon, Fri 1030–1730, Tues, Thurs 1030–2000, Wed 1300–2000. Public holidays closed.

Enquiries: By telephone, post, fax or e-mail (payment required for longer enquiries).
Admission: Non-members are admitted for reference purposes (payment required).
Lending: No.
Inter-library loans: No, but does supply photocopies of articles and chapters.
Union record: ARLIS, BUCOP.
Catalogues: OLib automated catalogue and SIFT (Summary of Information on Film and Television) on-line database.
Classification: Universal Decimal Classification.

Electronic facilities for non-members:

Microcomputing facilities: No.
On-line search facilities: Yes (payment required).
CD-ROM facilities: Yes.
Internet access: No.
Portable computers: Use permitted; power points available.

Other facilities for non-members:

Photocopying: Yes (payment required).
Microform holdings: Yes.
Reader-printer facilities: Yes (payment required).

Publications:

Information from the BFI SIFT (Summary of Information on Film and Television) database is published in *Film Index International* (Cambridge: Chadwyck-Healey), CD-ROM.

81 British Film Institute (*BFI*)

National Film and Television Archive, 21 Stephen Street, London W1P 2LN

Tel.: 020 7255 1444. Holdings enquiries 020 7255 1444 ext. 2319
Fax: 020 7580 7503
E-mail: olwen.terris@bfi.org.uk
WWW: http://www.bfi.org/collections/about/
Established: 1935

Chief Cataloguer: Olwen Terris

Collections:

The Archive has collected Latin American films and video recordings since its foundation. It now holds over 20 feature films and 16 documentaries produced in the region, together with over 300 documentaries on Latin America and the Caribbean produced outside the region. Most of the material is held at the J. Paul Getty Conservation Centre, Berkhamsted, Hertfordshire, while nitrate film, which is being copied onto modern safety film stock, is kept at Gaydon, Warwickshire.

Access to collections:

Opening hours: Mon–Fri 1000–1730. Public holidays closed.

Enquiries: By telephone, post, fax or e-mail.
Admission: Non-members are admitted for reference purposes.
Lending: No.
Inter-library loans: No.
Catalogue: SIFT (Summary of Information on Film and Television) online database.
Classification: Universal Decimal Classification for documentaries and news films.

Electronic facilities for non-members:

Microcomputing facilities: No.
On-line search facilities: No.
CD-ROM facilities: No.
Internet access: No.
Portable computers: Use permitted; power points available.

Other facilities for non-members:

Photocopying: Yes (payment required)

82 British Film Institute (*BFI*)

BFI Stills, Posters and Designs, 21 Stephen Street, London W1P 2LN

Tel.: 020 7957 4797
Fax: 020 7323 9260
E-mail: stills.films@bfi.org.uk
WWW: http://www.bfi.org.uk/collections/stills/index.html

Established: 1950

Senior Stills Officer: Vanessa Marshall

Collections:

The collection includes over 7,000,000 stills and colour slides, 15,000 film posters and 2,000 production and costume designs. Latin American and Caribbean material forms a minor part of the collection: approximately 3,000 stills, 130 posters and a small number of slides. The material is on closed access.

Access to collections:

Opening hours: Tues–Thurs 1100–1600. Public holidays closed.

Enquiries: By telephone, post, fax or e-mail.
Admission: Non-members are admitted for reference purposes (appointment required).
Lending: No.
Inter-library loans: No.
Catalogue: SIFT (Summary of Information on Film and Television) online database.
Classification: Material arranged in alphabetical order of original title.

Electronic facilities for non-members:

Microcomputing facilities: No.
On-line search facilities: No.
CD-ROM facilities: No.
Internet access: No.
Portable computers: Use not permitted.

Other facilities for non-members:

Photocopying: No.

Publications:

National Film Archive, *Catalogue of Stills, Posters, and Designs* (London: British Film Institute, 1982).

83 British Library, National Sound Archive

The Recorded Sound Information Service, 96 Euston Road, London NW1 2DB

Tel.: 020 7412 7440
Fax: 020 7412 7441
E-mail: nsa@bl.uk
Web catalogue: http://www.bl.uk/collections/sound-archive/cat.html
WWW: http://www.bl.uk/collections/sound-archive/nsa.html
Established: 1948 (as the British Institute of Recorded Sound)

Director: A.C. Jewitt
Curator, International Music Collection: Janet Topp Fargion
Specialist's tel.: 020 7412 7427
Specialist's e-mail address: NSA-IMC@bl.uk
Curator, Jazz: Andrew Simons
Specialist's tel.: 020 7412 7434
Specialist's e-mail address: NSA-Jazz@bl.uk
Curator, Popular Music: Andy Linehan
Specialist's tel.: 020 7412 7433
Specialist's e-mail address: NSA-Pop@bl.uk
Curator, Oral History: Dr Rob Perks
Specialist's tel.: 020 7412 7405
Specialist's e-mail address: NSA-Oral@bl.uk
Curator, Literature and Drama: Toby Oakes
Specialist's tel.: 020 7412 7436
Specialist's e-mail address: NSA-Drama@bl.uk
Curator, Wildlife Sounds: Richard Ranft
Specialist's tel.: 020 7412 7402
Specialist's e-mail address: NSA-Wildsound@bl.uk

Collections:

The Recorded Sound Information Service is based in the Humanities 2 Reading Room of the British Library. A large part of the collection of reference works, magazines, periodicals, discographies and record company catalogues is available on open access. A small number of monographs and periodicals relate to Latin America and the Caribbean. The Listening & Viewing Service is based in the Rare Books and Music Reading Room. An appointment is necessary, whether for individual or group listening. The Latin American and Caribbean collections include recordings of classical

Electronic facilities for non-members:

Microcomputing facilities: No.
On-line search facilities: No.
CD-ROM facilities: Yes.
Internet access: Yes.
Portable computers: Use permitted; power points available.

Other facilities for non-members:

Photocopying: Copies can be ordered in the Reading Rooms, or by post if full publication details can be provided (payment required).
Microform holdings: Yes.
Reader-printer facilities: Yes (payment required).

Publications:

Catalogue of the Newspaper Library, Colindale (London: British Museum Publications for the British Library, 1975), 8 vols.

85 British Library, Reader Services & Collection Development
96 Euston Road, London NW1 2DB

Tel.: 020 7412 7000. Admissions 020 7412 7677
Fax: 020 7412 7784. Admissions 020 7412 7794
E-mail: Hispanic Section hisp-enquiries@bl.uk; Admissions reader-admissions@bl.uk
Web catalogue: http://blpc.bl.uk/
WWW: http://www.bl.uk/collections/westeuropean/hispanic.html
Established: 1753 (1973 as the British Library)

Director General (Collections & Services): David Bradbury, MA, ALA
Head of the Hispanic Section: Geoffrey R. West, BA, MA, PhD
Subject enquiries to:
Hispanic Caribbean, Central America, excluding Mexico: Geoffrey R. West, BA, MA, PhD
Specialist's tel.: 020 7412 7569
Mexico, northern South America: Alison M. Hill, BA, PGCE, DipLib
Specialist's tel.: 020 7412 7569
Brazil, Southern Cone, Hispanic Collections, 1501–1850: Barry Taylor, BA, PhD
Specialist's tel.: 020 7412 7576

Specialist's e-mail: hisp-enquiries@bl.uk
Anglophone Caribbean: C. Holden, BSc, DipLib
Specialist's tel.: 020 7412 7597
Science and Technology tel.: 020 7412 7494/6
Life Sciences tel.: 020 7412 7288
Business Information Service tel.: 020 7412 7454
Business Information Service fax: 020 7412 7453
The British Library – Lloyds TSB Business Line: 020 7412 7454/7977

Collections:

Hispanic Section. Although it has no separate collection specifically devoted to Latin America, the British Library, Reader Services & Collection Development, has undoubtedly the largest and most significant holdings on the area in the British Isles and has been collecting material since its foundation in 1753. The Library has publications from the earliest times on most topics and seeks to develop an all-round collection of contemporary material from all countries, in addition to British imprints, received by copyright deposit. Currently, its collection development policy stresses language, literary texts and criticism, history (social, political and economic), contemporary politics and society, folk traditions, popular culture, and women's and gay studies. Among its historical holdings, it has a particularly good collection of early Mexican and Peruvian books, and strong holdings on the Independence movements of the early nineteenth century. The Library takes well over 600 serials from Latin America and subscribes to 17 newspapers, which are kept in the Newspaper Library at Colindale (no. 84). Government publications are well represented in the Official Publications and Social Sciences reading area. As well as substantial collections of government publications received from foreign states, some official publications originally received in British government department libraries have been transferred to the Library. As the national collection, the Library is outstandingly strong in materials on the former British colonies and territories in the Caribbean and on the mainland of Latin America. Many thousands of both current and retrospective titles are added annually to the collections. About two per cent of acquisitions are of non-current material. The Library also maintains a number of special collections, which include relevant material. These are available in the appropriate sections: the Manuscript Department, Philatelic Collections, Music Library and Map Library.

Science & Technology. The combined Science, Technology and Business (STB) collections constitute the national library for modern science, technology and commerce and are one of the best reference collections in the field in the western world. The collections cover (a) the life sciences and technologies: biotechnology, medicine and agriculture, mathematics, astronomy and earth sciences; (b) engineering, physical and industrial sciences and technologies. The Latin American holdings, which are not kept separate, are relatively small and relevant material is mostly contained in the general periodical literature. Research-level Latin American periodicals are acquired if they fall within the Library's field of interest. STB acquires books on the zoology, botany, agriculture and geology of Latin American countries where the country of publication is recognised as having specialised knowledge. An increasingly large range of material is available on CD-ROM.

Business Information Service. The BIS holds the most comprehensive collection of business information literature in the United Kingdom. Business literature published outside the United Kingdom is collected selectively. BIS covers the following service sectors: financial services, energy, environment, transport, and food and drink. It provides information on companies, markets and products, and access to online and CD-ROM databases through its research service. BIS holds an extensive collection of Latin American patents and trademarks.

Recorded Sound. Sound recordings are held in the National Sound Archive (no. 83).

Library & Information Science. The British Library Information Sciences Service (previously Library Association Library) was transferred to the Euston Road site in January 1999. The collection aims at worldwide and comprehensive coverage of librarianship and information science, although material on and from Latin America, which has been collected since 1933, is acquired very selectively. Emphasis in current acquisitions is on recent trends in information technology. Biannual lists of selected acquisitions in librarianship and information science are posted on the Library's web page.

Access to collections:

Opening hours: Mon 1000–2000, Tues–Thurs 0930–2000, Fri–Sat 0930–1700. Maps and Manuscripts: Mon 1000–1700, Tues–Sat

0930–1700. Business Information Service Research Service: Mon–Fri 0930–1300, 1400–1700.

Enquiries: By telephone, post, fax or e-mail.
Admission: Bona fide researchers (usually over 18) on application at the Reader Admissions Office (tel.: 020 7412 7677; fax: 020 7412 7794; e-mail: reader-admissions@bl.uk) Mon 1000–1800, Tues–Thurs 0930–1800, Fri–Sat 0930–1630.
Lending: No.
Inter-library loans: Via British Library Document Supply Service (BLDSC, no. 10).
Union record: BLDSC, BUCLA, BUCOP, COLALAS, *Serials in the British Library*.
Catalogue: British Library Public Catalogue in-house automated catalogue.
Classification: Dewey Decimal Classification for open-access material.

Electronic facilities:

Microcomputing facilities: No.
On-line search facilities: Only in STB (payment required).
CD-ROM facilities: Yes.
Internet access: Yes.
Portable computers: Use permitted; power points available.

Other facilities:

Photocopying: Yes (payment required).
Microform holdings: Yes.
Reader-printer facilities: Yes (payment required).

Publications:

The British Library General Catalogue of Printed Books to 1975 (London: Bingley & Saur, 1979–87), 360 vols.
The British Library General Catalogue of Printed Books, 1976 to 1982 (London: Saur, 1985), 50 vols.
The British Library General Catalogue of Printed Books, 1982 to 1985 (London: Saur, 1986), 26 vols. [Also available on microfiches; 175 fiches.]
General Catalogue of Printed Books, 1976–1985 (1986), 470 fiches.
The British Library General Subject Catalogue, 1975–1985 (London: Saur, 1986–), 75 vols. [Also available on microfiches; 1466 fiches.]

Subject Index of Modern Books, 1946–1950 [4 vols]; *1951–1955* [6 vols]; *1961–1970* [12 vols]; *1971–1975* [15 vols].

Henry Thomas (ed.), *Short-title Catalogues of Portuguese and of Spanish- American Books Printed before 1601 Now in the British Museum* (London: B. Quaritch, 1926).

V.F. Goldsmith, *A Short Title Catalogue of Spanish and Portuguese Books, 1601–1700 in the Library of the British Museum* (*the British Library, Reference Division*) (Folkestone: Dawsons, 1974).

Serials in the British Library (London: National Bibliographic Service, 1981–). Quarterly with annual cumulation.

86 British Museum
Department of Ethnography Library

Address until 2003: Museum of Mankind Library, Reading Room, Ethnography Department of the British Museum, 6 Burlington Gardens, London W1X 2EX
Tel.: 020 7323 8031
Fax: 020 7323 8013
E-mail: ethnography@thebritishmuseum.ac.uk
WWW: http://www.rai.anthropology.org.uk/mom/mom.html
Established: 1843

Acting Senior Librarian: Sheila MacKie, BA, DipLib, ALA
RAI Library Officer: Beverly Emery
Tel.: 020 7323 8052
Fax: 020 7383 4235
E-mail: rai@cix.compulink.co.uk

Collections:

The Library of the Royal Anthropological Institute (RAI) of Great Britain and Ireland was transferred to the British Museum by deed of gift in 1976 and incorporated into the library of the Department of Ethnography as the Museum of Mankind Library. The Library also includes the Sir Eric Thompson Library of 2,000 items on Mesoamerican archaeology, with an emphasis on the Maya. The total collection includes 110,000 volumes and 1,400 current periodicals. The RAI maintains a close connection with the Library, donates books and periodicals to enlarge the collection and supplies its journals in exchange for journals sent to the Library. Grants from the William Buller Fagg Charitable Trust have benefited the acquisitions programme. Latin American and Caribbean material has been collected since 1843 and the collection of material relating to the region includes an estimated 15,000 books and pamphlets, and 100 current and 400 non-current periodical titles; 900 volumes are added each year. The Library also collects theses, manuscripts, microform material and maps. Current acquisitions are strongest on the archaeology and ethnography of Mesoamerica. Subjects covered in the collection include physical anthropology, archaeology, cultural and social anthropology, ethnography, folklore and linguistics. The manuscript and archive collections of the Royal Anthropological Institute of Great Britain and Ireland share the Reading Room with the Library. The collections are on closed access.

Access to collections:

Opening hours: Mon–Fri 1000–1645. Public holidays closed.

Enquiries: By telephone, post, fax or e-mail.
Admission: Non-members are admitted for reference purposes if the material required is unavailable elsewhere (appointment required).
Lending: No.
Inter-library loans: No.
Union record: BLDSC, BUCLA, COLALAS.
Catalogues: Author, classified subject and tribal card catalogues for accessions until December 1988. Automated catalogue from January 1989.
Classification: Bliss Bibliographic Classification.

Electronic facilities for non-members:

Microcomputing facilities: No.
On-line search facilities: Yes (payment required).
CD-ROM facilities: No.
Internet access: No.
Portable computers: Use permitted; power points available.

Other facilities for non-members:

Photocopying: Yes (payment required).
Microform holdings: Yes.
Reader-printer facilities: No.

Publications:

The Museum of Mankind Library Catalogue on Microfiche (Bath: Mindata in association with the Trustees of the British Museum, 1990), 763 fiches.

Index to Current Periodicals Received in the Library (London: Royal Anthropological Institute, 1963–68).

Anthropological Index to Current Periodicals in the Library (London: Royal Anthropological Institute, 1968–95).

Anthropological Index Online (London: Royal Anthropological Institute, 1997–), http://lucy.ukc.ac.uk/AIO.html

87 British Standards Institution (BSI)
BSI Library, 389 Chiswick High Road, London W4 4AL

Tel.: 020 8996 7004
Fax: 020 8996 7005
E-mail: library@bsi-global.com
WWW: http://www.bsi-global.com/Resource+Centre/BSI+Library/
Established: 1901

Librarian: Mary E. Yates, BSc, DipLib

Collections:

The Library holds catalogues of standards from Latin American and Caribbean standards organisations, selected standards and some related technical legislation. The collection is on open access.

Access to collections:

Opening hours: Mon–Fri 0900–1700. Public holidays closed.

Enquiries: By telephone, post, fax or e-mail (payment required for longer enquiries).
Admission: Non-members are admitted for reference purposes (payment required).
Lending: No.
Inter-library loans: No.
Catalogue: Alphabetical subject card catalogue and an optical coincidence punched card system of information retrieval.
Classification: None; the general arrangement is alphabetical by country of origin.

Electronic facilities for non-members:
Microcomputing facilities: Yes (payment required).
On-line search facilities: Yes (payment required).
CD-ROM facilities: Yes (payment required).
Internet access: Yes.
Portable computers: Use not permitted.

Other facilities for non-members:
Photocopying: Yes (payment required).
Microform holdings: Yes.
Reader-printer facilities: No.

88 Catholic Central Library
Lancing Street, London NW1 1ND

Tel.: 020 7383 4333
Fax: 020 7388 6675
E-mail: librarian@catholic-library.org.uk
WWW: http://www.catholic-library.org.uk/
Established: 1959

Librarian: Joan Bond

Collections:

The Library has a collection of 65,000 books and periodicals on theology, spirituality, biography and history, including a small number of books in English concerning the Church and Christian sociology in Latin America. The collection is predominantly on open access.

Access to collections:

Opening hours: Mon–Tues, Thurs–Fri 1030–1700, Wed 1030–1900.

Enquiries: By telephone, post or e-mail.
Admission: Temporary or annual membership available (payment required).
Lending: Ordinary annual members have borrowing rights.
Inter-library loans: Does not lend to other libraries.
Union record: BLDSC.

Catalogues: Author, title, alphabetical subject and classified subject card catalogues. Automated catalogue in preparation.
Classification: Dewey Decimal Classification.

Electronic facilities for non-members:

Microcomputing facilities: No.
On-line search facilities: No.
CD-ROM facilities: Available shortly.
Internet access: No.
Portable computers: Use permitted; power points available.

Other facilities for non-members:

Photocopying: Yes (payment required).

89 Catholic Institute for International Relations (CIIR)
Library, Unit 3, Canonbury Yard, 190a New North Road, London N1 7BJ

Address for correspondence: Freepost ND 6366, London N1 7BR
Tel.: 020 7354 0883
Fax: 020 7359 0017
E-mail: ciir@ciir.org
WWW: http://www.ciir.org/
Established: 1940

Communications manager: Miranda Godfrey
E-mail address: miranda@ciir.org

Collections:

CIIR is a charity that builds links between people in the poor and rich worlds working for local and global change; its advocacy programme co-operates with partner organisations in Latin America and elsewhere to influence national policy and decision-making. CIIR's technical assistance programme, International Co-operation for Development (ICD), is active in seven countries of Latin America: the Dominican Republic, Ecuador, El Salvador, Haiti, Honduras, Nicaragua and Peru. The Library has approximately 2,000 volumes on the politics, economics and sociology of Latin America and the Caribbean, with an emphasis on social movements, local communities and religion (particularly the activities of the Church in the region, and liberation theology).

Access to collections:

Opening hours: Mon–Fri 0930–1730.

Enquiries: By telephone, post, fax or e-mail.
Admission: By appointment.
Lending: No.
Inter-library loans: No.
Catalogue: Manual catalogue under construction.
Classification: Own classification.

Electronic facilities for non-members:

Microcomputing facilities: No.
On-line search facilities: No.
CD-ROM facilities: Yes.
Internet access: Yes.
Portable computers: Use permitted; power points available.

Other facilities for non-members:

Photocopying: Yes (payment required).

90 Centre for Information on Language Teaching and Research (CILT)
CILT Resources Library, 20 Bedfordbury, London WC2N 4LB

Tel.: 020 7379 5110
Fax: 020 7379 5082
E-mail: library@cilt.org.uk
WWW: http://www.cilt.org.uk/
Established: 1966

Librarian: John Hawkins, BA, PGCE, DipLib

Collections:

CILT's central aim is 'to promote a greater national capability in languages'. One of its main objectives is to support language professionals through a range of activities: training, publications, information and advice. The Resources Library is open to all individuals concerned with the study, learning and teaching of languages. It holds teaching resources (including text, audio, video and ICT), research facilities (including periodicals, abstracting and indexing journals, and the CILT register of current research projects in language teaching and learning), ICT, satellite TV, video and audio facilities, a collection of Computer Assisted Language Learning software, facilities for listening to audio cassettes and on-line access to the Internet. There is a comprehensive collection of current Spanish-language teaching and learning materials (including some titles on the teaching of languages in Latin America and some Latin American Spanish courses) and a small section on the Portuguese language. The collections are on open access.

Access to collections:

Opening hours: Mon–Fri 1030–1700, Wed 1030–2000, Sat 1000–1300, Sun closed during term time. Christmas to New Year and public holidays closed.

Enquiries: By telephone, post, fax or e-mail.
Admission: Open to the general public.
Lending: No.
Inter-library loans: No.
Catalogue: EOS International GOPAC automated catalogue.
Classification: Own classification.

Electronic facilities:

Microcomputing facilities: No.
On-line search facilities: No.
CD-ROM facilities: Yes.
Internet access: Yes.
Portable computers: Power points for the use of portable computers to be installed.

Other facilities for non-members:

Photocopying: Yes (payment required).
Microform holdings: Yes.
Reader-printer facilities: No.

91 Chartered Institute of Bankers (CIB)
IFS Information Service, 90 Bishopsgate, London EC2N 4DQ

Tel.: 020 7444 7100
Fax: 020 7444 7109

E-mail: library@ifslearning.com
Web catalogue: http://www.ifsis.org.uk/catalogue.htm
WWW: http://www.ifsis.org.uk/libab.htm
Established: 1879

Manager, IFS Information Service: Susana Vazquez, BA

Collections:

The CIB Library & Information Service (now IFS Information Service) was founded in 1879 and has built up one of the most comprehensive collections in the United Kingdom on banking, finance and financial services, including 30,000 books, 200 current periodicals, annual reports from banks and central banks, press cuttings and subject files on banking and related subjects. Material on Latin America and the Caribbean forms a minor part of the overall stock. The collection is on open access. The Library also has a Business Research & Information Service, which provides a professional fee-based service for companies and consultants.

Access to collections:

Opening hours: Mon, Wed, Fri 0900–1700, Tues, Thurs 0900–1800. Public holidays closed.

Enquiries: By telephone, post, fax or e-mail (payment required).
Admission: Non-members are admitted for reference purposes (payment required).
Lending: Yes (payment required).
Inter-library loans: Lends to other libraries.
Catalogue: SIRSI Unicorn automated catalogue.
Classification: Universal Decimal Classification.

Electronic facilities for non-members:

Microcomputing facilities: No.
On-line search facilities: Yes (payment required).
CD-ROM facilities: Yes.
Internet access: Yes.
Portable computers: Use permitted; power points available.

Other facilities for non-members:

Photocopying: Yes (payment required).

92 Chartered Insurance Institute
Library, 20 Aldermanbury, London, EC2V 7HY

Tel.: 020 7417 4416. Holdings enquiries 020 7417 4415
Fax: 020 7972 0110
E-mail: library@cii.co.uk
WWW: http://www.ciilo.org
Established: 1897

Head of Libraries and Information: Robert Cunnew, BA, FLA

Collections:

The Library is the largest insurance library in the United Kingdom and one of the largest in the world. Latin American and Caribbean material, which the Library began collecting in 1934, forms a minor part of the overall stock; 92 books and pamphlets, and 18 current and 4 non-current serials are held. In addition, the Library indexes articles on the region appearing in other items. All countries of the region are represented. The collection is on open access.

Access to collections:

Opening hours: Mon, Tues, Thurs 0900–1700, Wed 1000–1700, Fri 0900–1645. Public holidays closed. Closes early before a public holiday.

Enquiries: By telephone, post, fax or e-mail.
Admission: Non-members are admitted for reference purposes (payment required).
Lending: No.
Inter-library loans: To subscribing libraries only.
Union record: BUCOP, COLALAS.
Catalogue: SIRSI Unicorn automated catalogue.
Classification: Own classification.

Electronic facilities for non-members:

Microcomputing facilities: No.
On-line search facilities: Yes (payment required).
CD-ROM facilities: Yes.
Internet access: Yes (payment required for printing).
Portable computers: Use permitted; power points available.

Other facilities for non-members:
Photocopying: Yes (payment required).

93 Christian Aid
Library, 35 Lower Marsh, London SE1 7RT

Tel.: 020 7620 4444. Holdings enquiries 020 7523 2413/2414
Fax: 020 7620 0719
E-mail: info@christian-aid.org
WWW: http://www.christian-aid.org.uk/
Established: 1970 (1948 as part of the British Council of Churches' Inter-Church Aid and Refugee Service)

Librarian: Sarah Heery, DipLib, ALA
E-mail address: library@christian-aid.org

Collections:

Christian Aid is the official agency of 40 church denominations in the United Kingdom and Ireland, working in more than 70 countries of the world through 700 local organisations whose programmes aim to strengthen the poor by helping them to become self-sufficient. Latin American and Caribbean material forms a major part of the Library's collections: 800 books and documents and 40 current periodicals are held. An internal database also holds 13,000 abstracts of journal articles. Approximately 300 items are added to the Library annually (books, documents, serials, annuals and journal abstracts). The material is shelved with the main collection and is predominantly on open access. The geographical emphasis is on Bolivia, Brazil, Colombia, the Dominican Republic, El Salvador, Guatemala, Haiti, Honduras, Jamaica, Montserrat, Nicaragua and Peru.

Access to collections:

Opening hours: Mon–Fri 1000–1700.

Enquiries: By telephone, post, fax or e-mail.
Admission: By appointment.
Lending: No.
Inter-library loans: Lends to other libraries.
Catalogue: DB/TextWorks automated catalogue.
Classification: Universal Decimal Classification.

Electronic facilities for non-members:
Microcomputing facilities: No.
On-line search facilities: No.
CD-ROM facilities: Yes (payment required).
Internet access: Yes (payment required).
Portable computers: Use permitted; power points available.

Other facilities for non-members:
Photocopying: Yes (payment required).

Publications:
Press Report.

94 Commonwealth Institute

Commonwealth Resource Centre, Kensington High Street, London W8 6NQ

Tel.: 020 7603 4535 ext. 210
Fax: 020 7603 2807
E-mail: crc@commonwealth.org.uk
WWW: http://www.commonwealth.org.uk/
Established: 1962

Head of Library Services: Marie Bastiampillai

Collections:

The Library, founded in 1962, has a collection of 10,000 volumes and about 20 current periodical titles, together with audio and video recordings, posters, wallcharts, maps, press cuttings and information files on Commonwealth organisations. The reference collection includes bibliographies, directories, yearbooks, encyclopaedias, dictionaries, travel guides, atlases and biographies. Material on Guyana, Belize and the Commonwealth Caribbean forms a major part of the collection, which is especially strong in imaginative literature and the arts. History and geography are also collected. About 400 volumes are added each year. The collection is on open access.

Access to collections:
Opening hours: Mon–Sat 1000–1600. Public holidays closed.

Enquiries: By telephone, post (include A4 stamped addressed envelope), fax or e-mail.
Admission: Non-members are admitted for reference purposes.
Lending: Yes (payment required).
Inter-library loans: Yes.
Union record: BLDSC, BUCOP.
Catalogue: Heritage automated catalogue, available through the website.
Classification: Bliss Bibliographic Classification.

Electronic facilities for non-members:

Microcomputing facilities: No.
On-line search facilities: No.
CD-ROM facilities: Yes.
Internet access: No.
Portable computers: Use permitted; power points available.

Other facilities for non-members:

Photocopying: Yes (payment required).

95 Commonwealth Parliamentary Association

Parliamentary Information and Reference Centre, Headquarters Secretariat, Suite 700, Westminster House, 7 Millbank, London SW1P 3JA

Tel.: 020 7799 1460
Fax: 020 7222 6073
E-mail: pirc@comparlhq.org.uk
WWW: http://www.comparlhq.org.uk/
Established: 1971

Director of Information Services: Andrew Imlach, BA

Collections:

The Parliamentary Information and Reference Centre was established in 1971. It has built up, with the cooperation of Members and officials of Commonwealth parliaments and legislatures, an unparalleled collection of Commonwealth parliamentary and constitutional material. This is used in providing an information service for members of Parliament, parliamentary officials, the media and academics, and can be made accessible to those engaged in the study of Parliament. Material on the region includes all Commonwealth Caribbean countries, Belize, Guyana and the Falkland Islands. The collection includes books, press cuttings, pamphlets, official statements, debates and articles; information is maintained on election results, constitutions, cabinet changes and High Commissioners. The material is on open access.

Access to collections:

Opening hours: Mon–Fri 1000–1700. Public holidays closed.

Enquiries: By telephone, post, fax or e-mail.
Admission: Non-members are admitted for reference purposes (written application required).
Lending: No.
Inter-library loans: No.
Catalogue: Microsoft Access automated catalogue.
Classification: Own classification.

Electronic facilities for non-members:

Microcomputing facilities: No.
On-line search facilities: Yes (payment required).
CD-ROM facilities: No.
Internet access: No.
Portable computers: Use permitted; power points available.

Other facilities for non-members:

Photocopying: Yes (payment required).

96 Commonwealth Secretariat
Library & Archives, Marlborough House, Pall Mall, London SW1Y 5HX

Tel.: 020 7747 6164
Fax: 020 7747 6168
E-mail: library@commonwealth.int
WWW: http://www.thecommonwealth.org/htm/info/inaction/
Established: 1965

Librarian: David Blake, BA, MSc, DipLib, ALA
Librarian's e-mail address: d.blake@commonwealth.int

Deputy Librarian and Archivist: Jay Gilbert, BA, MAS, MSc
E-mail address: j.gilbert@commonwealth.int

Collections:

The Library has a collection of 30,000 books and pamphlets and 4,500 periodical titles. Subjects covered include economics, trade, industry, agriculture, politics, international relations, environment, education, health, gender, youth, science and technology. The collection includes official statistical publications and development plans, publications from international organisations, and a complete set of the Secretariat's publications. The stock covers mainly the last ten years and is predominantly on open access. Material on the Caribbean forms a minor part of the collection. The archives of the Secretariat date from the mid-1960s and since 1997 have been released under a 30-year rule (viewing by appointment; apply to the Deputy Librarian & Archivist).

Access to collections:

Opening hours: Mon–Fri 1000–1645. Public holidays closed.

Enquiries: By telephone, post or e-mail.
Admission: Non-members are admitted for reference purposes (advance application to the Librarian required).
Lending: No.
Inter-library loans: Lends to other libraries.
Catalogue: Unesco CDS/ISIS author/subject automated catalogue.
Classification: The UNBIS Thesaurus is used for subject headings and classification.

Electronic facilities for non-members:

Microcomputing facilities: No.
On-line search facilities: No.
CD-ROM facilities: Yes.
Internet access: Limited access.
Portable computers: Battery-operated portable computers may be used.

Other facilities for non-members:

Photocopying: Yes (payment required).
Microform holdings: Yes.
Reader-printer facilities: No.

Publications:

A Bibliography of Commonwealth Secretariat Publications on Women, 1975–1994 (London: Library, Commonwealth Secretariat, 1994).

97 Corporation of London City Business Library
1 Brewers' Hall Garden, London EC2V 5BX

Tel.: 020 7332 1812
Fax: 020 7332 1847
Business Information Focus tel.: 020 7600 1461
Business Information Focus fax: 020 7600 1185
WWW: http://www.cityoflondon.gov.uk/leisure_heritage/libraries_archives_museums_galleries/city_london_libraries/cbl.htm
Established: 1970

Librarian: Garry Humphreys

Collections:

The Library was created in 1970, partly with material transferred from the Guildhall Library. In order to maintain the currency of the collection, older material is continually discarded or relegated; earlier holdings of some periodicals are transferred to the Guildhall Library. There are 750 current periodicals and 90 newspapers, together with indexing and abstracting services. The collection of directories (including overseas publications) is outstanding; companies information (annual reports, etc.) is collected. There is good coverage of management, law, banking, insurance, statistics and investment. A fee-based research service, Business Information Focus, is also available. Information on Latin America and the Caribbean is a minor aspect of the Library's overall stock; particularly useful are the publications of the Economist Intelligence Unit. The collection is on open access.

Access to collections:

Opening hours: Mon–Fri 0930–1700. Public holidays closed.

Enquiries: By telephone, post or fax.
Admission: Open to the general public.
Lending: Reference library only.
Inter-library loans: No.

Union record: BLCMP, BLDSC, COLALAS, LASER.
Catalogue: BLCMP Talis automated catalogue.
Classification: Dewey Decimal Classification. Own classification for directories and periodicals.

Electronic facilities for non-members:

Microcomputing facilities: No.
On-line search facilities: No.
CD-ROM facilities: Yes (payment required for printing).
Internet access: Yes.
Portable computers: Use permitted; power points available.

Other facilities for non-members:

Photocopying: Yes (payment required).

98 *Corporation of London Guildhall Library*
Aldermanbury, London EC2P 2EJ

Tel.: 020 7332 1868/1870
Fax: 020 7600 3384
E-mail: printedbooks.guildhall@corpoflondon.gov.uk
WWW: http://www.cityoflondon.gov.uk/leisure_heritage/libraries_archives_museums_galleries/city_london_libraries/guildhall_lib.htm
Established: 1423

Guildhall Librarian and Director of Libraries and Art Galleries: Melvyn P.K. Barnes, OBE, DMA, ALA, FBIM, FRSA

Collections:

The Library holds the records of major London commercial institutions. An important resource for nineteenth- and early twentieth-century Latin America are the papers of the Council of Foreign Bondholders. These include annual reports, records, committee papers and press cuttings files. The press cuttings files, although primarily composed of newspaper cuttings, also contain pamphlets, prospectuses, circulars, government reports and messages, and printed speeches. They cover the years 1869–1920 and are in the form of bound cuttings books for each of the countries in which the Council was interested. They were produced to provide a service for the

Council's negotiators and information for the area reports in the Council's annual report. Latin American countries were not reported extensively in the British press and all available information was collected, including political commentary. The files contain much material on the development of railways in Latin America. The collection is on closed access and the cuttings files have been microfilmed by Microform Imaging Ltd.

Access to collections:

Opening hours: Mon–Sat 0930–1700. Public holidays closed (including previous Saturdays).

Enquiries: By telephone, post or e-mail. The Library also provides a fee-based research service (tel.: 020 7332 1854; e-mail: search.guildhall@corpoflondon.gov.uk).
Admission: Open to the general public.
Lending: Reference library only.
Inter-library loans: No.
Union record: BLCMP.
Catalogue: BLCMP Talis automated catalogue.
Classification: Dewey Decimal Classification.

Electronic facilities for non-members:

Microcomputing facilities: No.
On-line search facilities: No.
CD-ROM facilities: Yes (payment required for printing).
Internet access: No.
Portable computers: Use permitted; power points available.

Other facilities for non-members:

Photocopying: Yes (payment required).
Microform holdings: Yes.
Reader-printer facilities: Yes (payment required).

Publications

The Newspaper Cuttings Files of the Council of Foreign Bondholders (Wakefield: Microform Academic Publishers).

99 Council for Education in World Citizenship
Resource Centre, Sir John Lyon House, 5 High Timber Street, London EC4V 3PA

Tel.: 020 7329 1500
Fax: 020 7329 8160
E-mail: info@cewc.org.uk
WWW: http://www.cewc.org.uk/
Established: 1939

Information Officer: Heather Brown
E-mail address: gabby@cewc.org.uk

Collections:

CEWC is an independent organisation which helps young people in the United Kingdom understand and confront global issues and challenges through publications, seminars and workshops, activities and projects, a speaker service, information and advice. The Resource Centre holds material relating to drugs and development in Latin America and the Caribbean.

Access to collections:

Opening hours: By appointment.

Enquiries: By telephone, post or e-mail.
Admission: Open to the general public; a small donation is requested.
Lending: No.
Inter-library loans: No.
Union record: None.
Catalogue: None.
Classification: None.

Electronic facilities for non-members:

Microcomputing facilities: No.
On-line search facilities: No.
CD-ROM facilities: No.
Internet access: No.
Portable computers: Use not permitted.

Other facilities for non-members:

Photocopying: Yes (payment required).

100 Department for International Development (DFID)
Library, 94 Victoria Street, London SW1E 5JL

Tel.: 020 7917 7000
Fax: 020 7917 0019
WWW: http://www.dfid.gov.uk/
Established: 1997 (1964 as Ministry of Overseas Development Library, 1970 as Overseas Development Administration Library)

The Library acts as an enquiry point for the main DFID library (no. 50), from which material can be requested.

101 Department of Trade and Industry, British Trade International, Trade Partners UK
Trade Partners UK Information Centre, 66–74 Victoria Street, London SW1E 6SW

Tel.: 020 7215 5444/5445
Fax: 020 7215 4231
E-mail: info@tradepartners.gov.uk
Web catalogue: http://www.tradepartners.gov.uk/information_centre/catalogue_search/
WWW: http://www.tradepartners.gov.uk/information_centre/home/welcome
Established: 1962 (Statistics and Market Intelligence Library), 1990 (Export Market Information Centre), 2000 (Trade Partners UK Information Centre)

Librarian: Andrew Strachan

Collections:

The Information Centre has collected material on Latin America and the Caribbean since 1962, but statistical serials are transferred to BLDSC (no. 10) after five years and older directories are withdrawn. The collection of current overseas trade statistics and directories is the largest in the United Kingdom. The Information Centre also holds other industrial, financial, labour, employment, demographic and social statistics, market research reports, classified telephone directories, development plans and information from the multilateral development agencies, and gives access to such online databases as the Economist Intelligence Unit and Euromonitor. The material is predominantly on open access.

Access to collections:

Opening hours: Mon–Fri 0900–2000, Sat 0900–1730. Public holidays closed.

Enquiries: By telephone, post, fax or e-mail.
Admission: Exporters and their representatives, market researchers and consultants are admitted without an appointment. Students should telephone to make an appointment and show their student identity cards on arrival at the Centre.
Lending: No.
Inter-library loans: No.
Union record: BLDSC (statistical series only).
Catalogue: SIRSI Unicorn automated catalogue.
Classification: Own classification. Material is arranged geographically.

Electronic facilities for non-members:

Microcomputing facilities: No.
On-line search facilities: Yes (payment required for printing; booking in advance may be required).
CD-ROM facilities: Yes (payment required for printing; booking in advance may be required).
Internet access: Yes (payment required for printing).
Portable computers: Battery-operated portable computers may be used.

Other facilities for non-members:

Photocopying: Yes (payment required).
Microform holdings: Yes.
Reader-printer facilities: Yes (payment required for printing).

102 Development Planning Unit (DPU), University College London, University of London
DPU Documentation Centre, 9 Endsleigh Gardens, London WC1H 0ED

Tel.: 020 7388 7581
Fax: 020 7387 4541
E-mail: f.liew@ucl.ac.uk
WWW: http://www.ucl.ac.uk/dpu/
Established: 1964 (at the Architectural Association), 1971 (at UCL)

Documentalist: Frankie Liew, BA, MSc

Collections:

The collections of the DPU Documentation Centre have been built up over a period of nearly forty years and now include over 10,000 volumes; there are 20 current periodicals. In addition to teaching materials, the collections include government planning documents, town plans, consultants' reports, urban bylaws and academic research papers. Subjects covered include demography, economics, environment and sociology; the main strengths are in urban and regional development and planning, including city development, housing and urban poverty. The material is arranged geographically by continent, subdivided by countries; in the Latin American section the strongest collections are those on Brazil, Colombia and Mexico. There are approximately 1,000 books and 1,000 manuscripts, official publications and consultancy reports. The material is on open access.

Access to collections:

Opening hours: Term: Mon–Fri 1100–1745. Public holidays closed. Vacation: Appointment must be made well in advance by telephone or e-mail.

Enquiries: By telephone, post, fax or e-mail.
Admission: Non-members are admitted for reference purposes.
Lending: No.
Inter-library loans: No.
Union record: BUCLA.
Catalogue: Author and classified subject card catalogue.
Classification: Universal Decimal Classification (modified).

Electronic facilities for non-members:

Microcomputing facilities: No.
On-line search facilities: No.
CD-ROM facilities: Yes.
Internet access: No.
Portable computers: Use permitted.

Other facilities for non-members:

Photocopying: Yes (payment required).

103 The Fawcett Library: the National Library of Women
Women's Library, Old Castle Street, London E1 7NT

Tel.: 020 7320 1189
Fax: 020 7320 1188
E-mail: fawcett@lgu.ac.uk
WWW: http://www.lgu.ac.uk/fawcett/
Established: 1926 (1953 name changed to The Fawcett Library)

Fawcett Development Librarian: Christine Wise, BA, DipLib, ALA
Subject enquiries to: Reference Librarian

Collections:

The Fawcett Library was established in 1926 as the library of the London Society for Women's Service (formerly Suffrage), a non-militant organisation led by Millicent Fawcett. The Library was run by the Fawcett Society until 1977, when it moved to London Guildhall University. As the national research library for women's history, it is the United Kingdom's oldest and most comprehensive research library on all aspects of women in society, including: feminism, work, education, health, the family, law, arts, science, technology, language, sexuality, fashion and the home. The Library holds over 60,000 books and pamphlets, 2,500 periodical titles, over 200 archival collections, extensive newspaper cuttings, ephemera and a wide range of visual materials such as posters, postcards and banners. The emphasis is on women in Britain, but many other countries are represented. The Latin American and Caribbean material forms a minor part of the overall collection. Modern books are on open access, special collections on closed access and periodicals mostly on open access. The Library closed in April 2001 and will reopen in January 2002 as the Women's Library in a new building in Old Castle Street, adjacent to Calcutta House.

Access to collections:

Opening hours: Term: Mon 1015–2030, Wed 0900–2030, Thurs–Fri 0900–1700. Vacation: Mon, Wed–Fri 0900–1700, Tuesdays and public holidays closed. Christmas, New Year and Easter closed.

Enquiries: By telephone, post or e-mail.
Admission: Open to the general public. Access is free to members of staff and students of London Guildhall University and to bona fide researchers employed in higher education institutions. Others may join as annual members or by paying a day fee.

Lending: Annual members may borrow certain books published after 1980.
Inter-library loans: No.
Catalogue: Libertas automated catalogue (records for books, pamphlets and periodicals form part of the London Guildhall University catalogue; the Library's archival catalogue and records of visual materials are currently being automated).
Classification: Dewey Decimal Classification for published materials.

Electronic facilities for non-members:

Microcomputing facilities: No.
On-line search facilities: No.
CD-ROM facilities: Yes.
Internet access: Yes.
Portable computers: Use permitted; power points available.

Other facilities for non-members:

Photocopying: Yes (payment required).
Microform holdings: Yes.
Reader-printer facilities: Yes.

Publications:

Researchers' Resource Guide.
Student Resource Guide.
Library Newsletter.
Miscellaneous reading lists.

104 Folklore Society Library
University College London, Bloomsbury Science Library, 2nd Floor, D.M.S. Watson Building, London, WC1

Address for correspondence: Folklore Society, The Warburg Institute, Woburn Square, London, WC1H 0AB
Tel.: 020 7387 5894
E-mail: c.oates@talk21.com

Web catalogue: http://library.ucl.ac.uk (Folklore Society holdings are prefixed by classmark FLS)
WWW: http://www.folklore-society.com

Established: 1878

Honorary Librarian: William F. Ryan, MA, DPhil
Subject enquiries to: Caroline F. Oates, MPhil, PhD, Information Officer / Librarian, at the Folklore Society's Office in The Warburg Institute, Woburn Square, London WC1H 0AB

Collections:

The Library of the Folklore Society was deposited at the College in 1911. It is one of the best collections on this subject in the world, holding 12,000 volumes and over 100 current serials. Materials on the region form a minor part of the overall stock and additions are usually made only by donation. There are 200 books and 4 current and 10 non-current periodical titles; 10–20 volumes are added each year. Mexico is the best represented country. The material is held in UCL's store and is fetched on request (minimum 24 hours' notice). The Frederick Starr collection of Mexican folklore objects is held at the Cambridge University Museum of Archaeology and Anthropology.

Access to collections:

Opening hours: Term: Mon–Thurs 0845–1030, Fri 0845–1900, Sat 0930–1630. Christmas and Easter Vacations: Mon–Fri 0930–1845, Sat closed. Summer Vacation: Mon–Fri 0930–1700, Sat closed. Christmas, New Year, Easter and public holidays closed.

Enquiries: By telephone, post or e-mail.
Admission: Non-members are admitted for reference purposes. Application should be made to University College London, Science Library Reader Admissions, for access to stock held in store. For bibliographical enquiries, contact the Folklore Society Librarian. Academic users are normally admitted free of charge; payment is usually required from those working for a company, charity or other organisation; payment may be required for members of the public and private researchers.
Lending: Lending to Folklore Society members and University College students and staff. Items over 100 years old, serials, rare books and pamphlets are not loaned.
Inter-library loans: Lends to other libraries.
Union record: BLDSC, BUCOP.
Catalogue: Ex Libris Aleph automated catalogue.
Classification: Own classification.

Electronic facilities for non-members:

Microcomputing facilities: No.
On-line search facilities: No.
CD-ROM facilities: No.
Internet access: No.
Portable computers: Battery-operated portable computers may be used.

Other facilities for non-members:

Photocopying: Yes (payment required).

105 Foreign and Commonwealth Office (FCO)
Library, Room E213, FCO, King Charles Street, London SW1A 2AL

Tel.: 020 7270 3025. Holdings enquiries and admissions 020 7270 3023
Fax: 020 7270 3015
WWW: http://www.fco.gov.uk
Established: 1968 (as FCO)

Librarian: Joy Herring, BA, ALA, DipLib
Subject enquiries to: Americas Team
Americas Team tel.: 020 7270 3021

Collections:

The FCO was formed in 1968, when the Commonwealth Office (formerly the Colonial and Commonwealth Relations Offices) and the Foreign Office were amalgamated. The Library is strong in international law (held in the Legal Library, Room K168), in British treaties and in official publications. Other subjects covered include diplomacy, international politics, and the politics, history, administration, economics and law of overseas countries. Other printed material for which the Library is notable includes early works in travel and exploration, and on the former British colonies in the Caribbean and there is a collection of photographs from the colonial period. Greater emphasis in current acquisitions is given to Commonwealth countries and United Kingdom overseas territories. The collection is on closed access. The website includes material relevant to Latin America and the Caribbean: speeches, statements, press releases, and consular and travel advice.

Access to collections:

Opening hours: Mon–Fri 0930–1730. Public holidays closed.

Enquiries: By telephone, post or fax.
Admission: Non-members are admitted for reference purposes (appointment required).
Lending: No.
Inter-library loans: Lends to other libraries.
Union record: BLDSC.
Catalogues: Author, title, alphabetical subject and classified subject printed catalogues for older material. SIRSI Unicorn automated catalogue for current acquisitions.
Classification: Library of Congress Classification.

Electronic facilities for non-members:

Microcomputing facilities: No.
On-line search facilities: No.
CD-ROM facilities: Yes.
Internet access: No.
Portable computers: Use permitted; power points available.

Other facilities for non-members:

Photocopying: Yes (payment required).
Microform holdings: Yes.
Reader-printer facilities: Yes.

Publications:

Catalogue of the Colonial Office Library (Boston, Mass.: G.K. Hall, 1964), 15 vols.
Catalogue of the Colonial Office Library: First Supplement, 1963–1967 (Boston, Mass.: G.K. Hall, 1967).
Catalogue of the Colonial Office Library: Second Supplement (Boston, Mass.: G.K. Hall, 1972), 2 vols.
Catalogue of the Foreign Office Library, 1926–1968 (Boston, Mass.: G.K. Hall, 1972), 8 vols.
Foreign and Commonwealth Office: Accessions to the Library, May 1971–June 1977 (Boston, Mass.: G.K. Hall, 1979), 4 vols.

106 Goldsmiths College, University of London
Goldsmiths College Library, New Cross, London SE14 6NW

Tel.: 020 7919 7150. Holdings enquiries 020 7919 7151
Fax: 020 7919 7165
E-mail: library@gold.ac.uk
Web catalogue: http://newlibra.gold.ac.uk
WWW: http://www.goldsmiths.ac.uk/infos/
Established: 1905

Director of Information Services: Joan Pateman, BSc
Subject enquiries to: Christine Jenkinson, ALA, Assistant Librarian, Cataloguer and Subject Librarian for European Languages
Specialist's tel.: 020 7919 7151
Specialist's e-mail address: c.jenkinson@gold.ac.uk

Collections:

The Library began collecting Caribbean material with the foundation of the Caribbean Studies Centre in 1980. Material on Latin America has also been collected since the 1980s, with a special emphasis on social anthropology. Other subjects include demography, economics, environment, geography, history, literature, political science and sociology. The Library holds 2,000 books and 13 current periodicals on the region. The collection is on open access.

Access to collections:

Opening hours: Term: Mon–Fri 0830–2100, Sat 0930–1730. Vacation: Mon–Fri 0830–1700, Sat closed. Public holidays closed.

Enquiries: By telephone, post or e-mail.
Admission: Non-members are admitted for reference purposes (proof of identity required). During term time up to three one-day reference tickets may be applied for in one term. Readers requiring a long-term reference ticket should write to the Deputy Librarian stating the reasons for their request. Vacation reference tickets are valid for one vacation only.
Lending: No.
Inter-library loans: Lends to other libraries.
Union record: University of London Union List of Serials.
Catalogue: Ex Libris Aleph automated catalogue.
Classification: Dewey Decimal Classification.

Electronic facilities for non-members:
Microcomputing facilities: No.
On-line search facilities: No.
CD-ROM facilities: No.
Internet access: No.
Portable computers: Use not permitted.

Other facilities for non-members:
Photocopying: Yes (payment required).
Microform holdings: Yes.
Reader-printer facilities: Yes (payment required).

107 Healthlink Worldwide (formerly AHRTAG)
Resource Centre, Cityside, 40 Adler Street, London E1 1EE

Tel.: 020 7539 1570
Fax: 020 7539 1580
E-mail: info@healthlink.org.uk
WWW: http://www.healthlink.org.uk/resource.html
Established: 1998 (1977 as AHRTAG)

Information Systems Officer: Victoria Richardson
Subject enquiries to: Christine Kahume, Information Production and Management Team Leader

Collections:

Healthlink Worldwide was originally founded in 1977 as AHRTAG (Appropriate Health Resources & Technologies Action Group), out of the health panel of the Intermediate Technology Development Group (ITDG). Healthlink Worldwide works to improve the health of poor and vulnerable communities by strengthening the provision, use and impact of information in developing countries. It works with partner organisations in Latin America, East, West and Southern Africa, Asia-Pacific and South-East Asia, on health communication projects including child health, AIDS and sexual health, disability and continuing education for health workers. These projects include the production of international and regional publications and information services. A bibliographic database, *Healthlink*

On-line, provides access to 16,000 records of materials held by Healthlink Worldwide's Resource Centre (books, manuals, journal articles, training materials and reports) on the management and practice of primary healthcare and disability in developing countries; about 100 new records are added each month; the database is available free on the Internet. The Latin American and Caribbean material held by the Resource Centre forms a minor part of the total collection; it is held predominantly on open access.

Access to collections:

Opening hours: By appointment only.

Enquiries: By telephone, post or e-mail (payment required).
Admission: Open to the general public (payment required).
Lending: No.
Inter-library loans: No.
Catalogue: DB/TextWorks automated catalogue.
Classification: Own classification.

Electronic facilities for non-members:

Microcomputing facilities: Yes (payment required).
On-line search facilities: Yes (payment required).
CD-ROM facilities: Yes (payment required).
Internet access: Yes.
Portable computers: Use permitted; power points available.

Other facilities for non-members:

Photocopying: Yes (payment required).

Publications:

Essential AIDS Resource Lists.
FIN Free International Newsletters. [Directory of free or low-cost health-related newsletters and magazines; available on-line at http://www.healthlink.org.uk/PDFnotes.html.]
Resource Centre manual. Available on-line at http://www.healthlink.org.uk/rcman/rchome.html.

108 Helpage International

1st Floor, York House, 207–22 Pentonville Road, London N1 9UZ
Address for correspondence: PO Box 32832, London N1 9UZ

Tel.: 020 7278 7778
Fax: 020 7843 1840
E-mail: hai@helpage.org
WWW: http://www.helpage.org/
Established: 1986

Information Officer: Austin Hall, MA, ALA
Information Officer's e-mail address: ahall@helpage.org

Collections:

Helpage International is a specialised development agency working to help the elderly in developing countries. The information department contains books and journals on the elderly in all countries including those of Latin America and the Caribbean. A large amount of grey literature is also collected, much of it produced in the region. All countries of Latin America and the Caribbean are covered.

Access to collections:

Opening hours: Mon–Fri 0900–1600.

Enquiries: By telephone, post or e-mail.
Admission: By appointment (telephone one week in advance of intended visit).
Lending: No.
Inter-library loans: No.
Catalogue: Microsoft Access automated catalogue.
Classification: Own classification.

Electronic facilities for non-members:

Microcomputing facilities: No.
On-line search facilities: No.
CD-ROM facilities: Yes.
Internet access: No.
Portable computers: Use permitted; power points available.

Other facilities for non-members:

Photocopying: No.

109 Heythrop College, University of London

Heythrop College Library, Kensington Square, London W8 5HQ

Tel.: 020 7795 4250
Fax: 020 7794 4253
E-mail: library@heythrop.ac.uk
Telnet catalogue: 193.63.81.240
Web catalogue: http://193.63.81.240/
WWW: http://www.heythrop.ac.uk/
Established: 1614

Librarian: Fr Christopher Pedley, SJ

Collections:

The Library was founded in 1614 and now holds 250,000 volumes on philosophy, theology, canon law and ecclesiastical history. In 1970 the College became legally independent of the Society of Jesus, but the Library has continued to be funded by an annual grant from the Society. The College was incorporated in the University of London in 1971. It moved to its present site in 1993. Materials on Latin America form a minor part of the overall stock, and focus on church history, the missions, Roman Catholic religious orders, liberation theology and current religious developments. In particular, a comprehensive collection is held relating to the history of the Jesuits in Latin America. There are 2,000 books and 5 current periodical titles; 20 volumes are added each year. The collection is predominantly on open access.

Access to collections:

Opening hours: Term: Mon–Fri 0930–1900, Sat 0930–1630. Vacation: Mon–Fri 0930–1730, Sat closed. Public holidays closed.

Enquiries: By post or e-mail.
Admission: Non-members are admitted for reference purposes (payment required, except for academic users).
Lending: Academic staff and research students of the University of London can gain borrowing rights. No other categories may borrow.
Inter-library loans: Lends to other libraries.
Union record: BUCOP, University of London Union List of Serials.
Catalogues: Card dictionary catalogue to 1989. From 1990 Innopac automated catalogue. Retrospective conversion of the card catalogue is expected to be completed in 2004.
Classification: Lynn-Peterson Classification.

Electronic facilities for non-members:
Microcomputing facilities: No.
On-line search facilities: No.
CD-ROM facilities: No.
Internet access: No.
Portable computers: Use permitted; power points available.

Other facilities for non-members:
Photocopying: Yes (payment required).
Microform holdings: Yes.
Reader-printer facilities: No.

110 Hispanic and Luso-Brazilian Council
Canning House Library, 2 Belgrave Square, London SW1X 8PJ

Tel.: 020 7235 2303
Fax: 020 7235 3587
E-mail: enquiries.library@canninghouse.com
WWW: http://www.canninghouse.com/library/index.html
Established: 1947

Librarian: Carmen Suárez Pérez, BA, MA

Collections:
Founded in 1947, Canning House is devoted specifically to the cultures of the Spanish- and Portuguese-speaking world, in Europe, Africa and Asia, as well as in Latin America. It is supported by the contributions of firms and individuals who have an interest in these areas, and has also been helped by foundation money. Much of its material is acquired from close contacts between the Council and the London embassies of the various Iberian and Latin American countries, and by exchange agreements. The collection shows some bias towards modern aspects of Latin America, being strong in the humanities and social sciences — anthropology, economics, sociology, history and linguistics — and with a special economics section containing up-to-date financial and business information, but there is also material across the whole spectrum of Latin American studies. Total book stock is in excess of 55,000 volumes; about 2,000 new volumes are added annually. The collections also include sheet music, a reference col-

lection of Spanish and Portuguese technical and specialist dictionaries and a small number of videos. Regular exhibitions of Latin American artists are held in the Library. The collections are predominantly on open access.

Access to collections:

Opening hours: Mon 1400–1830, Tues–Fri 0930–1300, 1400–1730. One week at Christmas and public holidays closed.

Enquiries: By telephone, post or e-mail.
Admission: Non-members are admitted for reference purposes.
Lending: Yes (payment required).
Inter-library loans: Lends to other libraries.
Union record: BLDSC, BUCLA, BUCOP, COLALAS.
Catalogue: Dynix Horizon automated catalogue (retroconversion in progress).
Classification: Library of Congress Classification.

Electronic facilities for non-members:

Microcomputing facilities: Yes (payment required).
On-line search facilities: No.
CD-ROM facilities: Yes (payment required for printing).
Internet access: No.
Portable computers: Use permitted; limited number of power points available.

Other facilities for non-members:

Photocopying: Yes (payment required).

Publications:

Canning House Library. Hispanic Council. Author Catalogue (Boston, Mass.: G.K. Hall, 1967), 2 vols.
Canning House Library. Hispanic Council. Subject Catalogue (Boston, Mass.: G.K. Hall, 1967), 2 vols.
Canning House Library. Luso-Brazilian Council. Author Catalogue and Subject Catalogue (Boston, Mass.: G.K. Hall, 1967).
Canning House Library. Hispanic and Luso-Brazilian Council, London. First Supplement. [Hispanic] Author Catalogue and Subject Catalogue (Boston, Mass.: G.K. Hall, 1973).

Canning House Library. Hispanic and Luso-Brazilian Council, London. First Supplement. [*Luso-Brazilian*] *Author Catalogue and Subject Catalogue* (Boston, Mass.: G.K. Hall, 1973).
British Bulletin of Publications on Latin America, the Caribbean, Portugal and Spain (1947–). Semi-annual, April and October.
Canning House Library (pamphlet available in English, Spanish and Portuguese).

111 Horniman Museum and Gardens

Horniman Library, 100 London Road, Forest Hill, London SE23 3PQ

Tel.: 020 8291 8681
Fax: 020 8291 5506
E-mail: enquiry@horniman.demon.co.uk
WWW: http://www.horniman.demon.co.uk/
Established: The Collections, including the Library, were given to London County Council in 1901

Librarian: David W. Allen, BSc, ALA, MIInfSci

Collections:

The Library acquires material in the three main subject areas of the Museum collections (ethnography, natural history and musicology) and now has 25,000 books, and 100 current and 150 non-current periodical titles. It has been collecting Latin American material since the 1890s and has over 1,000 books, with an annual growth of 20 volumes, and a small number of periodicals. Audio and video recordings are also collected. The collections are on closed access.

Access to collections:

Opening hours: Tues–Sat 1030–1730, Sun 1400–1730, Mon closed. Public holidays closed. Annual closure two weeks in December.

Enquiries: By telephone, post or e-mail.
Admission: Open to the general public.
Lending: No.
Inter-library loans: Lends to other libraries.
Union record: BLDSC.
Catalogue: Alice automated catalogue.
Classification: Universal Decimal Classification.

Electronic facilities for non-members:

Microcomputing facilities: No.
On-line search facilities: No.
CD-ROM facilities: No.
Internet access: No.
Portable computers: Battery-operated portable computers may be used.

Other facilities for non-members:

Photocopying: Yes (payment required).
Microform holdings: Yes.
Reader-printer facilities: No.

112 Hulton|Archive

Unique House, 21–31 Woodfield Road, London W9 2BA

Tel.: Sales enquiries 020 7266 2662. Research enquiries 020 7579 5777
Fax: 020 7266 2414/3154
E-mail: hultonresearch@getty-images.com
WWW: http://www.hultongetty.com
Established: 1947 (as Hulton Picture Library), 1958–88 (BBC Radio Times Hulton Picture Library), 1988 (as Hulton–Deutsch Picture Library), 1996 (as Hulton Getty Picture Collection), 2000 (as Hulton|Archive).

Collections:

Hulton|Archive was formed in 2000 after Getty Images acquired Archive Photos in New York. The Hulton, formerly the Hulton Getty Picture Collection, is one of the greatest libraries of photojournalism in the world. The collection includes 18,000,000 photographs, prints and engravings. Pictures of Latin America and the Caribbean form a minor part of the overall stock.

Access to collections:

Opening hours: Mon–Fri 0900–1800.

Enquiries: By telephone, post, fax or e-mail.
Admission: Non-members are admitted for reference purposes (appointment required).

Lending: Yes.
Inter-library loans: No.
Catalogue: Over 200,000 searchable images available digitally on the website.
Classification: Own classification.

113 Hutchison Picture Library
118b Holland Park Avenue, London W11 4UA

Tel.: 020 7229 2743
Fax: 020 7792 0259
E-mail: library@hutchisonpic.demon.co.uk
WWW: http://hutchisonpictures.co.uk/
Established: 1972

Subject enquiries to: Kate Pink
Specialist's e-mail address: katepink@hutchisonpic.freeserve.co.uk

Collections:

The Hutchison Picture Library was started in 1972 as a collection of photographs by foreign correspondents and now has a collection of more than 600,000 images, constantly updated and augmented with new work by more than 200 photographers. The Library specialises in documentary photographs of people, culture and places from most countries of the world. Subjects covered include the environment and climate, family life, conventional and alternative medicine, music around the world, and religions and belief systems. There is a special Disappearing World Archive, recording vanishing peoples of the world. The Latin American holdings constitute the largest part of the picture library — with especially large holdings on Bolivia, Brazil, Chile, Colombia, Ecuador, Mexico and Peru — but other countries (including the Caribbean islands) are also strongly represented.

Access to collections:

Opening hours: Mon–Fri 1000–1800.

Enquiries: By telephone, post or e-mail.
Search fee: Normally £25–£40; no fee for quick search or for searches made by library users. Commissions undertaken.

Admission: By appointment.
Lending: Yes (standard loan period of one month, extended loans by arrangement).
Catalogue: Automated catalogue.
Classification: Images are filed by country, subdivided by subject. Also files on general subjects (e.g. environment).

Electronic facilities for non-members:

Microcomputing facilities: Yes.
On-line search facilities: No.
CD-ROM facilities: No.
Internet access: No.
Portable computers: Use permitted.

Other facilities for non-members:

Photocopying: Yes.

Publications:

Brochure.

114 Inland Revenue, International Division
4th Floor, Victory House, 30–34 Kingsway, London WC2B 6ES

Tel.: 020 7438 6643
Fax: 020 7438 6106
E-mail: David.Reidy@ir.gsi.gov.uk, David.Brant@ir.gsi.gov.uk
Established: 1978 as International Division Library (originally part of the Board's Library)
Head of Section: Michael Gregory
Librarian: David Reidy

Collections:

The International Tax Library maintains an up-to-date collection of legislation and other material relating to direct taxation. Legislation is held from 1940s onwards and there are files of tax and company legislation for each country. Material on the region forms a minor part of the overall stock: 200 books and 3 current periodical titles are held. The region is also covered in comprehensive monographs and serials. Acquisitions are restricted mainly to new legislation. The collection is predominantly on open access, but older material is held in repository.

Access to collections:

Opening hours: Mon–Fri 1000–1600. Public holidays closed.

Enquiries: By telephone, post or e-mail.
Admission: Open to the general public (appointment required).
Lending: No.
Inter-library loans: Lends to other libraries.
Catalogue: Catalogue subdivided under general and country headings, on Word 7.0.
Classification: Own classification.

Electronic facilities for non-members:

Microcomputing facilities: No.
On-line search facilities: No.
CD-ROM facilities: No.
Internet access: No.
Portable computers: Battery-operated portable computers may be used.

Other facilities for non-members:

Photocopying: Yes (payment required).

115 Institute of Advanced Legal Studies, School of Advanced Study, University of London

Institute of Advanced Legal Studies Library, 17 Russell Square, London WC1B 5DR

Tel.: 020 7862 5800. Holdings enquiries 020 7862 5790. Admissions 020 7862 5801
Fax: 020 7862 5770/5775
E-mail: ials.lib@sas.ac.uk
Telnet catalogue: library.sas.ac.uk or 193.62.18.239
Web catalogue: http://lib.sas.ac.uk/
WWW: http://ials.sas.ac.uk/library.htm
Established: 1947

Head of Libraries and Information: Jules R. Winterton, BA, LLB, DipLib, ALA
Subject enquiries to: Paul Norman, Senior Assistant Librarian (Reference)

Specialist's tel.: 020 7862 5823
Specialist's e-mail address: Paul.Norman@sas.ac.uk

Collections:

The Library began collecting material on the region in 1947 and concentrates on the acquisition of primary legal materials (legislation and law reports) and periodicals. Material on Latin America forms a minor part of the overall stock. With the acquisition of the Commonwealth Law Library of the Foreign and Commonwealth Office, material on the Commonwealth Caribbean has become a major part of the collection. There are 1,600 books and 235 periodical titles (104 current); additions to the collection are very few: only 10 books are added each year. The collection of law reports includes 14 from Latin America and 17 from the Caribbean. Legislation for the Commonwealth Caribbean is well covered; for Latin America (except for Argentina and Brazil) coverage is less consistent. The material is predominantly on open access.

Access to collections:

Opening hours: Mon–Fri 0930–2000, Sat 1000–1730. Public holidays closed. Annual closure: two weeks in the latter half of September.

Enquiries: By telephone, post, fax or e-mail.
Admission: Academic staff of the University of London are admitted (proof of identity required). Research postgraduate students and taught postgraduate law students of the University of London are admitted (proof of registration required). Other students of the University of London, academic staff of other universities, library, administrative and technical staff of the University of London and of other universities, research postgraduate students and taught postgraduate students of other universities, may be admitted at the Director's discretion. Undergraduate students and students preparing for professional examinations are not admitted. Individuals may be admitted at the Director's discretion (payment required).
Lending: No.
Inter-library loans: Lends to other libraries (to a very limited extent).
Union record: BUCLA, BUCOP, CURL, *Union List of Legal Periodicals, Union List of Commonwealth and South African Law*, University of London Union List of Serials.

Catalogues: Card catalogue to 1981. From 1981 Innopac online catalogue. Retrospective conversion of the card catalogue in progress 2001.
Classification: Own classification.

Electronic facilities for non-members:

Microcomputing facilities: Yes.
On-line search facilities: Yes (for academic users). No (for other users).
CD-ROM facilities: Yes.
Internet access: Yes.
Portable computers: Use permitted; power points available.

Other facilities for non-members:

Photocopying: Yes (payment required).
Microform holdings: Yes.
Reader-printer facilities: Yes (payment required).

Publications:

Catalogue of the Library of the Institute of Advanced Legal Studies, University of London (Boston, Mass.: G.K. Hall, 1978), 6 vols.
Union List of Commonwealth and South African Law: a Location Guide to Commonwealth and South African Legislation, Law Reports and Digests Held by Libraries in the United Kingdom at May 1963 (London: Institute of Advanced Legal Studies, 1963).
Union List of Legal Periodicals: a Location Guide to Holdings of Legal Periodicals in Libraries in the United Kingdom, 4th ed. (London: Institute of Advanced Legal Studies, 1978).

116 Institute of Commonwealth Studies, School of Advanced Study, University of London

Institute of Commonwealth Studies Library, 28 Russell Square, London WC1B 5DS

Tel.: 020 7862 8842
Fax: 020 7862 8820
E-mail: icommlib@sas.ac.uk
Telnet catalogue: library.sas.ac.uk or 193.62.18.239
Web catalogue: http://lib.sas.ac.uk/
WWW: http://www.sas.ac.uk/commonwealthstudies/library/library.html

Established: 1949
Information Resources Manager: Erika Gwynnett, BA, DipLib
Subject enquiries to: Julie Evans, BA, MA, Deputy Information Resources Manager
Specialist's tel.: 020 7862 8833
Specialist's e-mail address: Julie.Evans@sas.ac.uk

Collections:

The Library has collected material on the Commonwealth Caribbean since its foundation and these holdings form a major part of the overall stock. The acquisition of the Library of the West India Committee in 1977 greatly increased the historical holdings and there are now 35,000 books, and 350 current and 1,000 non-current periodical titles; 600 volumes are added each year. The collections are strong in history, politics, and economic and social development (including education, tourism and women's studies). There is a good collection of official publications, including statistical digests, annual reports and census reports. The Archives and Special Collections include the minutes and archives of the West India Committee, the papers of the eighteenth-century sugar tycoon, Simon Taylor, the papers of the political activists C.L.R. James and (on microfiche) Richard Hart, early pamphlets on sugar and slavery, and political party, trades union and pressure group material. Current news sources are also collected. The collections are on closed access.

Access to collections:

Opening hours: Term: Mon–Fri 0930–1830. Vacation: Mon–Fri 0930–1730. Public holidays closed. Annual closure: two weeks in August.

Enquiries: By telephone, post or e-mail.
Admission: Academic staff and postgraduate students of any university are admitted for reference use. Undergraduate students of any university are admitted if the material they require is not available elsewhere. Others are admitted at the discretion of the Director (payment required).
Lending: No.
Inter-library loans: Lends to other libraries.
Union record: BUCLA, BUCOP, COLALAS, CURL, University of London Union List of Serials.
Catalogue: Innopac automated catalogue.
Classification: Library of Congress Classification.

Electronic facilities for non-members:

Microcomputing facilities: No.
On-line search facilities: Yes.
CD-ROM facilities: No.
Internet access: Yes.
Portable computers: Use permitted; power points available.

Other facilities for non-members:

Photocopying: Yes (payment required).
Microform holdings: Yes.
Reader-printer facilities: No.

117 Institute of Contemporary History and Wiener Library
4 Devonshire Street, London W1N 2BH

Tel.: 020 7636 7247
Fax: 020 7436 6428
E-mail: lib@wl.u-net.com
WWW: http://www.wienerlibrary.co.uk/
Established: 1933

Librarian: Margot Trask

Collections:

The Library was founded in Amsterdam in 1933 and moved to London in 1939. It began collecting Latin American material in the 1940s. The main themes of the collection are the history of the Third Reich and the recent history of Jewry and of anti-Semitism. There is a small amount of material on the Nazi influence in Latin America and on anti-Semitism there. Some of the pamphlet material is very rare and there is a large collection of press cuttings, some of them from Latin American newspapers. Argentina is well represented in this collection, but there is also some material on Chile, Venezuela, Uruguay and other countries of the region. Latin American materials form a minor part of the overall stock; 200–300 books are held and very few are added annually. The collections are on partially closed access.

Access to collections:

Opening hours: Mon–Fri 1000–1730. Public holidays closed.

Enquiries: By post and telephone.
Admission: Non-members are admitted for reference purposes (letter of introduction required). Membership is available (payment required).
Lending: No.
Inter-library loans: No.
Union record: BLDSC.
Catalogues: Card catalogue for older material. Genesis automated catalogue for current acquisitions.
Classification: Own classification.

Electronic facilities for non-members:

Microcomputing facilities: No.
On-line search facilities: Yes.
CD-ROM facilities: Yes.
Internet access: No.
Portable computers: Use permitted; power points available.

Other facilities for non-members:

Photocopying: Yes (payment required).
Microform holdings: Yes.
Reader-printer facilities: Yes (payment required).

Publications:

Journal of Contemporary History (London: Sage Publications, 1966–).

118 Institute of Education, University of London
Information Services, 20 Bedford Way, London WC1H 0AL

Tel.: 020 7612 6080. Admissions 020 7612 6081
Fax: 020 7612 6093
E-mail: lib.enquiries@ioe.ac.uk
Web catalogue: http://libserv.ioe.ac.uk
WWW: http://www.ioe.ac.uk/infoserv/ishome.htm
Established: 1902

Librarian and Head of Information Services: Anne Peters, BA
Subject enquiries to: Diana Guthrie, MA, ALA
Specialist's tel.: 020 7612 6087
Specialist's e-mail address: d.guthrie@ioe.ac.uk

Collections:

Latin American and Caribbean materials form a minor part of the overall stock of the Library; the books, journals and statistics are held in the Comparative Education collection. There is some material on Latin America, but the main geographical strength is the Anglophone Caribbean. There are 930 books, 6 current and 6 non-current periodical titles, 2 CD-ROMs and a small amount of microfiche material. About 20–30 volumes are acquired annually; some ten per cent of acquisitions are of non-current material. About half of the collection is on open access.

Access to collections:

Opening hours: Term, Christmas and Easter Vacations: Mon–Thurs 0930–2100, Fri 1030–1900, Sat 0930–1700. Summer Vacation: Mon–Fri 0930–1800, Sat closed. Public holidays closed.

Enquiries: By telephone, post or e-mail.

Admission: Non-members are admitted for reference purposes (payment required). Some special categories are eligible for free Reference Membership.

Lending: Limited borrowing rights are granted to Associate Members (payment required). Some special categories are eligible for free Associate Membership.

Inter-library loans: Lends to other libraries.

Union record: BLDSC, BUCLA, BUCOP, COLALAS, LASER, University of London Union List of Serials.

Catalogues: Card catalogue for material acquired before 1981. SIRSI Unicorn automated catalogue 1981– .

Classification: London Education Classification.

Electronic facilities for non-members:

Microcomputing facilities: No.
On-line search facilities: No.
CD-ROM facilities: Yes.
Internet access: No.
Portable computers: Use permitted; power points available.

Other facilities for non-members:

Photocopying: Yes (payment required).
Microform holdings: Yes.
Reader-printer facilities: Yes (payment required).

Descriptions of Libraries and Collections 171

Publications:

Catalogue of the Collection of Education in Tropical Areas (Boston, Mass.: G.K. Hall, 1964), 3 vols.

Catalogue of the Comparative Education Library, University of London Institute of Education (Boston, Mass.: G.K. Hall, 1971), 6 vols.

Catalogue of the Comparative Education Library, University of London Institute of Education: First Supplement, 1969–1974 (Boston, Mass.: G.K. Hall, 1974), 3 vols.

Education Libraries Bulletin (London: University of London, Institute of Education Library, 1958–88).

Education Libraries Journal (London: University of London, Institute of Education Library, 1989–93).

119 Institute of Historical Research, School of Advanced Study, University of London

Institute of Historical Research Library, Senate House, Malet Street, London WC1E 7HU

Tel.: 020 7862 8760. Admissions 020 7862 8740
Fax: 020 7862 8762
E-mail: ihrlib@sas.ac.uk
Telnet catalogue: library.sas.ac.uk or 193.62.18.239
Web catalogue: http://lib.sas.ac.uk/
WWW: http://ihr.sas.ac.uk/cwis/library.html
Established: 1921

Librarian: Robert Lyons, BA, DipLib
Subject enquiries to: Donald Munro, MA, DipLib, Assistant Librarian
Specialist's tel.: 020 7862 8767
Specialist's e-mail address: dmunro@sas.ac.uk

Collections:

The Library has collected material on Latin America from its foundation in 1921 and now holds more than 12,000 books (with annual acquisitions of approximately 170 volumes, of which twenty per cent are of non-current material). There are 17 current and 37 non-current periodicals. The Institute specialises in primary historical materials, leaving the acquisition of secondary materials to other libraries of the University. The combined collections form one of the strongest research resources in the field of history in the United Kingdom. The collection consists mainly of bibliographies, guides to manuscripts and archives and collections of printed source materials. The following sets are particularly noteworthy: *Colección de documentos ... del Real Archivo de Indias* (44 vols), *Documentos históricos* from the Biblioteca Nacional do Brasil (110 vols), *Publicações* of the Arquivo Nacional do Brasil (68 vols), *Documentos para la historia argentina* (45 vols), *Colección documental de la independencia del Perú* (48 vols), *Biblioteca de la Academia Nacional de la Historia de Venezuela* (more than 170 vols, in progress), and *Biblioteca de historia nacional colombiana* (more than 120 vols, in progress). Biographical dictionaries and other reference works are also collected and copies of most University of London theses in the field of history are deposited in the Library. Some material is acquired in exchange for *Historical Research*. The collection is on open access and arranged by geographical area. Latin American material (mainly dealing with New Spain and South America) is shelved in the basement.

Access to collections:

Opening hours: Mon–Fri 0900–2045, Sat 0900–1645. Public holidays in May 0900–1645. Christmas to New Year, Good Friday to Easter Monday, and August Bank Holiday week closed.

Enquiries: By telephone, post or e-mail.
Admission: Membership free to staff and postgraduate students of most European Union Universities and subscribing institutions. Others may be admitted on payment of a fee.
Lending: The library is reference only.
Inter-library loans: No.
Union record: BUCLA, BUCOP, COLALAS, CURL, University of London Union List of Serials.
Catalogue: Innopac automated catalogue.
Classification: Own classification.

Electronic facilities for non-members:

Microcomputing facilities: Yes.
On-line search facilities: No.
CD-ROM facilities: Yes.
Internet access: Yes.

Portable computers: Readers who wish to use portable computers should contact library staff in advance.

Other facilities for non-members:
Photocopying: Yes (payment required).
Microform holdings: Yes.
Reader-printer facilities: Yes (payment required).

120 Institute of International Visual Arts (inIVA)
6–8 Standard Place, Rivington Street, London EC2A 3BE

Tel.: 020 7729 9616
Fax: 020 7729 9509
E-mail: institute@iniva.org
WWW: http://www.iniva.org/library
Established: 1994

Librarian / Information Manager: Ariede Migliavacca
Librarian's e-mail address: ariede@iniva.org

Collections:

The Institute of International Visual Arts (inIVA) was established in December 1994 with a specific brief to promote the work of contemporary artists from diverse cultural backgrounds. Primary activities include exhibitions, research, publishing and education. Key resources include the Library and the website. The reference Library has a rapidly growing collection on contemporary arts and cultural studies. The emphasis is on contemporary art from Latin America, Asia and Africa, and on British artists from different cultural backgrounds. The collections consist of over 4,000 exhibition catalogues, arranged both by country and individual artist, approximately 1,000 monographs covering culture, politics, gender and media studies, and 150 periodicals, of which half are current. Some 4,500 slides are maintained in a collection of active artists' files. Recent acquisitions and current journals are listed on the website.

Access to collections:

Opening hours: Mon–Fri 1000–1700.

Enquiries: By telephone, post or e-mail.

Admission: Open to the general public, by appointment (payment required).
Lending: No.
Inter-library loans: No.
Catalogue: CALM 2000 automated catalogue, indexed by author, subject, title, curator, artist and individual contributors, with an abstract for each entry recorded.
Classification: Own classification.

Electronic facilities for non-members:
Microcomputing facilities: No.
On-line search facilities: No.
CD-ROM facilities: Yes.
Internet access: Yes.
Portable computers: Use permitted.

Other facilities for non-members:
Photocopying: Yes (payment required).

Publications:
Library reference guides: Periodicals, Audiovisual, Cultural Studies, Exhibition Catalogues.

121 Institute of Latin American Studies, School of Advanced Study, University of London

Institute of Latin American Studies Library, 35 Tavistock Square, London WC1

Address for correspondence: Institute of Latin American Studies Library, 31 Tavistock Square, London WC1H 9HA
Tel.: 020 7862 8501
Fax: 020 7862 8971
E-mail: ilas.lib@sas.ac.uk
Telnet catalogue: library.sas.ac.uk or 193.62.18.239
Web catalogue: http://lib.sas.ac.uk/
WWW: http://www.sas.ac.uk/ilas/library.htm
Established: 1965

Information Resources Manager: Erika Gwynnett, BA, DipLib

Subject enquiries to: Alan Biggins, BSc, DipLib, ALA, Latin American Bibliographer
Specialist's tel.: 020 7862 8504
Specialist's e-mail address: Alan.Biggins@sas.ac.uk

Collections:

The Library holds the main reference collection for Latin America in the University, including bibliographies, dictionaries, directories, encyclopaedias, guides to research and indexes. It was developed in part as a subject index to the British Union Catalogue of Latin Americana (see below) and now numbers approximately 7,000 volumes. Some of these materials are held in electronic format. There are 260 current and 1,500 non-current periodical titles. These include academic journals in the social sciences dealing with the region, published in Europe and the Americas; news sources from and about the region (including a microfilm set of the Buenos Aires daily *La Nación* 1951–88); and newsletters and annual reports from universities and other organisations and institutions in, or working on, the region. Many of the earlier issues of the news sources have been received as donations, initially from the Contemporary Archive on Latin America (CALA), which closed in 1981, and, more recently, from Amnesty International, Latin American Newsletters, the Latin America Bureau, Survival, the Central American Human Rights Committee and other organisations and individuals. A collection of press cuttings (mainly from British publications) on Latin America from the 1930s to the present is maintained; much of this material was received as donations from Norman Macdonald and the Latin America Bureau, and by the purchase of the George Pendle collection. Political pamphlets and other ephemera were received as part of the CALA gift and have been supplemented by subsequent acquisitions; about 2,000 items are held. There is a collection of approximately 3,000 research papers and reports from academic centres, non-governmental organisations, and other institutions in Europe and the Americas; and approximately 4,000 monographs, primarily for the use of the Institute's Master's students, the main subject collections being held elsewhere in the University. In 1992 the Library received a bequest of video recordings of Latin American feature films from the late Nissa Torrents. This collection has been enlarged and enhanced by subsequent donations from Channel Four and Robert Pring-Mill, by purchase and by the off-air recording of documentaries on the region; 350 videocassettes are held.

A full set of dissertations for the University of London intercollegiate MA in Area Studies (Latin America) is held, together with those for the MSc in Latin American Politics, the MSc in Environmental Issues in Latin America, the MA in Latin American Literature and Culture and the MA in Brazilian Studies; the Institute's first PhD student graduated in 1998 and copies of his thesis, and of those of subsequent students, are held. The Library maintains the Institute's website, which provides a gateway to a wide range of Internet resources for Latin American studies.

Access to collections:

Opening hours: Mon, Thurs 0930–1730, Tues 0930–2000, Wed 1000–1830, Fri 0930–1700. Public holidays closed.

Enquiries: By telephone, post, fax or e-mail. The Library provides a referral service supplying information on publications, library resources and experts on Latin America.

Admission: Non-members are admitted for reference purposes (undergraduates must submit a letter of introduction from their home institution).

Lending: No.

Inter-library loans: Does not lend books, but provides photocopies of periodical articles.

Union record: BLDSC, BUCLA, COLALAS, CURL, University of London Union List of Serials.

Catalogues: British Union Catalogue of Latin Americana (author card catalogue of Latin American collections in the United Kingdom, recording 204,000 titles and 374,000 locations), closed to new accessions in September 1988. Innopac automated catalogue.

Classification: Dewey Decimal Classification (modified).

Electronic facilities for non-members:

Microcomputing facilities: No.
On-line search facilities: No.
CD-ROM facilities: Yes.
Internet access: Yes.
Portable computers: Battery-operated portable computers may be used.

Other facilities for non-members:

Photocopying: Yes (payment required).
Microform holdings: Yes.
Reader-printer facilities: No.

country and include biographical information on important
in the industry. These have also been available electronically
ginning of 2000. Latin American and Caribbean material forms
of the overall collection and very few items are acquired annu-
llection is predominantly on open access.

collections:

urs: Mon–Fri 0930–1700. Public holidays closed.

By telephone, post, fax or e-mail (payment required).
Non-members are admitted for reference purposes (payment
). Reduced entrance fee for students (letter of introduction
or and proof of status required).
No.
ry loans: Lends to other libraries.
s: Author and subject catalogues of acquisitions to 1987.
monographs database and Library periodicals database on
tWorks include all acquisitions since 1987 and some of the
naterial.
ation: UREN.

ic facilities for non-members:

mputing facilities: Yes (payment required).
search facilities: Yes (payment required).
M facilities: Yes (payment required).
access: Yes.
e computers: Use permitted; power points available.

facilities for non-members:

opying: Yes (payment required).
orm holdings: Yes.
r-printer facilities: No.

Institute of Race Relations

iry, 2–6 Leeke Street, King's Cross Road, London WC1X 9HS

020 7833 2010/7837 0041
: 020 7278 0623
iail: info@irr.org.uk

WWW: http://www.irr.org.uk/library/
Established: 1958

Librarian: Hazel Waters, MA, ALA

Collections:

The Library holds a unique collection of material on race relations and racis[m] worldwide. The collection includes 20,000 books and pamphlets. Material [on] Latin America and the Caribbean, and on people of Caribbean origin [in] Britain, are included in the overall stock. The collection is on closed acces[s.]

Access to collections:

Opening hours: Mon–Thurs 1000–1300, 1400–1700. Public holidays close[d.]

Enquiries: By telephone, post, fax or e-mail.
Admission: Non-members are admitted for reference purposes at t[he] Librarian's discretion (appointment required).
Lending: No.
Inter-library loans: No.
Catalogue: Author, classified subject and regional catalogues.
Classification: Own classification.

Electronic facilities for non-members:

Microcomputing facilities: No.
On-line search facilities: No.
CD-ROM facilities: No.
Internet access: No.
Portable computers: Use not permitted.

Other facilities for non-members:

Photocopying: Yes (payment required).

Publications:

Library Catalogue of the Institute of Race Relations, London (Boston, Mass.: G.K. Hall, 1981), 6 vols.

125 Institution of Civil Engineers (ICE)
Library, 1 Great George Street, London SW1P 3AA

Tel.: 020 7222 7722. Archives 020 7665 2043. Admissions 020 7665 2252
Fax: 020 7976 7610
E-mail: library@ice.org.uk and archive@ice.org.uk
WWW: http://www.ice.org.uk
Established: 1818

Librarian: Michael M. Chrimes, BA, MLS, ALA

Collections:

The ICE's library is the largest civil engineering and construction library in the United Kingdom. The Latin American and Caribbean material is largely in the area of civil engineering (especially the development of railways and ports and harbours) and forms a very small part of the overall collection of over 100,000 books and 900 current periodicals. It is integrated with the main collections: 700 books, 10 current and 30 non-current periodical titles from the region, manuscript material including the diaries of engineers active in South America and a number of unpublished papers, and some slides and photographs. The geographical coverage emphasises Argentina, Brazil, Chile, Cuba, Guyana, Mexico, Peru, Trinidad and Uruguay. About 15 new titles are acquired annually.

Access to collections:

Opening hours: Mon 1030–1730, Tues–Fri 0915–1730. Closed between Christmas and New Year.

Enquiries: By post or e-mail.
Admission: Freely available to all members of the Institution and to members of other United Kingdom and overseas engineering institutions. Other visitors are admitted by appointment or with a letter of introduction from a member; non-members without an appointment will be charged a day fee (reduced for students).
Lending: To members of ICE and the Institution of Mechanical Engineers only.
Inter-library loans: Yes.
Catalogue: Librarian automated catalogue. The Library's catalogue is avail- able on the Internet.
Classification: Universal Decimal Classification.

Electronic facilities for non-members:

Microcomputing facilities: Yes
On-line search facilities: Yes (payment required).
CD-ROM facilities: Yes (payment required).
Internet access: No.
Portable computers: Use permitted; power points available.

Other facilities for non-members:

Photocopying: Yes (payment required).
Microform holdings: Yes.
Reader-printer facilities: Yes.

126 Institution of Mechanical Engineers
Information and Library Service, 1 Birdcage Walk, London SW1H 9JJ

Tel.: 020 7973 1266/1267. Archives 020 7973 1265
Fax: 020 7222 8762
E-mail: ils@imeche.org.uk
WWW: http://www.imeche.org.uk
Established: 1847 (Royal Charter 1930)

Senior Librarian and Archivist: Keith Moore, MA, DipLib
Librarian's e-mail address: k_moore@imeche.org.uk

Collections:

The Institution's Information and Library Service contains one of the world's largest collections on mechanical engineering and related disciplines in the United Kingdom. Book and journal holdings are international in scope. The department administers the Institution's archives and manuscript holdings, which include photographs, paintings and artefacts. Latin American holdings are a minor part of the collections, but contain information on the work of British engineers in South America and South American members. These include, for example, Robert Stephenson (1803–59), second President of the Institution, active in Bogotá, Colombia, 1825–27. Among company records is an important archive of James Livesey & Company (founded 1865) and successor companies (Livesey, Son & Henderson, etc.), railway consultants and contractors throughout

Central and South America and the Caribbean, nineteenth to twentieth centuries. The Institution itself had a River Plate branch (covering Argentina and Uruguay), 1926–50, and a Caribbean branch (West Indies, British Guiana, Venezuela and Colombia), 1938–74.

Access to collections:

Opening hours: Mon–Fri 0915–1730.

Enquiries: By telephone, post, fax or e-mail.
Admission: By appointment.
Lending: To IMechE members and to members of engineering bodies with reciprocal loan arrangements.
Inter-library loans: No.
Catalogues: CAIRS-LMS database containing post-1989 loan stock and pre-1955 historical book stock (a total of more than 16,500 records). Full catalogue conversion in progress. CAIRS-LMS archive database (currently 4,000 records and expanding). Other current technical databases.
Classification: Dewey Decimal Classification.

Electronic facilities for non-members:

Microcomputing facilities: No.
On-line search facilities: Yes (payment normally required).
CD-ROM facilities: Yes.
Internet access: Yes.
Portable computers: Use permitted; power points available.

Other facilities for non-members:

Photocopying: Yes (payment required).
Microform holdings: Yes.
Reader-printer facilities: Yes.

Publications:

John Pullin, *Progress through Mechanical Engineering: the First 150 years of the Institution of Mechanical Engineers* (London: Quiller Press, 1997).
Bibliographies, guides and catalogue information produced on demand.

127 Institution of Mining and Metallurgy
Library and Information Services, 77 Hallam Street, London W1W 5BS

Tel.: 020 7307 5401
Fax: 020 7436 5388
E-mail: LIS@imm.org.uk
WWW: http://www.imm.org.uk/index1.htm
Established: 1894
Head of Library and Information Service: Michael McGarr, BSc

Collections:

The Library provides information services on economic geography, mining technology, mineral processing and extractive metallurgy relating to non-ferrous metals and non-coal industrial minerals. The total stock includes 50,000 volumes and 1,100 current periodical titles; Latin American materials form a minor part of this collection. Periodicals are indexed for *Imm Abstracts* and *IMMAGE*. The Library also provides, through its website, a literature search and document delivery service with a same-day photocopy service for material held in stock. The Library's collections are on open access.

Access to collections:

Opening hours: Mon–Fri 1000–1700. Public holidays closed.

Enquiries: Telephone, post, fax and e-mail.
Admission: Non-members are admitted for reference purposes (payment required for all except students).
Lending: No.
Inter-library loans: No.
Catalogues: Author and classified subject catalogues. IMMAGE reference database from 1979.
Classification: Universal Decimal Classification.

Electronic facilities for non-members:

Microcomputing facilities: No.
On-line search facilities: No.
CD-ROM facilities: Yes.
Internet access: No.
Portable computers: Use permitted; power points available.

Other facilities for non-members:

Photocopying: Yes (payment required).
Microform holdings: Yes.
Reader-printer facilities: No.

Publications:

IMM Index to Mining and Metallurgy, 1894–1949 [includes, in country section, *Other America*, 5 fiches].
IMM Abstracts (London: Institution of Mining and Metallurgy, 1951–).
IMMAGE [Information on Mining, Metallurgy and Geological Exploration] (London: Institution of Mining and Metallurgy, 1980–). CD-ROM, or online database at http://www.eins.org/

128 International Coffee Organization (ICO)
Library, 22 Berners Street, London W1P 4DD

Tel.: 020 7612 0610
Fax: 020 7580 6129
E-mail: library@ico.org
WWW: http://www.ico.org/
Established: 1962

Library Administrator: Martin Wattam, BA

Collections:

The Library has a collection of 10,000 books, 250 periodical titles, over 9,000 slides, and maps, films and video recordings. A small amount of material relates to international cooperation before the signing of the International Coffee Agreement of 1962. Subject coverage emphasises the economic aspects of coffee production, marketing and consumption; material on the economies of the coffee-producing countries, on technical aspects of coffee production and on general trade and development issues, is also acquired. The Library began collecting material on Latin America and the Caribbean in 1972 and all coffee-producing countries are represented. Publications of international bodies such as the Organization of American States and the Economic Commission for Latin America and the Caribbean are held. The collection is predominantly on open access.

Access to collections:

Opening hours: Mon–Fri 0900–1700. Public holidays closed.

Enquiries: By telephone, post, fax and e-mail.
Admission: Non-members are admitted for reference purposes (appointment required).
Lending: No.
Inter-library loans: No.
Union record: Serials in the British Library.
Catalogue: Coffeeline; also available online through subscription to iCoffee at http://www.icoffee.com.
Classification: Own classification.

Electronic facilities for non-members:

Microcomputing facilities: No.
On-line search facilities: Yes.
CD-ROM facilities: No.
Internet access: Yes.
Portable computers: Use permitted; power points available.

Other facilities for non-members:

Photocopying: Yes (payment required).
Microform holdings: Yes.
Reader-printer facilities: No.

Publications:

Coffeeline (London: ICO).
Library Monthly Entries Bulletin (London: ICO). Six per annum.

129 International Institute for Strategic Studies
Library, Arundel House, 13–15 Arundel Street, Temple Place, London WC2R 3DX

Tel.: 020 7395 9122
Fax: 020 7836 3108
E-mail: library@iiss.org.uk
WWW: http://www.iiss.org/pub/iisslib.asp

Established: 1958

Chief Librarian: Ellen Peacock, BA

Collections:

The Library holds a collection of 6,700 books, 11,000 pamphlets, 76 periodical titles, and press and journal cuttings, dating from 1958 to the present. Subjects covered include international affairs, defence, politics, regional security, defence economics, arms control, war theory, weapons and strategy. Latin American materials have been collected since the foundation of the Library, but form a minor part of the overall stock. The collection is on open access.

Access to collections:

Opening hours: Mon–Fri 1000–1700. Public holidays closed.

Enquiries: By telephone, post, fax or e-mail.
Admission: Non-members are admitted for reference purposes (payment required).
Lending: No.
Inter-library loans: Lends to other libraries.
Union record: BLDSC.
Catalogue: SIRSI Unicorn automated catalogue.
Classification: Own classification.

Electronic facilities for non-members:

Microcomputing facilities: Yes (payment required).
On-line search facilities: Yes (payment required).
CD-ROM facilities: Yes (payment required).
Internet access: Yes (payment required).
Portable computers: Use permitted; power points available.

Other facilities for non-members:

Photocopying: Yes (payment required).
Microform holdings: Yes.
Reader-printer facilities: Yes (payment required).

130 International Labour Office (ILO)
Library, Millbank Tower, 21–24 Millbank, London SW1P 4QP

Tel.: 020 7828 6401
Fax: 020 7233 5925
E-mail: ipu@ilo-london.org.uk
WWW: http://www.ilo.org/public/english/support/lib/contact/gbr.htm
Established: 1919

Head of Publications and Information: Nick Evans
E-mail address: evansn@ilo-london.org.uk

Collections:

The Library holds a reference collection of ILO material published in English since 1919. This constitutes 2,000 volumes of ILO books, reports and working papers, together with ILO institutional documents. The Latin American material, much of which is contained in ILO working papers, is kept in a separate sequence, and on open access.

Access to collections:

Opening hours: Mon–Fri 1000–1300, 1400–1630.

Enquiries: By telephone, post or fax.
Admission: Open to the general public by appointment.
Lending: No.
Inter-library loans: No.
Catalogues: ILOLEX and NATLEX CD-ROMs and a subset of the LABORDOC database (books, reports and journal articles). A printed copy of the database, for stock held in the London office, is also maintained.
Classification: Own classification.

Electronic facilities for non-members:

Microcomputing facilities: No.
On-line search facilities: No.
CD-ROM facilities: Yes (payment required for printing).
Internet access: No.
Portable computers: Use not permitted.

Other facilities for non-members:

Photocopying: Yes (payment required).

131 International Planned Parenthood Federation (IPPF)

Library, Regent's College, Inner Circle, Regent's Park, London NW1 4NS

Tel.: 020 7487 7855
Fax: 020 7487 7950
E-mail: info@ippf.org
WWW: http://www.ippf.org/
Established: 1952

Librarian: Rita A. Ward, ALA

Collections:

The IPPF Library contains 6,000 books, 2,000 pamphlets, 3,500 microforms, 50 audio recordings, 400 video recordings and 90 periodical titles dealing with birth control, sex education and population studies, and material on Latin America and the Caribbean has been acquired since 1965. The material is held on open access.

Access to collections:

Opening hours: Mon–Fri 1000–1700. Public holidays closed.

Enquiries: By telephone, post, fax or e-mail.
Admission: Non-members are admitted for reference purposes (appointment required).
Lending: No.
Inter-library loans: Lends to other libraries.
Union record: BLDSC.
Catalogue: InMagic automated catalogue.
Classification: Own classification.

Electronic facilities for non-members:

Microcomputing facilities: By arrangement.
On-line search facilities: No.
CD-ROM facilities: Yes.
Internet access: No.
Portable computers: Use permitted; power points available.

Other facilities for non-members:

Photocopying: Yes (payment required).
Microform holdings: Yes.
Reader-printer facilities: No.

132 International Rubber Study Group
1st Floor, Heron House, 109–115 Wembley Hill Road, London HA9 8DA

Tel.: 020 8903 7727
Fax: 020 8903 2848
E-mail: economics@rubberstudy.com
WWW: http://www.rubberstudy.com
Established: 1944

Subject enquiries to: Darren Cooper, Chief Statistician
Specialist's e-mail address: Statistics@rubberstudy.com

Collections:

The International Rubber Study Group is an intergovernmental organisation, which provides a forum for the discussion of matters affecting the supply and demand for natural and synthetic rubber. This covers all aspects of the world rubber industry, including marketing, shipping distribution, trade in raw materials and the manufacture and sale of rubber products. The material on Latin America forms a minor part of the collection: 20 books and 2 current periodical titles, with an emphasis on Brazil. A range of historical statistical series on natural rubber dating back to 1822 is also held.

Access to collections:

Opening hours: Mon–Fri 0900–1700.

Enquiries: By telephone, post (payment required) or e-mail.
Admission: By appointment; letter of introduction required.
Lending: No.
Inter-library loans: No.

Electronic facilities for non-members:

Microcomputing facilities: No.
On-line search facilities: No.
CD-ROM facilities: No.
Internet access: No.
Portable computers: Use permitted; power points available.

Other facilities for non-members:

Photocopying: Yes (payment required).

133 International Sugar Organization
1 Canada Square, Canary Wharf, London E14 5AA

Tel.: 020 7513 1144
Fax: 020 7513 1146
E-mail: hcole@isosugar.org
WWW: http://www.isosugar.org/
Established: 1977

Librarian: Hilary Cole, BA

Collections:

The Library holds a collection of periodicals, yearbooks, statistical series and reports on the sugar industry, with worldwide coverage. Latin American and Caribbean materials form a minor part of the overall stock. The material is on open access.

Access to collections:

Opening hours: Mon–Fri 1000–1600.

Enquiries: By telephone, post, fax or e-mail.
Admission: Open to the general public by appointment; a Canary Wharf security pass is issued on entry to the building.
Lending: No.
Inter-library loans: No.
Catalogue: Manual catalogue.
Classification: Material arranged in country sections.

Electronic facilities for non-members:

Microcomputing facilities: Yes.
On-line search facilities: No.
CD-ROM facilities: Yes.
Internet access: No.
Portable computers: Use permitted; power points available.

Other facilities for non-members:

Photocopying: Yes (payment required).

134 King's College London (KCL), University of London

Chancery Lane Library and Information Services Centre, Chancery Lane, London WC2A 1LR

Tel.: 020 7848 2139. Holdings enquiries and admissions 020 7848 2424
Fax: 020 7848 1777
E-mail: libraryenquiry@kcl.ac.uk
Web catalogue: http://library.kcl.ac.uk/
WWW: http://www.kcl.ac.uk/library/
Established: 1829

Director of Library Services: Anne Bell, BA, MA, ALA
Subject enquiries to: Martin Hodgson, BA, DipLIS, MA, ALA
Specialist's tel.: 020 7848 2186
Specialist's e-mail address: martin.hodgson@kcl.ac.uk

Collections:

The Library began collecting in the field in the 1960s. The collection comprises some 7,000 volumes, together with approximately 25 current and 65 non-current periodical titles; present acquisitions total about 100 volumes a year. The holdings are particularly strong in Latin American (including Brazilian) literature and linguistics. The Library also contains material on colonial and modern history, travel works and economic geography. Some material on Brazil is included in 200 microform reels of Lusophone material. All collections are predominantly on open access.

Access to collections:

Opening hours: Term: Mon–Fri 0900–2000, Sat 0930–1730. Vacation: Mon–Fri 0930–1700, Sat closed. Christmas and Easter closed.

Enquiries: By telephone, post or e-mail.
Admission: Non-members are admitted for reference purposes (written application required).
Lending: Yes (written application and payment required).
Inter-library loans: Lends to other libraries.
Union record: BLDSC, BUCLA, BUCOP, COLALAS, CURL, *Serials in the British Library*, University of London Union List of Serials.
Catalogue: Author, classified and alphabetical subject catalogue on microform for some pre-1980 material. Ex Libris Aleph automated catalogue.
Classification: Library of Congress Classification.

Electronic facilities for non-members:

Microcomputing facilities: No.
On-line search facilities: No.
CD-ROM facilities: No.
Internet access: No.
Portable computers: Use permitted.

Other facilities for non-members:

Photocopying: Yes (payment required).
Microform holdings: Yes.
Reader-printer facilities: Yes (payment required for printing).

135 London Borough of Bromley

Central Library, High Street, Bromley, Kent BR1 1EX

Tel.: 020 8460 9955
Fax: 020 8313 9975
Web catalogue: http://library.bromley.gov.uk/
WWW: http://www.bromley.gov.uk/
Established: 1894
Librarian: Barry Walkinshaw, BA, ALA

Collections:

In 1976, Bromley took over from the London Borough of Hackney the responsibility for purchasing current British publications on Latin American and Caribbean history, geography and travel, for the LASER subject specialisation scheme for public libraries in South East England. The library system now holds 1,500 books and acquires about 100 volumes each year. The material forms part of the general reference and lending stock and is held on open access.

Access to collections:

Opening hours: Mon, Wed, Fri 0930–1800, Tues, Thurs 0930–2000, Sat 0930–1700. Public holidays closed.

Enquiries: By telephone, post, fax or e-mail.
Admission: Non-members are admitted for reference purposes.
Lending: No.

Inter-library loans: Lends to other libraries.
Union record: BLDSC, LASER.
Catalogue: Geac automated catalogue.
Classification: Dewey Decimal Classification.

Electronic facilities for non-members:

Microcomputing facilities: Yes (payment required).
On-line search facilities: No.
CD-ROM facilities: Yes (payment required).
Internet access: Yes (payment required).
Portable computers: Use permitted, provided that it does not disturb other readers; limited power points available.

Other facilities for non-members:

Photocopying: Yes (payment required).
Microform holdings: Yes.
Reader-printer facilities: Yes (payment required).

136 London Borough of Hackney

C.L.R. James Library, 24–30 Dalston Lane, Hackney, London E8 3AZ

Tel.: 020 8356 1665
Fax: 020 7254 4655

Homerton Library, Homerton High Street, Hackney, London E9 6AS
Tel.: 020 8356 2572
Fax: 020 8525 7945
WWW: http://www.hackney.gov.uk/educate/data/ed_lib1.htm

Executive Librarian: Bethan Williams, ALA
E-mail address: bwilliams@hackney.gov.uk

Collections:

From 1946 to 1975 (when the responsibility was transferred to Bromley) Hackney public library authority accepted responsibility for purchasing current British publications on Latin American and Caribbean history, geography and travel under a subject specialisation scheme begun by the metropolitan libraries in 1946 and later extended to cover all public libraries in South East England (LASER). The collection totals about

1,000 volumes and is held at the Homerton Library on closed access. The Three Continents Liberation Collection, reflecting the liberation struggles in Africa, Asia, and Latin America and the Caribbean, is held at the C.L.R. James Library on open access.

Access to collections:

Opening hours: Mon–Tues, Thurs–Fri 1000–2000, Sat 0900–1700, Wed closed. Public holidays closed.

Enquiries: By telephone, post or fax.
Admission: Non-members are admitted for reference purposes.
Lending: No.
Inter-library loans: Lends to other libraries.
Union record: BUCOP, COLALAS, LASER.
Catalogue: Dynix automated catalogue.
Classification: Dewey Decimal Classification.

Electronic facilities for non-members:

Microcomputing facilities: Yes (payment required).
On-line search facilities: Yes (payment required).
CD-ROM facilities: Yes.
Internet access: Yes (payment required).
Portable computers: Use not permitted.

Other facilities for non-members:

Photocopying: Yes (payment required).
Microform holdings: Yes.
Reader-printer facilities: Yes (payment required).

137 London Borough of Tower Hamlets
Limehouse Library, 638 Commercial Road, London E14 7HS

Tel.: 020 7364 2527
Fax: 020 7364 2502

Head of Libraries: Anne Cunningham, ALA
Acting Library Resources Co-ordinator: Donald Chitty, BA, ALA
Tel.: 020 7364 2537

Collections:

Tower Hamlets has responsibility for purchasing literature in Portuguese, and works in English on Portuguese and Brazilian literature and language, under the LASER subject specialisation scheme for public libraries in South East England. Some translations of Portuguese and Brazilian literary works are also purchased. Limehouse Library now holds 1,080 books (mainly twentieth-century literature). The collection is on open access.

Access to collections:

Opening hours: Mon 0900–2000, Fri 0900–1800, Sat 0900–1200, Tues–Thurs closed. Public holidays closed.

Enquiries: By telephone, post or fax.
Admission: Non-members are admitted for reference purposes.
Lending: No.
Inter-library loans: Lends to other libraries.
Union record: BLDSC, LASER.
Catalogue: DS automated catalogue.
Classification: Dewey Decimal Classification.

Electronic facilities for non-members:

Microcomputing facilities: No.
On-line search facilities: No.
CD-ROM facilities: No.
Internet access: No.
Portable computers: Use not permitted.

Other facilities for non-members:

Photocopying: Yes (payment required).

138 London Chamber of Commerce and Industry

Business Information Centre, 33 Queen Street, London EC4R 1AP

Tel.: 020 7248 4444
Fax: 020 7489 0391
E-mail: info@londonchamber.co.uk
WWW: http://www.londonchamber.co.uk/
Established: 1881

Head of Information: Marita Ewins

Collections:

The Business Information Centre collects trade journals, United Kingdom and overseas business directories, newspapers, marketing data, international statistics and management literature. Latin American and Caribbean materials form a minor part of the collection, consisting mainly of general introductions to doing business in individual countries, trade directories and lists of suppliers or manufacturers of goods and services. The collection is on open access.

Access to collections:

Opening hours: Mon–Fri 0900–1730. Public holidays closed.

Enquiries: By telephone, post, fax or e-mail (payment required).
Admission: Non-members are admitted for reference purposes (payment required).
Lending: No.
Inter-library loans: No.
Catalogue: Author, title and alphabetical subject catalogue.
Classification: Own classification.

Electronic facilities for non-members:

Microcomputing facilities: No.
On-line search facilities: Yes (payment required).
CD-ROM facilities: Yes (payment required).
Internet access: No.
Portable computers: Application to Head of Information required.

Other facilities for non-members:

Photocopying: No.
Microform holdings: Yes.
Reader-printer facilities: Yes (payment required).

139 The London Library
14 St James's Square, London SW1Y 4LG

Tel.: General 020 7930 7705. Holdings enquiries 020 7766 4747. Admissions 020 7766 4720
Fax: 020 7766 4766

E-mail: Membership membership@londonlibrary.co.uk;
  Enquiries inquiries@londonlibrary.co.uk
Web catalogue: http://www.londonlibrary.co.uk/webpacj/library.html
WWW: http://www.londonlibrary.co.uk/
Established: 1841

Librarian: Inez T.P.A. Lynn, BA, MLitt, ALA
Subject enquiries to: Gillian Turner, MA, DipLib, Acquisitions Support Librarian
Specialist's tel.: 020 7766 4735
Specialist's e-mail address: gill.turner@londonlibrary.co.uk

Collections:

The Library has a collection of 1,000,000 books, 4,000 pamphlets and over 500 current periodical titles, mainly in the humanities and social sciences. Latin American and Caribbean materials form a minor part of this collection, probably numbering about 10,000 volumes. The geographical coverage of the collection is stronger on Latin America than on the Caribbean; Argentina, Brazil, Mexico and Peru are the best represented countries. Materials on the region have been collected since the foundation of the Library and, in 1936, it benefited from a bequest of literary works from the collection of R.B. Cunninghame Graham. Current acquisitions (some 200–300 volumes a year in Spanish and over 100 a year in English) are mainly in the field of literature; other subjects represented in the collection are history, politics, biography, topography, travel, anthropology and economics. The collections are on open access.

Access to collections:

Opening hours: Mon, Fri–Sat 0930–1730, Tues–Thurs 0930–1930, Sun closed. Public holidays and Saturdays preceding public holidays closed.

Enquiries: By telephone, post, fax or e-mail.

Admission: Non-members and certain temporary types of membership admitted for reference purposes where material is not readily accessible elsewhere (payment required), but may not have access to the stacks. Non-members may request titles to view by special arrangement.

Lending: No. (All members may borrow all categories of stock subject to specific title restrictions. Membership subscription for individual, institutional and life-membership categories.)

Inter-library loans: Lends to other libraries that are members of the London Library.
Catalogue: A retrospective conversion programme is in progress: twenty-five per cent of titles are currently on the automated catalogue, including all post-1983 acquisitions. The published catalogues do not include material acquired 1950–82, for which information is available only through the Library. Dynix automated catalogue.
Classification: Own classification.

Electronic facilities for non-members:

Microcomputing facilities: No.
On-line search facilities: No.
CD-ROM facilities: Yes (payment required).
Internet access: Yes.
Portable computers: Use permitted; power points available.

Other facilities for non-members:

Photocopying: Yes (payment required).

Publications:

Catalogue of the London Library, St James's Square, London, revised edition (London: The Library, 1913–14), 2 vols.
Catalogue of the London Library, St James's Square, London: Supplement, 1913–1920 (London: The Library, 1920).
Catalogue of the London Library, St James's Square, London: Supplement, 1920–1928 (London: The Library, 1929).
Catalogue of the London Library, St James's Square, London: Supplement, 1928–1950 (London: The Library, 1953).
Subject-index of the London Library, St James's Square, London (London: Williams & Norgate, 1909).
Subject-index of the London Library, St James's Square, London: Additions, 1909–1922 (London: The Library, 1923).
Subject-index of the London Library, St James's Square, London: Additions, 1923–1938 (London: The Library, 1938).
Subject-index of the London Library, St James's Square, London: Additions, 1938–1954 (London: The Library, 1955).

140 London School of Economics, University of London

British Library of Political and Economic Science, 10 Portugal Street, London WC2A 2HD

Tel.: 020 7955 7229. Admissions 020 7955 6733
Fax: 020 7955 7454
E-mail: library@lse.ac.uk
Web catalogue: http://blpes.lse.ac.uk/
WWW: http://www.lse.ac.uk/library/
Established: 1896

Librarian and Director of Information Services: Jean Sykes, MA, MLitt, DipLib, ALA
Subject enquiries (non-official publications) to: Graham Camfield, BA, MA, Senior Assistant Librarian
Specialist's tel.: 020 7955 7942
Specialist's e-mail address: g.camfield@lse.ac.uk
Subject enquiries (official publications) to: Chris James, MA, ALA, Assistant Librarian
Specialist's tel.: 020 7955 7943
Specialist's e-mail address: c.james@lse.ac.uk

Collections:

The Library has collected material on the region since 1896. Latin American and Caribbean material form a minor part of the overall stock of the Library, but there are more than 30,000 books and pamphlets and over 400 periodical titles. The collection is particularly strong in politics, economics and sociology. In addition social anthropology, demography, psychology, and nineteenth- and twentieth-century political and economic history are collected. There are extensive holdings of official publications: especially statistics and constitutional, criminal and labour law. The Library is a depository library for the United Nations and some of its agencies, the Organization of American States and other international bodies. The collection is mainly on open access.

Access to collections:

Opening hours: Term and Easter Vacation: Mon–Fri 0900–2300, Sat–Sun 1100–2100. Christmas and Summer Vacations: Mon–Fri 0900–2000, Sat–Sun closed. Public holidays closed.

Enquiries: By telephone or e-mail.

Admission: University of London: academic staff and students may apply for a permit for reference use. Other academic institutions: academic staff and research students may apply for a permit for reference use; taught students preparing a substantial dissertation may apply for a permit for reference use for one term (including vacation); other taught students will be admitted free of charge during vacations (payment required for term-time use). Embassies in London: staff may use the Library for reference purposes (proof of identity required). All other visitors must pay a fee.

Lending: Academic staff and research students of the University of London may apply for an external borrower's card.

Inter-library loans: No.

Union record: BLDSC, BUCLA, BUCOP, COLALAS, CURL, University of London Union List of Serials.

Catalogue: SIRSI Unicorn automated catalogue.

Classification: Library of Congress Classification.

Electronic facilities for non-members:

Microcomputing facilities: No.
On-line search facilities: Yes.
CD-ROM facilities: No.
Internet access: No.
Portable computers: Use permitted; power points available.

Other facilities for non-members:

Photocopying: Yes (payment required).
Microform holdings: Yes.
Reader-printer facilities: Yes.

Publications:

A London Bibliography of the Social Sciences (London: London School of Economics and Political Science, 1931–89), 47 vols.

International Bibliography of the Social Sciences. Available at http://www.bids.ac.uk/

141 London School of Hygiene and Tropical Medicine, University of London

Library, Keppel Street, London WC1E 7HT

Tel.: 020 7927 2283
Fax: 020 7927 2273
E-mail: library@lshtm.ac.uk
Web catalogue: http://unicorn.lshtm.ac.uk/uhtbin/webcat
WWW: http://www.lshtm.ac.uk/as/library/
Established: 1899
Librarian & Director of Information Services: R. Brian Furner, BA, MSc, MIInfSc

Collections:

The Library has one of the strongest collections in Britain in the field of public health, epidemiology and tropical medicine, including 50,000 books, 15,000 pamphlets and 800 periodical titles. Latin American and Caribbean materials form a minor part of the overall stock, including over 1,500 books, 100 periodical titles and 400 volumes of official reports. The Library holds many publications of the Pan American Health Organization, some maps, and reports of twentieth-century expeditions. The collections are mainly on open access.

Access to collections:

Opening hours: Mon–Fri 0830–2025, Sat 0900–1230.

Enquiries: By telephone, post, fax or e-mail.
Admission: Non-members are admitted for reference purposes (proof of identity required).
Lending: No.
Inter-library loans: Lends to other libraries.
Union record: BLDSC, BUCLA, BUCOP, CURL, LASER, University of London Union List of Serials, WLSP.
Catalogue: SIRSI Unicorn automated catalogue.
Classification: Barnard Classification.

Electronic facilities for non-members:

Microcomputing facilities: No.
On-line search facilities: No.
CD-ROM facilities: No.

Internet access: No.
Portable computers: Use not permitted.

Other facilities for non-members:
Photocopying: Yes (payment required).
Microform holdings: Yes.
Reader-printer facilities: Yes (payment required).

Publications:

Dictionary Catalogue of the London School of Hygiene and Tropical Medicine, University of London (Boston, Mass.: G.K. Hall, 1965), 7 vols.
Dictionary Catalogue of the London School of Hygiene and Tropical Medicine, University of London: First Supplement, 1971 (Boston, Mass.: G.K. Hall, 1971).
A Catalogue of the Ross Archives (London: The School, 1983), 34 microfiches.

142 Marx Memorial Library
Marx House, 37a Clerkenwell Green, London EC1R 0DU

Tel.: 020 7253 1485/7251 4706
Fax: 020 7251 6039
E-mail: marx.library@britishlibrary.net
WWW: http://www.marxmemoriallibrary.sageweb.co.uk
Established: 1933

Librarian: Tish Collins, BA, MSc

Collections:

The Library was founded in 1933 but includes earlier material and holds 100,000 books, 50,000 pamphlets, 120 current periodical titles, 30,000 periodical volumes, 25 microforms, 10 videos and many photographs and illustrations. The collection covers the labour movement worldwide (including Marxist, socialist, communist and radical movements), trades unions, cooperatives, and social issues. Latin American and Caribbean material forms a minor part of the overall stock, but includes pamphlet collections on Cuba, Jamaica and Guyana, together with other pamphlets on the region. The Library has an extensive International Brigade Archive relating to the Spanish Civil War. The collections are on open access.

Access to collections:

Opening hours: Mon 1300–1800, Tues–Thurs 1300–2000, Sat 1000–1300, Fri closed.

Enquiries: By telephone, post, fax or e-mail.
Admission: Membership and affiliation available.
Lending: Members may borrow.
Inter-library loans: No.
Catalogues: Card index. Retrospective conversion project in progress. The automated catalogue will be made available on the Internet.
Classification: Own classification.

Electronic facilities for non-members:

Microcomputing facilities: No.
On-line search facilities: No.
CD-ROM facilities: Yes.
Internet access: No.
Portable computers: Use permitted; power points available (payment required).

Other facilities for non-members:

Photocopying: Yes (payment required).
Microform holdings: Yes.
Reader-printer facilities: No.

Publications:

Catalogue of the Marx Memorial Library, London (Boston, Mass.: G.K. Hall, 1979), 3 vols.
Catalogue: J.D. Bernal Peace Collection, Marx Memorial Library (London: The Library, 1981).
International Brigade Memorial Archive: Catalogue, 1986 (London: Marx Memorial Library, 1986).
International Brigade Memorial Archive: Catalogue, 1990 (London: Marx Memorial Library, 1990).
International Brigade Memorial Archive: Catalogue, 1994 (London: Marx Memorial Library, 1994).
Marx Memorial Library Bulletin (London: The Library, 1957–).

143 Maya: the Guatemalan Indian Centre

Reference Library, 94 Wandsworth Bridge Road, London SW6 2TF

Tel./Fax: 020 7371 5291
E-mail: maya@ukonline.co.uk
Web catalogue: http://web.ukonline.co.uk/maya/html/librarydb.htm
WWW: http://web.ukonline.co.uk/maya/html/library.htm or
    http://www.maya.org.uk
Established: 1990

Curator: Jamie Marshall
Curator's e-mail address: jamie.marshall@ukonline.co.uk

Collections:

The Library is one of the largest and most comprehensive collections of Guatemalan material in the United Kingdom. Although the Centre was founded in 1990, the collection was started in the 1970s. Almost 2,000 monograph titles cover all aspects of Guatemala and the Maya, with special emphasis on anthropology, archaeology and ethnography. There are 2 current and 7 non-current periodical titles, newspapers and weekly newspacks, press cuttings from 1980 to the present, maps, photographs, slides, theses and sound recordings. A video archive of approximately 100 documentaries and feature films covering human rights, history, politics, anthropology and archaeology can be viewed at the Centre. In addition, the Centre holds the largest collection of Guatemalan Indian textiles outside Guatemala (some 7,000 items) and mounts exhibitions on Mayan life and dress. The collection is on open access.

Access to collections:

Opening hours: Tues, Thurs 1400–1800, Sat 1000–1800, Mon, Wed, Fri, Sun closed. Public holidays closed. Closed in January, August and for two weeks at Easter.

Enquiries: By telephone, post, fax or e-mail (payment may be required).
Admission: Non-members are admitted for reference purposes (payment and appointment required).
Lending: No.
Inter-library loans: No.
Catalogues: Author / subject card catalogue. Automated author catalogue (also available through the website).
Classification: Own classification.

Electronic facilities for non-members:

Microcomputing facilities: No.
On-line search facilities: No.
CD-ROM facilities: No.
Internet access: No.
Portable computers: Use permitted; power points available.

Other facilities for non-members:

Photocopying: Limited off-site photocopying can be arranged.
Microform holdings: Yes.
Reader-printer facilities: No.

144 Mexicolore
28 Warriner Gardens, London SW11 4EB

Tel.: 020 7622 9577
Fax: 020 7498 3643
E-mail: Ian.Mursell@btinternet.com
WWW: http://www.mexicolore.co.uk/photolib.htm
Established: 1980

Subject enquiries to: Ian Mursell

Collections:

Mexicolore is a specialist commercial picture library containing several thousand original colour images of Mexico since 1980. A unique part of the collection are the slides illustrating Aztec civilisation and its legacy today, covering: archaeological sites, excavations and ruins, pyramids, statues and monuments, sculptures, murals, calendars, codices and manuscripts, musical instruments, costumes, arts and crafts, food and farming, everyday artefacts, ceremonies and jewellery. All pictures are available in low- or high-resolution digital format.

Access to collections:

Opening hours: Mon–Fri 0900–1800. Weekends by appointment.

Enquiries: By telephone, post, fax or e-mail.
Admission: By appointment.
Search/service fee: £25 + VAT. Commissions undertaken.

Lending: Pictures are supplied on a commercial basis only.

Electronic facilities for non-members:
Portable computers: Use permitted.

Other facilities for non-members:
Copying: Photocopying, slide duplication (payment required).

Publications:
Brochure.

145 Middlesex University
Library, Tottenham Campus, White Hart Lane, London N17 8HR

Tel.: 020 8411 5165. Holdings enquiries 020 8411 5651
Fax: 020 8411 6068
Web catalogue: http://library.mdx.ac.uk/
WWW: http://www.ilrs.mdx.ac.uk/lib/
Established: 1973 (as Middlesex Polytechnic), 1992 (as University)

Head of Information and Learning Resource Services and University Librarian: William Marsterson, MA, ALA
Subject enquiries to: Vicky Sharp, BA, ALA, Subject Librarian for Modern Languages
Specialist's tel.: 020 8411 6087
Specialist's e-mail address: v.sharp@mdx.ac.uk

Collections:

Latin American and Caribbean materials are held in two of the campus libraries of the University: history, languages and literature at Tottenham and social sciences at Enfield (tel.: 020 8411 5334/5991). The best represented countries are Chile, Cuba and Peru. More than 500 books are available throughout the system and 100 titles are added each year. There are 3 current periodical titles and some videos. The material is on open access.

Access to collections:

Opening hours: Term: Mon–Tues 0900–2200, Wed–Thurs 0900–2400, Fri 1000–1800, Sat 1000–1600. Vacation: Mon–Thurs 0930–1700, Fri 1000–1700, Sat closed. Public holidays closed.

Enquiries: By telephone, post, fax or e-mail.
Admission: Non-members are admitted for reference purposes (proof of identity and of need to use the library required).
Lending: No.
Inter-library loans: Lends to other libraries.
Union record: BLDSC.
Catalogue: Dynix Horizon automated catalogue.
Classification: Dewey Decimal Classification.

Electronic facilities for non-members:

Microcomputing facilities: No.
On-line search facilities: No.
CD-ROM facilities: No.
Internet access: No.
Portable computers: Use permitted; power points available.

Other facilities for non-members:

Photocopying: Yes (payment required).

146 Ministry of Defence (MOD)
Admiralty Library, 3–5 Great Scotland Yard, London SW1A 2HW

Tel.: 020 7218 5446
Fax: 020 7218 8210
WWW: http://www.mod.uk
Established: c. 1809

Librarian: J.M. Wraight, BLib, ALA, FRSA

Collections:

The total stock of over 160,000 volumes and 10,000 pamphlets is devoted to maritime history (and especially the history of the British Navy and its personnel), to shipbuilding and naval science, and to voyages and travels in general. These are now divided between four sites. The rich collection of early voyages, including a number of travel accounts relating to Latin America in the first half of the nineteenth century, hydrographical surveys, charts and maps (dating back mainly to the first half of the nineteenth century, but with several eighteenth-century items and a few from the seventeenth century), are in the care of the Hydrographic Office, Admiralty Way, Taunton, Somerset TA1 2DN (tel.: 01823 337900 ext. 3451). Material on naval campaigns and actions (including the Latin American theatre), strategy, tactics, administration, policy, doctrine, etc., currently remains in London (address as above). Social history, shipbuilding, sciences, biography, law and a broad range of other subjects are held at the Admiralty Library, Portsmouth, PP 85, Building 1/51, HM Naval Base, Portsmouth, Hampshire PO1 3NH (tel.: 023 9272 5490), which is staffed by the Royal Naval Museum. The collections of the Royal Naval Medical Service are housed at the Institute of Naval Medicine, Crescent Road, Alverstoke, Gosport, Hampshire PO12 2DL (tel.: 023 9276 8000).

Access to collections:

Opening hours: London collections: Mon–Fri by appointment. Public holidays closed.

Enquiries: By telephone, post or fax.
Admission: Open to the general public. Application in advance to the Librarian required.
Lending: No.
Inter-library loans: No.
Catalogue: SydneyPLUS automated catalogue.
Classification: Own classification.

Electronic facilities for non-members:

Microcomputing facilities: No.
On-line search facilities: No.
CD-ROM facilities: No.
Internet access: No.
Portable computers: Use permitted; power points available.

Other facilities for non-members:

Photocopying: Yes (payment required).
Microform holdings: Yes.
Reader-printer facilities: Yes (payment required).

147 Ministry of Defence (*MOD*)
Whitehall Library, 3–5 Great Scotland Yard, London SW1A 2HW

Tel.: 020 7218 4445
Fax: 020 7218 5413
E-mail: whitehall.lib.mod@dgics.gov.uk
WWW: http://www.mod.uk

Chief Librarian: G. Webster, BSc, FLA, MInstAM, MMS

Collections:

The Latin American material in the Library relates both to the military history of the region and to the current strategic situation. The historical collection has material both on the struggle for independence in the early nineteenth century and on the wars between the newly independent states. The memoirs of British soldiers who campaigned officially or unofficially in Latin America are a feature of the historical collection. The material is in the process of being transferred to the DISC (Defence Intelligence and Security Centre) Library, Chicksands, Shefford, Bedfordshire SG17 5PR. It will be available for consultation in due course.

Access to collections:

Opening hours: Mon–Fri 0930–1230, 1330–1630, by appointment. Public holidays closed.

Enquiries: By telephone, post, fax or e-mail.
Admission: Open to the general public if the material required is not available elsewhere. Written application in advance to the Chief Librarian and appointment required.
Lending: No.
Inter-library loans: Lends to other libraries.
Union record: BLDSC.
Catalogue: C2 automated catalogue.
Classification: Universal Decimal Classification and own classification.

Electronic facilities for non-members:

Microcomputing facilities: No.
On-line search facilities: No.
CD-ROM facilities: No.
Internet access: No.
Portable computers: Use not permitted.

Other facilities for non-members:

Photocopying: Yes (payment required).
Microform holdings: Yes.
Reader-printer facilities: No.

148 National Art Library, Victoria and Albert Museum

Cromwell Road, South Kensington, London SW7 2RL

Tel.: 020 7942 2400
Fax: 020 7942 2401
E-mail: nal.enquiries@vam.ac.uk
Telnet catalogue: library1.nal.vam.ac.uk
Web catalogue: http://www.nal.vam.ac.uk/nalcomct.html
WWW: http://www.nal.vam.ac.uk/
Established: 1837

Chief Librarian: Post vacant

Collections:

The Library's collections include 1,000,000 books, 1,000,000 manuscript items, 1,500 periodical titles, 8,000 information files and 19 videodiscs on all aspects of the fine and applied arts. Latin American and Caribbean materials form a minor part of the overall stock; Argentina, Brazil, Cuba and Mexico have the best coverage. The collections are on closed access.

Access to collections:

Opening hours: Tues–Sat 1000–1700, Sun–Mon closed. Public holidays and Saturdays before public holidays closed. Closed for three weeks following August Bank Holiday.

Enquiries: By telephone, post, fax or e-mail.
Admission: Open to the general public for reference purposes on production of identification. There is no charge to use the Library, but first-time readers are subject to the Museum's entry charges. Access to Special Collections requires a Reader's Ticket for Special Collections (referee required).
Lending: No.
Inter-library loans: No.

Catalogues: Exhibition Handlist for catalogues published 1890–1986; catalogues published 1980 and later may be on the automated catalogue. Sales catalogues up to 1986 are listed on a microfiche catalogue; from 1987 they are on the automated catalogue. Pre-1890 Author Catalogue MUEN to VOSM in six volumes; the remaining items from this catalogue are incorporated in the Main Author Catalogue. Main Author Catalogue on microfiche for all items acquired or catalogued 1891–1986. Dynix automated catalogue for all items acquired or catalogued since January 1987. Union List of Art, Architecture and Design Serials — a database of art and design periodicals held in academic, public, national and special libraries in the United Kingdom and Ireland — is being created by NAL staff in conjunction with the Art Libraries Society, and will be held on the NAL's automated catalogue.
Classification: Dewey Decimal Classification for open access reference material. Own classification for other materials.

Electronic facilities for non-members:

Microcomputing facilities: No.
On-line search facilities: Yes (appointment and payment required).
CD-ROM facilities: Yes.
Internet access: Yes.
Portable computers: Use permitted; limited number of power points available.

Other facilities for non-members:

Photocopying: Yes (payment required; copying undertaken by staff).
Microform holdings: Yes.
Reader-printer facilities: Yes (payment required).

149 National Maritime Museum
Caird Library, Romney Road, Greenwich, London SE10 9NF

Tel.: 020 8312 6528/6673. Admissions 020 8312 6672
Fax: 020 8312 6722
E-mail: library@nmm.ac.uk
Web catalogue: http://www.nmm.ac.uk/cgi-bin/empower?DB=library_index99
WWW: http://www.nmm.ac.uk/cmr/library.html
Established: 1934

Library and Information Resources Manager: Jill Davies, BSc, DipLib
Charts and Atlases tel.: 020 8312 6757
Manuscripts tel.: 020 8312 6691/6669
Manuscripts e-mail: manuscripts@nmm.ac.uk
Picture Library tel.: 020 8312 6631/6704
Picture Library e-mail: Lxpring@nmm.ac.uk
Research Enquiry Service tel.: 020 8312 6712
Research Enquiry Service e-mail: LXVeri@nmm.ac.uk

Collections:

The Caird Library is the largest reference library on maritime affairs in the world. There are over 100,000 books, 20,000 pamphlets, 25,000 bound volumes of periodicals, 500 current periodicals, microfilms and CD-ROMs. The main focus is British maritime history, and the collection has important material on the Caribbean, but material from and about other countries is also collected. The collections cover all aspects of seafaring — naval, merchant and recreational. Of particular importance are the collections on navigation, voyages and travel, and piracy, and there is also material of interest on naval history, biography, topography, merchant shipping, naval architecture and fisheries. Relevant material is also present in the Manuscript Collection, the Chart Collection (including atlases), and the Picture Library.

Access to collections:

Opening hours: Mon–Fri 1000–1645. Sat by appointment only. Public holidays closed.

Enquiries: By telephone, post, fax or e-mail.
Admission: Open to the general public for reference use (application for reader's ticket required). Notice may need to be given to consult certain items; telephone in advance.
Lending: No.
Inter-library loans: No.
Catalogue: TinLib automated catalogue.
Classification: Universal Decimal Classification.

Electronic facilities for non-members:

Microcomputing facilities: No.
On-line search facilities: Yes (payment required).

CD-ROM facilities: Yes.
Internet access: Yes.
Portable computers: Use permitted; power points available.

Other facilities for non-members:
Photocopying: Yes (payment required)
Microform holdings: Yes.
Reader-printer facilities: Yes (payment required).

Publications:
Catalogue of the Library (London: HMSO, 1968–76), 5 vols.

150 Natural History Museum
Department of Library and Information Services, Natural History Museum, Cromwell Road, London SW7 5BD

Tel.: 020 7942 5460
Fax: 020 7942 5559
E-mail: library@nhm.ac.uk
Telnet catalogue: unicorn.nhm.ac.uk (login: uniweb (no password))
Web catalogue: http://library.nhm.ac.uk/uhtbin/webcat
WWW: http://www.nhm.ac.uk/library/index.html
Established: 1881

Head of Library Services: R. Lester, BSc, PhD, FIInfSc
Botany Librarian: Malcolm Beasley
Botany Library tel.: 020 7942 5520
Botany Library e-mail: botlib@nhm.ac.uk
Earth Sciences Librarian: Ann Lum
Earth Sciences Library tel.: 020 7942 5269
Earth Sciences Library e-mail: earthscilib@nhm.ac.uk
Entomology Librarian: Julie Harvey, BSc, DipLib, FRES
Entomology Library tel.: 020 7942 5241
Entomology Library e-mail: entlib@nhm.ac.uk
Natural History Librarian: Carol Gokce, BSc, MSc
General Library tel.: 020 7942 5027/5460
General Library fax: 020 7942 5559
General Library e-mail: genlib@nhm.ac.uk
Librarian Ornithology and Rothschild Libraries, Tring: F.E. Warr

Ornithology and Rothschild Libraries, Tring, tel.: 020 7942 6156
Ornithology and Rothschild Libraries, Tring, fax: 020 7942 6150
Ornithology and Rothschild Libraries, Tring, e-mail: ornlib@nhm.ac.uk
Zoology Librarian: Ann Datta
Zoology Library tel.: 020 7942 5645
Zoology Library e-mail: zoolib@nhm.ac.uk
Museum Archivist: Susan Snell, BA, DAA
Museum Archivist tel.: 020 7942 5507
Museum Archivist e-mail: s.snell@nhm.ac.uk or archives@nhm.ac.uk

Collections:

The Libraries form one of the largest and most comprehensive collections on natural history and related subjects in the world. Latin American and Caribbean materials form a minor part of the overall stock and include 5,000 books, 250 current (500 non-current) periodical titles, 50 collections of manuscript material, 500 topographic maps and 2,500 other maps; about 550 volumes are added each year. The Libraries are particularly strong in scientific reports of voyages and expeditions concerning flora and fauna. There are manuscript and drawing collections relating to the Andes, Barbados, Brazil, British Guiana, Chile, Colombia, Demerara, Ecuador, Grenada, Jamaica, Paraguay, St Thomas, St Vincent and Trinidad. Among the most important are H.W. Bates's Amazon notebooks (1851–59); Lady Edith Blake's collection of drawings of Jamaican lepidoptera and plants (1889–98); F.D. Godman and O. Salvin's correspondence, note-books, drawings of insects and other manuscript material relating to *Biologia Centrali Americana*, published between 1879 and 1915; and four volumes of original pencil drawings of fishes of the Rio Negro by Alfred Russel Wallace, made between 1850 and 1852, together with manuscript descriptions of fishes and other animals of the Rio Negro and the Amazon. The collections are on closed access.

Access to collections:

Opening hours: Mon–Fri 1000–1630. Public holidays closed.

Enquiries: By telephone, post, fax or e-mail (payment required for commercial enquiries).
Admission: Bona fide researchers are admitted for reference purposes (appointment required).
Lending: No.
Inter-library loans: No.

Union record: BLDSC, BUCOP, COLALAS, WLSP.
Catalogue: SIRSI Unicorn automated catalogue.
Classification: Universal Decimal Classification and own classifications.

Electronic facilities for non-members:

Microcomputing facilities: No.
On-line search facilities: No.
CD-ROM facilities: Yes.
Internet access: Yes.
Portable computers: Use permitted; power points available.

Other facilities for non-members:

Photocopying: Yes (payment required).
Microform holdings: Yes.
Reader-printer facilities: Yes (payment required).

Publications:

Bernard Barham Woodward (comp.), *Catalogue of the Books, Manuscripts, Maps and Drawings in the British Museum (Natural History)* (London: British Museum, 1903–40), 8 vols.

Frederick C. Sawyer, *A Short History of the Libraries and List of Manuscripts and Original Drawings in the British Museum (Natural History)* (London: British Museum, 1971).

151 Office for National Statistics

Library, Office for National Statistics, Drummond Gate, London SW1V 2QQ

Postal enquiries: Library, Office for National Statistics, Cardiff Road, Newport NP10 8XG, Wales
Tel.: 020 7533 6266. Holdings enquiries 020 7533 6250 / 0845 601 3034
Fax: 01633 652747
E-mail: info@statistics.gov.uk
WWW: http://www.statistics.gov.uk/services/nslibraryservices.asp
Established: 1996 (as ONS)

Librarian: John Birch, BLib, PGCE, ALA
Deputy Librarian / Enquiry Manager [based at Newport]: Ian Bushnell, BA, ALA

Collections:

The Library is based on the collections of the former Office of Population Censuses and Surveys and the Central Statistical Office and includes material on economics, trade, labour markets, demography, vital registration, epidemiology, survey methodology and computing, and social and health services. In addition to United Kingdom statistics the Library holds a range of overseas statistical data. The Latin American and Caribbean material forms a minor part of the overall stock.

Access to collections:

Opening hours: Mon–Fri 0900–1700.

Enquiries: By telephone, post, fax or e-mail.
Admission: Open to the general public.
Lending: Yes.
Inter-library loans: Lends to other libraries.
Catalogue: Sydney automated catalogue.
Classification: Bliss Bibliographic Classification.

Electronic facilities for non-members:

Microcomputing facilities: Yes.
On-line search facilities: No.
CD-ROM facilities: Yes.
Internet access: Yes (subject to availability).
Portable computers: Use permitted on application.

Other facilities for non-members:

Photocopying: Yes (payment required).
Microform holdings: Yes.
Reader-printer facilities: No.

152 Overseas Development Institute (ODI)

Overseas Development Institute Library, 111 Westminster Bridge Road, London SE1 7JD

Tel.: 020 7922 0300
Fax: 020 7922 0399
E-mail: library@odi.org.uk

Web catalogue: http://nt1.ids.ac.uk/eldis/odi/index.htm
WWW: http://www.odi.org.uk/
Established: 1960

Librarian: Kate C. Kwafo-Akoto, BA, DipLib, MA, FLA
Librarian's e-mail address: k.kwafo-akoto@odi.org.uk

Collections:

Following a strategic review in 1998 the ODI Library is undergoing a period of transition from being predominantly document-based to becoming an information centre which combines document storage with information provision from other, mainly electronic, sources, in order to anticipate and be responsive to the changing needs of ODI researchers. Much Library stock has been withdrawn and there is currently an emphasis on the acquisition of electronic journals, online bibliographic and statistical databases, and CD-ROMs.

The ODI Library collects material in the areas of the Institute's research and policy programmes: rural policy and environment, poverty and public policy, forest policy and environment, international economic development, and humanitarian policy. There is a small collection of books, research papers, periodicals and items of grey literature. A small proportion of the collection relates to Latin America and the Caribbean. The collections are predominantly on open access.

Access to collections:

Opening hours: Mon–Fri 1000–1700. Public holidays closed.

Enquiries: By telephone, post, fax or e-mail.
Admission: Non-members are admitted for reference purposes. An appointment is required and readers are only admitted if the material that they need to consult is not available in other libraries in the United Kingdom.
Lending: No.
Inter-library loans: Lends to academic, research and government libraries.
Catalogue: DB/TextWorks automated catalogue.
Classification: Own classification. Modified combination of OECD/CAB/IIMI thesauri.

Electronic facilities for non-members:

Microcomputing facilities: No.
On-line search facilities: No.
CD-ROM facilities: Yes.
Internet access: No.
Portable computers: Use permitted; power points available.

Other facilities for non-members:

Photocopying: Yes (payment required).

153 Panos Pictures
1 Chapel Court, Borough High Street, London SE1 1HH

Tel.: 020 7234 0010
Fax: 020 7357 0094
E-mail: pics@panos.co.uk
WWW: http://www.panos.co.uk
Established: 1987

Subject enquiries to: Adrian Evans, Teresa Wolowiec

Collections:

A commercial picture library specialising in documentary photography (black-and-white and colour), with a focus on political, cultural, economic and social issues in Africa, Asia, Eastern Europe, the Middle East, and Latin America and the Caribbean. There is extensive coverage of Central and South America, including political events from the past ten years (religion, economics, culture, travel and geography), and similarly extensive coverage of the Caribbean islands, with particularly in-depth treatment of Cuba, Haiti and the Dominican Republic.

Access to collections:

Opening hours: Mon–Fri 1000–1800.

Enquiries: By telephone, post, fax or e-mail.
Admission: By appointment.
Search/service fee: £30. Commissions undertaken.
Lending: Yes.
Catalogues: Catalogues and newsletter updates.

Electronic facilities for non-members:
On-line search of images: Gallery site with a search engine.
On-line delivery of images: Upon request.
CD-ROM facilities: Yes.
Internet access: No.
Portable computers: Use not permitted.

Other facilities for non-members:
Copying: Allowed, with a reproduction fee.

Publications:
Catalogues and newsletter updates.

154 Peru Support Group
c/o Catholic Institute for International Relations (CIIR), Unit 3, Canonbury Yard, 190a New North Road, London N1 7BJ

Tel./Fax: 020 7354 9825
After-hours fax: 020 7359 0017
E-mail: perusupport@gn.apc.org
WWW: http://www.perusupportgroup.co.uk
Established: 1983

Coordinator: Marcia Walker

Collections:
The Peru Support Group was established in 1983 as an independent organisation, which works to support the people of Peru, particularly those from the poorest sectors, and to increase public awareness of Peru in Britain. It publishes books and newsletters, briefings and educational material on key issues concerning Peru (especially politics, human rights, society, the economy and the environment), and coordinates workshops, conferences and meetings. A small collection of books, reports, newsletters, magazines and other contemporary material is held, a large part of which originates in Peru. Of particular importance are the daily press-cuttings service and daily wire reports received from Peruvian news agencies.

Access to collections:
Opening hours: Mon–Fri 0930–1730.

Enquiries: By telephone, post or e-mail.
Admission: By appointment.
Lending: No.
Catalogue: A list of current periodicals appears on the website.

Electronic facilities for non-members:

Microcomputing facilities: No.
On-line search facilities: No.
CD-ROM facilities: No.
Internet access: No.
Portable computers: Use permitted.

Other facilities for non-members:

Photocopying: Yes (payment required).

155 *Philip Wolmuth*

19 Menelik Road, London NW2 3RJ

Tel./Fax: 020 7435 8651
E-mail: philipwolmuth@compuserve.com
WWW: Website under development
Established: 1977

Collections:

Philip Wolmuth has been contributing photographs and documentary material to development agencies, the media and other picture libraries for the past 20 years. His picture library contains black-and-white and colour photographs of the Caribbean on a range of social, political and economic issues, including in-depth coverage of the Eastern Caribbean banana industry, Haitian migrant labour in the Dominican Republic, and the Grenada revolution and its aftermath. The countries covered are Antigua, Barbados, Cuba, Dominica, the Dominican Republic, Grenada, Haiti, Puerto Rico, St Lucia and Trinidad.

Access to collections:

Opening hours: Mon–Fri 0900–1800.

Enquiries: By telephone, post or e-mail.
Admission: By appointment.

Search/service fee: £10 + VAT. Commissions undertaken.
Lending: By arrangement.
Catalogues: None.
Classification: By country.

Electronic facilities for non-members:

On-line search of images: No.
On-line delivery of images: Yes.
CD-ROM facilities: Yes.
Internet access: No.
Portable computers: Use not permitted.

Other facilities for non-members:

Copying: No.

156 Queen Mary, University of London
Main Library, Mile End Road, London E1 4NS

Tel.: 020 7882 3300
Fax: 020 8981 0028
E-mail: library-enquiries@qmw.ac.uk
Web catalogue: http://catalogue.library.qmw.ac.uk
WWW: http://www.library.qmw.ac.uk/
Established: 1887

Director, Academic Information Services: Brian Murphy, BA, ALA
Subject enquiries (social sciences) to: Eilis Rafferty, BA, MSc, ALA
Specialist's tel.: 020 7882 3327
Specialist's e-mail address: e.p.rafferty@qmw.ac.uk
Subject enquiries (history, languages and literature) to: Viv Aggett, BA, ALA
Specialist's tel.: 020 7882 3327
Specialist's e-mail address: v.aggett@qmw.ac.uk

Collections:

Queen Mary (formerly Queen Mary and Westfield College) was formed from the merger in 1989 of Queen Mary College (1934) and Westfield College (1882). The Library has been collecting material on the region since 1965 and now has a collection of 4,500 books and 14 current periodical titles (9 on language and literature and 5 on economics, politics and history). The main subject fields covered by the book stock are literature and literary criticism, history, economics, politics and geography. The collection is on open access.

Access to collections:

Opening hours: Term: Mon–Fri 0900–2100, Sat 1000–1600. Christmas and Summer Vacations: Mon–Fri 0900–1700, Sat closed. Easter Vacation: Mon–Fri 0900–1900, Sat closed. Christmas, New Year, Easter and August Bank Holiday closed.
Enquiries: By telephone, post, fax or e-mail.
Admission: Non-members are admitted for reference purposes after 1700 and on Saturdays in term-time, and during normal opening hours in vacation. Academic staff and students of the University of London and members of the M25 Access Scheme are admitted during normal opening hours. All visitors must show proof of identity.
Lending: No.
Inter-library loans: Lends to other libraries.
Union record: BLDSC, BUCLA, BUCOP, LASER, University of London Union List of Serials.
Catalogue: SIRSI Unicorn automated catalogue.
Classification: Library of Congress Classification.

Electronic facilities for non-members:

Microcomputing facilities: No.
On-line search facilities: No.
CD-ROM facilities: No.
Internet access: No.
Portable computers: Use permitted, provided other readers are not disturbed.

Other facilities for non-members:

Photocopying: Yes (payment required).
Microform holdings: Yes.
Reader-printer facilities: Yes (payment required).

157 Religious Society of Friends (*Quakers*)
Library, Friends House, 173 Euston Road, London NW1 2BJ

Tel.: 020 7663 1135
Fax: 020 7663 1001
E-mail: library@quaker.org.uk
WWW: http://www.quaker.org.uk/library/

Librarian: Heather Rowland

Collections:

Latin American and Caribbean material forms a minor part of the 28,000 volumes held by the Library. About 1,000 volumes on the region are held, together with a small range of periodicals. The strongest part of this collection is nineteenth-century anti-slavery material, mostly relating to the Caribbean. There is also some material on the international politics of Latin America. Some material is on open access, some on closed access.

Access to collections:

Opening hours: Mon–Tues, Thurs–Fri 1300–1700, Wed 1000–1700. Public holidays closed.

Enquiries: By telephone, post, fax or e-mail.
Admission: Non-members are admitted for reference purposes (letter of recommendation required).
Lending: Yes.
Inter-library loans: Lends to other libraries.
Union record: BLDSC.
Catalogues: Author, title, classified subject and place card catalogues for manuscripts and for printed books. TinLib automated catalogue for material published after 1988.
Classification: Own classification.

Electronic facilities for non-members:

Microcomputing facilities: No.
On-line search facilities: No.
CD-ROM facilities: No.
Internet access: No.
Portable computers: Use permitted; power points available.

Other facilities for non-members:
Photocopying: Yes (payment required).
Microform holdings: Yes.
Reader-printer facilities: Yes (payment required).

Publications:

Anna L. Littleboy, *A History of the Friends' Reference Library with Notes on Early Printers and Printing in the Society of Friends* (London: Society of Friends, 1921).
Muriel Hicks, 'Friends' Reference Library, 1901–1959', *Journal of the Friends' Historical Society*, vol. 49, no. 3 (1960), pp. 123–34.

158 Royal Anthropological Institute of Great Britain and Ireland
Photographic Library, Royal Anthropological Institute, 50 Fitzroy Street, London W1T 5BT

Tel.: 020 7387 0455
Fax: 020 7383 4235
E-mail: photo@therai.org.uk
WWW: http://www.rai.anthropology.org.uk/photo/Photo.html

Photographic Librarian: Arkadiusz Bentkowski

Collections:

The Institute's photographic collection contains an archive of 65,000 photographs dating from the period 1865–1960. Latin American material forms a minor part of the collection, but includes important work by Walter Garbe (Botocudos, Rio Doce, 1909), stylised depictions of Arawak, Warrau and Macusi by Sir Everard im Thurn (Guyana, 1883–97), postcards and catalogues of Guido Boggiani's 'Indian Types' (1889), 1,500 photographs by Sir Kenneth Grubb covering Central and South America in the 1930s, photographs of people of the Japura Valley in North West Amazonia by Thomas William Whiffen (1908–09) and a further 150 nineteenth-century photographs of Amazonia. The material is on closed access, with copy prints and contact prints on open access.

Access to collections:
Opening hours: Two days per week. Usually Mon–Tues 0930–1730.

Enquiries: By telephone, post, fax or e-mail.
Admission: Non-members are admitted for reference purposes (appointment required).
Lending: No.
Inter-library loans: No.
Union record: BLDSC, BUCOP, COLALAS.
Catalogues: Author, title, alphabetical subject and classified subject, illustrated card catalogue. Computer database in progress.
Classification: Bliss Bibliographic Classification.

Electronic facilities for non-members:

Microcomputing facilities: No.
On-line search facilities: No.
CD-ROM facilities: No.
Internet access: No.
Portable computers: Use permitted; power points available.

159 Royal Geographical Society (with The Institute of British Geographers)
Information Resources Division, 1 Kensington Gore, London SW7 2AR

Library
Tel.: 020 7591 3044
Fax: 020 7591 3001 (not in the Library)
E-mail: library@rgs.org

Map Room
Tel.: 020 7591 3050
Fax: 020 7591 3001
E-mail: maps@rgs.org

Picture Library
Tel.: 020 7591 3060
Fax: 020 7591 3061
E-mail: pictures@rgs.org

Expedition Advisory Centre
Tel.: 020 7591 3030
Fax: 020 7591 3031

E-mail: eac@rgs.org
WWW: http://www.rgs.org/
Established: 1830

Librarian: Eugene Rae, MA, DipLib
Curator of Maps: Francis Herbert, Hon.FRGS, FBCartS
Picture Library Manager: Joanna Wright, BA, MA
Head of Expedition Advisory Centre: Shane Winser, BSc, DipIfSc

Collections:

The combined collections of the Royal Geographical Society (with the Institute of British Geographers) held in the Library, Map Room, Picture Library and Archives, form one of world's most important sources of geographical information. Latin American and Caribbean materials have been collected since the foundation of the Society and now include over 3,500 volumes and 80 periodical titles on geography, topography, travel, exploration and history (including boundary disputes) in the Library; maps, atlases, gazetteers (many from the eighteenth century), charts (some dating from the sixteenth century) and expedition reports are held in the Map Room; and paintings and photographs are held in the Picture Library. There is also an Artefact Collection, containing scientific instruments, clothing, etc. The Expedition Advisory Centre, part of the Expedition and Field Work Division, maintains a database of expedition reports held by the RGS–IBG, together with planned and past expeditions, and can provide print-outs for particular destinations or subjects to assist in the early planning stages of proposed expeditions.

Access to collections:

Opening hours: Mon–Fri 1100–1700. Public holidays and three weeks in June closed. The Library and Map Room will be closed until late 2002, while work on the *Unlocking the Archives* project is carried out. The Picture Library will be open by appointment only Mon–Fri 1000–1300, 1400–1700.

Enquiries: By telephone, post, fax or e-mail.
Admission: Non-members are admitted for reference purposes if the material they require is not readily available elsewhere (payment required).
Lending: No.
Inter-library loans: Lends to other libraries.
Union record: BLDSC, BUCOP, COLALAS, WLSP.

Catalogue: Author and alphabetical subject card catalogue.
Classification: Own classification.

Electronic facilities for non-members:

Microcomputing facilities: No.
On-line search facilities: No.
CD-ROM facilities: Include *Geobase* and *National Geographic Magazine* and various guides and atlases.
Internet access: No.
Portable computers: Use permitted; power points available.

Other facilities for non-members:

Photocopying: Yes (payment required).
Microform holdings: Yes.
Reader-printer facilities: No.

Publications:

Hugh Robert Mill (comp.), *Catalogue of the Library of the Royal Geographical Society: Containing the Titles of All Works up to December 1893* (London: John Murray, 1895).

G.R. Crone, 'The Library of the Royal Geographical Society', *Geographical Journal,* vol. 121 (1955), pp. 27–32.

John Coles (comp.), *Catalogue of [the] Map Room of the Royal Geographical Society. March 1881* (London: Murray, 1882).

G.R. Crone and E.E.T. Day, 'The Map Room of the Royal Geographical Society', *Geographical Journal,* vol. 126 (1960), pp. 12–17.

160 Royal Institute of British Architects (RIBA)

British Architectural Library, 66 Portland Place, London W1B 1AD

Tel.: 020 7580 5533. Holdings enquiries 020 7307 3672. Public Information Line 0906 302 0400
Fax: 020 7631 1802
E-mail: bal@inst.riba.org
Web catalogue: http://site.yahoo.net/riba-library/oncat.html
WWW: http://site.yahoo.net/riba-library/
Established: 1834

Director and Sir Banister Fletcher Librarian: Ruth H. Kamen, BA, MAT, MLS, FLA, FRSA

Collections:

The British Architectural Library is the most comprehensive collection on all aspects of architecture throughout the world in the British Isles. It also covers related subjects such as building, civil engineering and structural engineering. It now holds 140,000 volumes, including books, pamphlets, reports, conference proceedings, exhibition catalogues and standards. There are 650,000 photographs in the Photographs Collection; 450,000 drawings are held in the Drawings Collection at 21 Portman Square (closed to personal users except on Monday afternoons; collection to be transferred to the Victoria and Albert Museum in 2004). Latin American materials form a minor part of the collection; over 1,000 books, 18 current and 59 non-current periodical titles, and some photographs and drawings. There is strong coverage of Brazilian architecture, and the holdings on Mexico (especially Mayan architecture and other historical aspects), Peru and Cuba are also significant. The collections are on open access.

Access to collections:

Opening hours: Mon 1330–1700, Tues 1000–1900, Wed 1000–1700, Thurs 1000–1900, Fri 1000–1700, Sat 1000–1330. Public holidays closed. August closed.

Enquiries: By telephone, post, fax or e-mail (payment required).
Admission: Non-members are admitted for reference purposes (payment required).
Lending: Yes (payment required).
Inter-library loans: Lends to other libraries.
Union record: BLDSC, BUCOP, *Serials in the British Library.*
Catalogue: SIRSI Unicorn automated catalogue.
Classification: Universal Decimal Classification.

Electronic facilities for non-members:

Microcomputing facilities: No.
On-line search facilities: Yes (payment required).
CD-ROM facilities: Yes (payment required).
Internet access: Yes.
Portable computers: Use permitted; power points available.

Other facilities for non-members:
Photocopying: Yes (payment required).
Microform holdings: Yes.
Reader-printer facilities: Yes (payment required).

Publications:

Catalogue of the Royal Institute of British Architects Library (London: RIBA, 1937–38), 2 vols.
Catalogue of the Drawings Collection of the Royal Institute of British Architects (Farnborough: Gregg International, 1968–89).
Early Printed Books, 1478–1840: Catalogue of the British Architectural Library Early Imprints Collection (London: Bowker-Saur, 1994–).
RIBA Library Bulletin (London: RIBA, 1945–72).
RIBA Annual Review of Periodical Articles (London: RIBA, 1965–72).
Architectural Publications Index (London: RIBA, 1972–).

161 Royal Institute of International Affairs (RIIA)

Chatham House Library, 10 St James's Square, London SW1Y 4LE

Tel.: 020 7957 5723
Fax: 020 7957 5710 (mark for attention of the Library)
E-mail: libenquire@riia.org
WWW: http://www.riia.org/library/libindex.html
Established: 1920

Head of Library and Information Service: Catherine Hume, BA, MSc, ALA
Subject enquiries to: Malcolm Madden, BA, MSc, Assistant Librarian
Specialist's tel.: 020 7314 3628
Specialist's e-mail address: mmadden@riia.org

Collections:

The Library collects material on all aspects of international affairs, with special emphasis on foreign policy, politics, economics and security issues. It still holds historic collections built up since its foundation in 1920, but now focuses on the last 30–35 years. Official publications from the European Union, the United Nations and its agencies (such as the Economic Commission for Latin America and the Caribbean), and the

Organization of American States are held. The total collection numbers 130,000 books and pamphlets, 300 current periodicals and newspapers and a large collection of press cuttings which are classified and cross-referenced in detail. In 1986 the Library donated four collections of press cuttings to the British Library, Newspaper Library (no. 84), but it still holds cuttings from 1924–39 on microfilm and the original cuttings from 1972–97; indexes for the files at Colindale are available. The Library has collected material on Latin America and the Caribbean since its foundation in 1920 and now has 6,500 books and 15 current periodical titles, in addition to useful material on political and economic developments in the region in the press cuttings. Only recent material is on open access.

Access to collections:

Opening hours: Mon–Fri 1100–1730. Public holidays closed.

Enquiries: By telephone, post, fax or e-mail.
Admission: Non-members are admitted for reference purposes (payment and letter of introduction required). Prior arrangement is required and readers must be graduates.
Lending: No.
Inter-library loans: Lends to other libraries.
Union record: BLDSC, BUCLA, BUCOP.
Catalogues: Author and classified card catalogue for material acquired up to 1989. TinLib automated catalogue (retrospective conversion in progress).
Classification: Own classification.

Electronic facilities for non-members:

Microcomputing facilities: Yes.
On-line search facilities: Yes (payment required).
CD-ROM facilities: Yes.
Internet access: Yes.
Portable computers: Use permitted; power points available.

Other facilities for non-members:

Photocopying: Yes (payment required).
Microform holdings: Yes.
Reader-printer facilities: Yes (payment required).

Publications:

The Classified Catalogue of the Library of the Royal Institute of International Affairs (Oxford: Oxford Microform and Publishing Services, 1981), 164 microfiches.

Index to Periodical Articles, 1950–1964, in the Library of the Royal Institute of International Affairs (Boston, Mass.: G.K. Hall, 1964), 2 vols.

Index to Periodical Articles, 1965–1972, in the Library of the Royal Institute of International Affairs (Boston, Mass.: G.K. Hall, 1973).

Jean Aitchison et al., *The Royal Institute of International Affairs Library Thesaurus* (London: RIIA, 1992), 2 vols.

162 Royal Society of Medicine

Library, 1 Wimpole Street, London W1G 0AE

Tel.: 020 7290 2940
Fax: 020 7290 2939
E-mail: library@rsm.ac.uk
Web catalogue: http://www.rsm.ac.uk/librar/libcat.htm
WWW: http://www.rsm.ac.uk/librar/library.htm
Established: 1805

Director of Information Services: Ian Snowley, BA, MBA, ALA, MIInfSc, MIMgt

Collections:

The Library has a total collection of 500,000 books, 25,000 pamphlets, and 2,000 current and 8,000 non-current periodical titles. Latin American materials have been collected since the mid-nineteenth century and form a minor part of the collection, consisting predominantly of periodicals. The collection is on open access.

Access to collections:

Opening hours: Mon–Fri 0900–2030, Sat 1000–1700. Public holidays closed.

Enquiries: By telephone, post, fax or e-mail (payment required).
Admission: Non-members are admitted for reference purposes (payment required).

Lending: No.
Inter-library loans: No.
Union record: BUCOP, COLALAS, WLSP.
Catalogues: Author and alphabetical subject catalogues for material acquired before 1984. SIRSI Unicorn automated catalogue for materials acquired from 1984 to the present.
Classification: Universal Decimal Classification to 1992. National Library of Medicine classification from 1992.

Electronic facilities for non-members:

Microcomputing facilities: Yes.
On-line search facilities: Yes (payment required).
CD-ROM facilities: Yes.
Internet access: Yes.
Portable computers: Use permitted; power points available.

Other facilities for non-members:

Photocopying: Yes (payment required).
Microform holdings: Yes.
Reader-printer facilities: Yes.

163 School of Oriental and African Studies, University of London
Library, Thornhaugh Street, Russell Square, London WC1H 0XG

Tel.: 020 7898 4163
Fax: 020 7898 4159
E-mail: libenquiry@soas.ac.uk. Membership: libmembership@soas.ac.uk
Telnet catalogue: lib.soas.ac.uk
Web catalogue: http://lib.soas.ac.uk/search/
WWW: http://www.soas.ac.uk/Library/
Established: 1916

Librarian: Keith Webster, BSc, MLib, ALA, MInfSc
Subject enquiries to: Angela Sabin, BA, DipLib, ALA, Principal Assistant Librarian (Social Sciences and General Subjects, including Maps)
Specialist's tel.: 020 7898 4155
Specialist's e-mail address: as13@soas.ac.uk

Collections:

The Library has collected material on Latin America since 1916, and since c. 1950 has built up a special collection on Amerindian languages of North, Central and South America, and on other aspects of Amerindian culture. Over 900 volumes are held; some 10 volumes are added each year, of which ten per cent are of non-current material. The collection is on open access.

Access to collections:

Opening hours: Term, Christmas and Easter Vacations: Mon–Thurs 0900–2045, Fri 0900–1900, Sat 0930–1300. Summer Vacation: Mon–Fri 0900–1700, Sat 0930–1700. Christmas, New Year, Easter and August Bank Holiday closed.

Enquiries: By telephone, post, fax or e-mail.
Admission: Non-members are admitted for reference purposes (payment required). British academic staff and research students, and overseas academics are admitted free of charge; British taught-course students are admitted free of charge in SOAS vacations.
Lending: No.
Inter-library loans: Lends to other libraries.
Union record: BLDSC, BUCLA, BUCOP, University of London Union List of Serials.
Catalogue: Author, title and alphabetical subject card catalogue for acquisitions to mid-1989. Innopac automated catalogue for acquisitions from mid-1989.
Classification: Dewey Decimal Classification (modified).

Electronic facilities for non-members:

Microcomputing facilities: No.
On-line search facilities: No.
CD-ROM facilities: Yes.
Internet access: Restricted access.
Portable computers: Use permitted in restricted areas.

Other facilities for non-members:

Photocopying: Yes (payment required).
Microform holdings: Yes.
Reader-printer facilities: Yes (payment required).

Publications:

Library Catalogue (Boston, Mass.: G.K. Hall, 1963), 28 vols.

Library Catalogue: First Supplement, 1963–1968 (Boston, Mass.: G.K. Hall, 1968), 16 vols.

Library Catalogue: Second Supplement, 1968–1973 (Boston, Mass.: G.K. Hall, 1973), 16 vols.

Library Catalogue: Third Supplement, 1973–1978 (Boston, Mass.: G.K. Hall, 1979), 19 vols.

Library Catalogue: Fourth Supplement, 1978–1984 (Zug: IDC, 1985), 363 fiches.

164 Thames Valley University
Learning Resource Centre (LRC), St Mary's Road, London W5 5RF

Address for correspondence: TVU (LRC SMR), Walpole House, 18–22 Bond Street, Ealing, London W5 5AA
Tel.: 020 8231 2248
Fax: 020 8231 2631
E-mail: lrc@tvu.ac.uk
Web catalogue: http://tvutalis.tvu.ac.uk/
WWW: http://www.tvu.ac.uk/lrs/lrc/index.html
Established: 1992 (as TVU). Formerly Ealing College

Head of Learning Resources: J.I. Wolstenholme, BA, MSc
LRC Manager: David McGrath
Subject enquiries to: Jennifer Bartlett, Subject Librarian, Languages
Specialist's tel.: 020 8231 2670
Specialist's e-mail address: Jennifer.Bartlett@tvu.ac.uk

Collections:

The acquisition of Latin American materials began in 1969. The collection was developed chiefly in support of the teaching of Hispanic studies and, until the 1990s, was mainly in Spanish. There are now over 2,000 volumes and 6 current periodical titles. The main subject areas are politics, economics, geography and history. All of Latin America is covered, but there is more material on Mexico than on any of the other countries. The collection is on open access.

Access to collections:

Opening hours: Term: Mon–Thurs 0830–2200, Fri–Sun 0830–1800. Vacation: Mon–Thurs 0830–1900, Fri 0830–1730, Sat–Sun closed. Public holidays closed.

Enquiries: By telephone, post or e-mail.
Admission: Members of the London Plus scheme are admitted for reference purposes. There is vacation reference access for students from other universities in the United Kingdom. Other non-members may be admitted for reference purposes (advance agreement with the LRC Manager required).
Lending: No.
Inter-library loans: Lends to other libraries.
Union record: BLCMP, BUCOP.
Catalogue: BLCMP Talis automated catalogue.
Classification: Dewey Decimal Classification.

Electronic facilities for non-members:

Microcomputing facilities: No.
On-line search facilities: No.
CD-ROM facilities: No.
Internet access: Yes.
Portable computers: Use permitted; power points available.

Other facilities for non-members:

Photocopying: Yes.
Microform holdings: Yes.
Reader-printer facilities: Yes.

165 Tourism Concern

Library, Stapleton House, 277–281 Holloway Road, London N7 8HN

Tel.: 020 7753 3330
Fax: 020 7753 3331
E-mail: info@tourismconcern.org.uk
WWW: http://www.tourismconcern.org.uk
Established: 1989

Librarian: Paul Smith

Collections:

Tourism Concern is a charity founded in 1989 to raise issues concerned with the impact of tourism on communities and the environment, both in the United Kingdom and worldwide. The organisation has an active publications programme (recent titles have included information packs on ecotourism in Ecuador and the Caribbean) and produces teaching materials. Tourism Concern has the most extensive specialised library in the United Kingdom on the impact of tourism. The Latin American and Caribbean holdings form a significant part of the total collections of several hundred books, reports and periodicals, several thousand articles from United Kingdom and international publications, and an extensive video collection.

Access to collections:

Opening hours: Mon–Fri 1000–1700.
Enquiries: By telephone, post or e-mail.
Admission: Non-members are admitted for reference purposes (payment and appointment required).
Lending: No.
Inter-library loans: No.
Catalogue: Manual catalogue.
Classification: The material is arranged by country/region and by subject.

Electronic facilities for non-members:

Microcomputing facilities: No.
On-line search facilities: No.
CD-ROM facilities: No.
Internet access: No.
Portable computers: Use permitted during off-peak periods; contact Library in advance; limited power points available.

Other facilities for non-members:

Photocopying: Yes (payment required).

166 Trades Union Congress Library Collections
The Learning Centre, University of North London, 236–250 Holloway Road, London N7 6PP

Tel.: 020 7753 3184

Fax: 020 7753 3191
E-mail: tuclib@unl.ac.uk
Web catalogue: http://opac.unl.ac.uk/
WWW: http://www.unl.ac.uk/library/tuc/
Established: 1922, transferred to UNL in 1996

Librarian: Christine M. Coates, MA, ALA
E-mail: c.coates@unl.ac.uk

Collections:

The Trades Union Congress Library Collections contain material acquired by the TUC up to 1993. Later material will be deposited annually and some current material will be acquired. The main subject areas are labour, trades unionism, and social, economic and working conditions throughout the world. Latin American and Caribbean materials form a minor part of the collection and are mainly pamphlets and serials produced by trades unions and other organisations in the region. The majority of the collections are on open access.

Access to collections:

Opening hours: Mon–Fri 0915–1645. Public holidays closed.

Enquiries: By telephone, post, fax or e-mail.
Admission: Non-members are admitted for reference purposes (appointment required). Undergraduate students must present written authorisation from their supervisors.
Lending: No.
Inter-library loans: No.
Catalogues: Author and alphabetical subject catalogues. Material acquired since January 1999 appears on the University of North London's BLCMP Talis automated catalogue.
Classification: Library of Congress Classification.

Electronic facilities for non-members:

Microcomputing facilities: No.
On-line search facilities: No.
CD-ROM facilities: No.
Internet access: No.
Portable computers: Use permitted; power points available.

Other facilities for non-members:

Photocopying: Yes (payment required).
Microform holdings: Yes.
Reader-printer facilities: Yes (payment required).

167 United Nations Information Centre

Reference Library, Millbank Tower (21st Floor), 21–24 Millbank, London SW1P 4QH

Tel.: 020 7630 1981
Fax: 020 7976 6478
E-mail: library@uniclondon.org
WWW: http://www.unitednations.org.uk/info/index.html
Established: 1947

Librarian: Karen Davies

Collections:

The Centre, one of 69 throughout the world, holds the official publications of the United Nations from 1946 onwards, including material from the Economic Commission for Latin America and the Caribbean (ECLAC). The collection is on open access.

Access to collections:

Opening hours: Mon–Fri 0900–1700. Public holidays and official UN holidays closed.

Enquiries: By telephone, post, fax or e-mail.
Admission: Open to the general public for reference purposes (appointment required).
Lending: No.
Inter-library loans: No.
Catalogues: United Nations documents indexes and publications catalogues. *UNBIS Plus* on CD-ROM.
Classification: The material is arranged by UN issuing body.

Electronic facilities for non-members:

Microcomputing facilities: No.
On-line search facilities: No.

CD-ROM facilities: Yes.
Internet access: Yes.
Portable computers: Use permitted; power points available.

Other facilities for non-members:
Photocopying: Yes (payment required).

168 University College London, University of London
University College London Library, Gower Street, London WC1E 6BT

Tel.: 020 7679 7700. Admissions 020 7679 7953. Holdings enquiries 020 7679 7793
Fax: 020 7679 7373
E-mail: library@ucl.ac.uk. Admissions: lib-membership@ucl.ac.uk
Web catalogue: http://library.ucl.ac.uk
WWW: http://www.ucl.ac.uk/library/
Established: 1828 (UCL), 1937 (Institute of Archaeology)

Director of Library Services: Paul Ayris, PhD, ALA
Subject enquiries (Anthropology) to: Kirstin Preest, Assistant Librarian
Specialist's tel.: 020 7679 2791
Specialist's e-mail address: k.preest@ucl.ac.uk
Subject enquiries (Archaeology) to: Robert T. Kirby, MA, Assistant Librarian
Specialist's tel.: 020 7679 7485
Specialist's e-mail address: r.kirby@ucl.ac.uk
Subject enquiries (Archives) to: Gillian Furlong, BA, DipArch
Specialist's tel.: 020 7679 7796
Specialist's e-mail address: g.furlong@ucl.ac.uk
Subject enquiries (Geography) to: Kirstin Preest, Assistant Librarian
Specialist's tel.: 020 7679 2791
Specialist's e-mail address: k.preest@ucl.ac.uk
Subject enquiries (History) to: Michael Jahn, MPhil, DipLib, Assistant Librarian
Specialist's tel.: 020 7679 2827
Specialist's e-mail address: m.jahn@ucl.ac.uk
Subject enquiries (Literature) to: Patricia Campbell, BA, DipInfSt
Specialist's tel.: 020 7682 9454
Specialist's e-mail address: p.campbell@ucl.ac.uk

Collections:

The Chair of Latin American History at University College London, the first academic post specifically dedicated to Latin American studies in the United Kingdom, was established in 1948. The collection of material on Latin American history was developed at the same time, and the Latin American History Library now includes material on the non-Hispanic Caribbean, including contemporary economic and social history, and PhD theses from the USA on microfilm. The Library collects mainly secondary material; primary material is collected by the Institute of Historical Research (no. 119), and, together with the material at UCL, forms one of the best collections in this field in the United Kingdom. There is also a collection of Latin American business archives, deposited in the Library in the 1960s and 1970s, and covering banking, railways, trade and shipping. The material includes maps, plans, photographs and ephemera, and is the largest collection of such archives outside Latin America (1,600 volumes and 350 boxes).

The Library has collected Spanish-American literature since the 1960s. The collection consists mainly of modern fiction and poetry; Argentine and Mexican writers are the best represented. The acquisition of anthropological and geographical material also began in the 1960s. The anthropology collection has a geographical emphasis on Brazil and Mexico, while the geography collection also includes Colombian material, and concentrates on human and economic geography.

The history and literature collections are located in the Main Library, while anthropology and geography are in the Science Library (DMS Watson Building). The combined Latin American and Caribbean collections total some 25,000 books, with 30–40 current periodicals (over 200 non-current) and about 30 video recordings. The collections are predominantly on open access.

The Institute of Archaeology Library (31–34 Gordon Square, London WC1H 0PY), which has a total collection of 80,000 books, 10,000 pamphlets and 800 current periodicals, has collected Latin American material since 1966. The collection now includes 5,000 books and pamphlets, 60 periodical titles, some maps, and microforms (mainly of theses). The main geographical emphasis is on Mexico, Peru and Ecuador, and, in addition to archaeology, the Library holds some material on anthropology and folklore. The main collection is on open access, but older and less-used material is in local and off-site stores.

Access to collections:

Opening hours:
Main Library. Term: Mon–Thurs 0845–2230, Fri 0845–1900, Sat 0930–1630, Sun 1100–1700. Christmas and Easter Vacations: Mon–Fri 0930–1900, Sat–Sun closed. Summer Vacation: Mon–Fri 0930–1845, Sat 0930–1630, Sun closed. Christmas, New Year, Easter and August Bank Holiday closed.
Science Library. Term: Mon–Thurs 0845–2230, Fri 0845–1900, Sat 0930–1630, Sun 1100–1700. Christmas and Easter Vacations: Mon–Fri 0930–1900, Sat–Sun closed. Summer Vacation: Mon–Fri 0930–1845, Sat 0930–1630, Sun closed. Christmas, New Year, Easter and August Bank Holiday closed.
Archives. Mon, Thurs–Fri 1000–1700, Tues, Wed 1000–1900. Christmas, New Year, Easter and August Bank Holiday closed.
Institute of Archaeology Library. Mon–Thurs 0930–2100, Fri 0930–1900, Sat 0930–1630. Christmas, New Year, Easter and August Bank Holiday closed.

Enquiries: By telephone, post, fax or e-mail.
Admission: Non-members are admitted for reference purposes. Taught-course students (except for those from the University of London) may use the Library only during UCL vacations. Overseas students, commercial and organisational users and private researchers should apply in advance to the Admissions Officer (payment may be required).
Lending: Academic staff and research postgraduates of the University of London may apply for a borrowing ticket (proof of status required).
Inter-library loans: Lends to other libraries.
Union record: BLDSC, BUCLA, BUCOP, COLALAS, CURL, University of London Union List of Serials.
Catalogues: Author and classified subject card catalogue for material catalogued before 1982. Ex Libris Aleph eUCLid automated catalogue for material catalogued since 1982 increasingly includes earlier material. The Institute of Archaeology also has an index to archaeological sites. Handlists are available for some of the Latin American Business Archives.
Classification: Garside classification. Institute of Archaeology has own classification.

Electronic facilities for non-members:

Microcomputing facilities: No.
On-line search facilities: No.

CD-ROM facilities: No.
Internet access: No.
Portable computers: Use permitted; power points available.

Other facilities for non-members:

Photocopying: Yes (payment acquired).
Microform holdings: Yes.
Reader-printer facilities: Yes (payment acquired).

Publications:

Janet Percival, *The Archives of the Peruvian Corporation: a Handlist* (London: Library, University College, University of London, 1980) (Occasional publications no. 7)

Manuscript Collections in the Library of University College, London, 2nd ed. (London: Library, University College, University of London, 1978) (Occasional publications no. 1)

169 University of London Library
Senate House, Malet Street, London WC1E 7HU

Tel.: 020 7862 8500. Holdings enquiries 020 7862 8461/8462. Admissions 020 7862 8439/8440
Fax: 020 7862 8480
E-mail: enquiries@ull.ac.uk
Telnet catalogue: 193.63.81.240
Web catalogue: http://193.63.81.240
WWW: http://www.ull.ac.uk
Established: 1838

Librarian: Emma Robinson, BSc, ALA
Subject enquiries to: Christine A. Anderson, BA, ALA
Specialist's tel.: 020 7862 8456
Specialist's e-mail address: canderson@ull.ac.uk

Collections:

Latin America was well represented in the historic collections of the Library before a Latin American collection was developed from 1968 in order to provide a specialist resource centre for Latin American studies. It is now the largest open-access, separately-shelved research collection for the region in the United Kingdom, with over 45,000 books and pamphlets and an annual growth rate of approximately 2,000 volumes. The material in the Latin American collection is mainly in the humanities and social sciences, with particular emphasis on history, politics, economics, anthropology and literature, and covers all the countries of Central and South America, together with the islands of the Caribbean, the South Atlantic, the Galapagos Islands and the Antarctic territories administered by Chile and Argentina. In addition, over 200 current and non-current periodicals are kept with the Library's periodicals collection. Maps of the region, including atlases, admiralty charts, town plans and wall maps, are kept in the Geography and Maps collection. There are over 250 books on Latin American music, together with approximately 200 scores and some recordings, in the Music Library. Bibliography is well represented in the Latin American collection and national bibliographies are held in the Middlesex South Library. The Goldsmiths' Collection contains a considerable number of early travel accounts and material on slavery and economic conditions before 1850. Manuscripts and archival material relating to Central America and the British West Indies are kept in the Palaeography Room.

The collections are predominantly open access, although manuscripts and rare books are in closed access and some other less-used material must be requested at the Stack Service Desk in the Main Hall.

Access to collections:

Opening hours: Term: Mon–Thurs 0900–2100, Fri 0900–1830, Sat 0930–1730. Vacation: Mon–Fri 0900–1800, Sat 0930–1730.
Special collections
Term: Mon 0930–2045, Tues–Fri 0930–1800, Sat 0930–1300, 1400–1715.
Vacation: Mon–Fri 0930–1700, Sat 0930–1300, 1400–1715.

Enquiries: By telephone, post or e-mail.
Admission: Charges are made for all use of the Library. In some circumstances, where access is required to certain named research collections, fees for short-term use of the Library may be waived. In most circumstances application should be made in writing to the Librarian.
Lending: Yes (on payment of fee).
Inter-library loans: Lends to other libraries.
Union record: BUCLA, BUCOP, COLALAS, CURL, RLIN, University of London Union List of Serials.

Catalogue: Innopac automated catalogue.
Classification: Bliss Bibliographic Classification.

Electronic facilities for non-members:

Microcomputing facilities: No.
On-line search facilities: Yes (payment required).
CD-ROM facilities: Yes.
Internet access: Yes.
Portable computers: Use permitted; power points available.

Other facilities for non-members:

Photocopying: Yes (payment required).
Microform holdings: Yes.
Reader-printer facilities: Yes (payment required).

Publications:

Latin American Studies.

170 Venezuelan Embassy / Embajada de los Estados Unidos de Venezuela

Biblioteca Latinoamericana Andrés Bello, 58 Grafton Way, London W1P 5LB

Tel.: 020 7388 5788
Fax: 020 7383 3253
E-mail: embvenuk-ccm@dial.pipex.com
WWW: http://www.venezlon.demon.co.uk/
Established: 1986; 1994 (as Biblioteca Latinoamericana Andrés Bello)

Subject enquiries to: Diana Gómez

Collections:

The Library has a collection of 3,500 books, 500 non-current periodical titles, video recordings and recorded music; 50–65 volumes are added each year. The main subject strength is Venezuelan history, but the Embassy is currently developing collections on Latin American and Venezuelan art and politics. Other subjects covered are economics, law and literature, and there is a strong collection of official publications. The material is predominantly on open access.

Access to collections:

Opening hours: Mon–Fri 0930–1530.

Enquiries: By telephone, post, fax or e-mail.
Admission: Open to the general public (appointment required).
Lending: No.
Inter-library loans: Lends to other libraries.
Catalogue: Author catalogue on Microsoft Access, in progress.
Classification: Dewey Decimal Classification.

Electronic facilities for non-members:

Microcomputing facilities: No.
On-line search facilities: No.
CD-ROM facilities: No.
Internet access: No.
Portable computers: Use not permitted.

Other facilities for non-members:

Photocopying: Yes (payment required).

171 Wellcome Library for the History and Understanding of Medicine

History of Medicine Library, Wellcome Library for the History and Understanding of Medicine, Wellcome Building, 183 Euston Road, London NW1 2BE

Tel.: 020 7611 8582
Fax: 020 7611 8369
E-mail: library@wellcome.ac.uk
Telnet catalogue: library.wellcome.ac.uk
Web catalogue: http://library.wellcome.ac.uk/
WWW: http://www.wellcome.ac.uk/library
Established: 1890 (opened to the public 1949)

Librarian: David R.S. Pearson, MA, ALA

Collections:

The Library, which has collected material on the history of medicine in Latin America since 1890, has an important collection of over 16,000 volumes which was maintained until 1990 in a special room, but is now dispersed among the General Collections. Much of the material derives from the collections of Dr Nicolás León (1859–1929), acquired in 1927, and those of Dr Francisco Guerra (1916–), acquired in 1962. The Library holds 130 periodical titles, 150 manuscripts of American origin (mainly of the colonial period), and over 800 pre-1851 Latin American imprints (including facsimiles of works not held in the collection). In addition to medical books and serials there are works on ethnology and travel, and on Amerindian medicine (including the culture and medicine of the Aztec, Maya and Inca civilisations, with reproductions of their illuminated codices). There is an almost complete collection of medical Mexicana from 1557 to 1833, and a fairly complete collection for the remainder of Latin America (particularly Peru) and the Caribbean during the colonial period. The collection also includes official publications, *guías de forasteros*, national histories of medicine, theses (particularly Mexican theses) on indigenous medicine, colonial newspapers and bibliographies of Latin American and Caribbean imprints. The collection is predominantly on closed access.

Access to collections:

Opening hours: Mon, Wed, Fri 0945–1715, Tues, Thurs 0945–1915, Sat 0945–1300. Bank Holiday weekends closed.

Enquiries: By telephone, post, fax or e-mail.
Admission: Open to the general public (proof of identity required).
Lending: The Library is reference only.
Inter-library loans: Lends to other libraries (with restrictions).
Union record: BUCLA, OCLC.
Catalogue: Innopac automated catalogue.
Classification: Barnard Classification (modified) and National Library of Medicine Classification.

Electronic facilities for non-members:

Microcomputing facilities: No.
On-line search facilities: No.
CD-ROM facilities: Yes.
Internet access: Yes.
Portable computers: Use permitted; power points available (reader must supply own adapter).

Other facilities for non-members:
Photocopying: Yes (payment required).
Microform holdings: Yes.
Reader-printer facilities: Yes.

Publications:

A Catalogue of Printed Books in the Wellcome Historical Medical Library.
Vol. 1. *Books Published before 1641,* rev. ed. (New York: Maurizio Martino, 1996) (Catalogue series PB1).
Vol. 2. *Books Printed from 1641–1850. A–E,* rev. ed. (New York: Maurizio Martino, 1966) (Catalogue series PB2).
Vol. 3. *Books Printed from 1641–1850. F–L* (London: Wellcome Institute for the History of Medicine, 1976) (Catalogue series PB3).
Vol. 4. *Books Printed from 1641–1850. M–R* (London: Wellcome Institute for the History of Medicine, 1995) (Catalogue series PB4).
Samuel Arthur Joseph Moorat, *Catalogue of Western Manuscripts on Medicine and Science in the Wellcome Historical Medical Library.*
Vol 1. *Mss Written before 1650 A.D.* (London: Wellcome Institute for the History of Medicine, 1962) (Catalogue series MS1).
Vol 2. *Mss Written after 1650 A.D.* (London: Wellcome Institute for the History of Medicine, 1973) (Catalogue series MS2-3).
Richard Palmer, *Catalogue of Western Manuscripts in the Wellcome Library for the History and Understanding of Medicine: Western Manuscripts 5120–6244* (London: The Library, 2000).
Frederick Noel Lawrence Poynter, *A Catalogue of Incunabula in the Wellcome Historical Medical Library* (London: Oxford University Press, 1954) (Publications of the Wellcome Historical Medical Museum. New series 5).
Subject Catalogue of the History of Medicine and Related Sciences (Munich: Kraus International Publications, 1980), 18 vols.
Robin Price, *An Annotated Catalogue of Medical Americana in the Library of the Wellcome Institute for the History of Medicine: Books and Printed Documents, 1557–1821, from Latin America and the Caribbean Islands and Manuscripts from the Americas, 1575–1927* (London: Wellcome Institute for the History of Medicine, 1983) (Catalogue series Amer1).
Robin Price, 'El Instituto Wellcome de la Historia de la Medicina', *Boletín de la Sociedad Mexicana de Historia y Filosofía de la Medicina,* vol. 2, nos 10–11 (1975), pp. 89–94.

Robin Price, 'Latin American Materials in the Wellcome Institute for the History of Medicine', *Bulletin of the Society for Latin American Studies*, vol. 23 (1975), pp. 17–22.

Robin Price, *The American Collections of the Wellcome Institute for the History of Medicine* (London: Wellcome Institute for the History of Medicine, 1986).

John Symons, *Wellcome Institute for the History of Medicine: a Short History* (London: The Wellcome Trust, 1993).

Wellcome Institute for the History of Medicine: a Brief Description, 5th ed. (London: Wellcome Institute for the History of Medicine, 1993).

Current Work in the History of Medicine: an International Bibliography (London: Wellcome Historical Medical Library, 1954–).

172 Westminster City Libraries

Westminster City Hall, Education and Leisure Department, 13th floor, 64 Victoria Street, London SW1E 6QP

Tel.: 020 7641 4632

Westminster Reference Library
35 St Martin's Street, London WC2H 7HP
Tel.: 020 7641 4636. Business and official publications 020 7641 4634. Arts 020 7641 4638
Fax: 020 7641 4606

Westminster Music Library
Victoria Library, 160 Buckingham Palace Road, London SW1W 9UD
Tel.: 020 7641 4292
Fax: 020 7641 4281
WWW: http://www.westminster.gov.uk/index/libraries.cfm/

Assistant Director, Lifetime Learning: David Ruse ALA, MIPM

Collections:

Westminster acquires much of the material published in the United Kingdom on Latin America and the Caribbean, together with a significant proportion of North American publications. Its foreign language acquisitions are also relatively high. Latin American and Caribbean holdings amount to over 3,000 books, 200 music scores, 100 records and a number of periodicals and newspapers. The library system has responsibility for the acquisition of Hispanic language and literature under the Inner London Subject Specialisation scheme, most of the stock being held at the Victoria Library. The Westminster Reference Library is notable for its worldwide map collection and its holdings of official publications of the United Kingdom and international organisations. The collections are on open access.

Access to collections:

Opening hours: Westminster Reference Library: Mon–Fri 1000–2000, Sat 1000–1700.
Victoria Library: Mon–Fri 0930–1900, Sat 0930–1300.
Westminster Music Library: Mon–Fri 1100–1900, Sat 1000–1700.
All libraries closed on public holidays.

Enquiries: By telephone, post or fax.
Admission: Open to the general public.
Lending: No.
Inter-library loans: Lends to other libraries.
Union record: BLDSC, BUCOP, GLASS, LASER.
Catalogues: Author and classified subject catalogue. Alphabetical subject catalogue (Westminster Reference Library). Geac automated catalogue.
Classification: Dewey Decimal Classification. Own classification for art. McColvin classification for music.

Electronic facilities for non-members:

Microcomputing facilities: No.
On-line search facilities: Yes (payment required).
CD-ROM facilities: Yes.
Internet access: Yes.
Portable computers: Use not permitted.

Other facilities for non-members:

Photocopying: Yes (payment required).
Microform holdings: Yes.
Reader-printer facilities: Yes (payment required).

173 Women's Art Library (MAKE Resource)

107–109 Charing Cross Road, London WC2H 0DU

Tel./Fax: 020 7514 8863
E-mail: womensart.lib@ukonline.co.uk
WWW: http://web.ukonline.co.uk/womensart.lib/index.html
Established: 1983

Librarian: Althea Greenan

Collections:

The Women's Art Library facilitates the study and appreciation of work by women artists. Together with its core activities of publishing and research, the Library is actively involved in arts and education initiatives that develop opportunities for women artists. It now has one of the largest archives on women artists in Europe, representing all facets of art created by more than 12,000 women artists. A major feature of the archive is the slide registry of work made by women artists worldwide, supplemented by books, periodicals and catalogues on women's art and its social and historical context, and the archives of individual artists. The Library also holds press cuttings, press releases, ephemera, catalogue extracts, video and audio recordings, and dissertations. For group exhibitions of Latin American women artists and individual women artists from Latin America and the Caribbean, information is held in the form of ephemera, unpublished dissertations, press cuttings, catalogues and slides.

Access to collections:

Opening hours: Tues–Fri 1000–1700.

Enquiries: By telephone, post, fax or e-mail.
Admission: Membership entitles users to admission to the Library, research assistance and other benefits. Membership categories are: artist, group, individual, corporate/institutional, Friends of WAL. Short-term access is also available through a day ticket.
Lending: All text materials are for reference only. Slides may be borrowed for educational use by members (payment required) and by commercial researchers (flat fee charged).
Inter-library loans: No.
Catalogue: Automated catalogue

Classification: Material in the library is mostly organised by individual artist and group exhibition. The automated catalogue provides access via subject, medium and nationality of artist.

Electronic facilities for non-members:

Microcomputing facilities: No.
On-line search facilities: No.
CD-ROM facilities: No.
Internet access: For queries and other contact use only.
Portable computers: Use permitted.

Other facilities for non-members:

Photocopying: Yes (payment required).

Publications:

Bulletin (membership newsletter, quarterly).
Make: the Magazine of Women's Art. Quarterly.

174 Worldaware
Resource Centre, 31–35 Kirby Street, London EC1N 8TE

Tel.: 020 7831 3844
Fax: 020 7831 1746
E-mail: info@worldaware.org.uk
WWW: http://www.worldaware.org.uk

Resource Administrator: Trisha Sharratt
E-mail address: trishasharatt@worldaware.org.uk

Collections:

Worldaware is an independent educational charity, which seeks to increase understanding in Britain of economic and social development issues worldwide. The Resource Centre holds printed and audio-visual materials produced by Worldaware and many other sources, including development NGOs and educational publishers. The material is arranged geographically, with a separate section on Latin America and the Caribbean. The collection is on open access.

Access to collections:

Opening hours: Mon–Fri 1000–1600. Public holidays closed.

Enquiries: By telephone, post, fax or e-mail.
Admission: Open to the general public (by appointment).
Lending: No.
Catalogue: Printed catalogue (to be available on the website).
Classification: Own classification.

Electronic facilities for non-members:

Microcomputing facilities: Yes (payment required for printing).
On-line search facilities: Yes (payment required for printing).
CD-ROM facilities: Yes (payment required for printing).
Internet access: Yes (payment required for printing).
Portable computers: Use permitted; power points available.

Other facilities for non-members:

Photocopying: Yes (payment required).

175 World Mission Association Ltd (WMA)
Partnership House Mission Studies Library, Partnership House, 157 Waterloo Road, London SE1 8XA

Tel.: 020 7928 8681
Fax: 020 7401 2731
E-mail: c.rowe@mailbox.ulcc.ac.uk
WWW: http://www.uspg.org.uk/phl.html
Established: 1987 (as Partnership House)

Librarian: Colin E. Rowe, BA, ALA

Collections:

The Library was formed by the amalgamation of the post-1945 collections of the United Society for the Propagation of the Gospel (USPG) and the Church Mission Society (CMS). The Library also holds the pre-1945 collection of the CMS, called the Max Warren Collection. The pre-1945 collection of the USPG is held at Rhodes House Library (no. 194). The archives of the CMS, 2,000,000 items currently, are being deposited in instalments in the University of Birmingham Library (no. 9). At present the papers from 1799 to 1949 are available for scholarly study.

The Church Mission Society began collecting material on Latin America in the second half of the nineteenth century and built up a small collection on the theology (including liberation theology) and history of the Church in the region. The USPG collection included post-1945 material on Guyana and the Caribbean, together with material on human rights, development issues and the Church in Latin America. Material on the region continues to form a minor part of the overall stock; 5 current periodical titles are held. The collection is predominantly on open access.

Access to collections:

Opening hours: Mon–Fri 0930–1700. Public holidays closed.

Enquiries: By telephone, post, fax or e-mail (payment may be required for long enquiries).
Admission: Non-members are admitted for reference purposes.
Lending: No.
Inter-library loans: Yes.
Union record: BLDSC.
Catalogues: Author, title and alphabetical subject catalogue. INMAGIC DB/TextWorks automated catalogue.
Classification: Dewey Decimal Classification.

Electronic facilities for non-members:

Microcomputing facilities: No.
On-line search facilities: No.
CD-ROM facilities: No.
Internet access: Yes (on application).
Portable computers: Use permitted; power points available.

Other facilities for non-members:

Photocopying: Yes (payment required).

176 Writers and Scholars Educational Trust (*Index on Censorship*)
Library, 33 Islington High Street, London N1 9LH
Tel.: 020 7278 2313
Fax: 020 7278 1878
E-mail: contact@indexoncensorship.org
WWW: http://www.indexoncensorship.org
Established: 1974

Subject enquiries to: Natasha Schmidt
Specialist's tel.: 020 7278 2313
Specialist's e-mail address: natasha@indexoncensorship.org

Collections:

The Trust's library, founded in 1974, includes a small separate collection of volumes and periodicals on Latin America, together with a collection of press cuttings related to censorship and human rights in Latin America and the Caribbean. Writers and Scholars International Ltd, which is associated with the Trust, publishes the journal *Index on Censorship*. The material is on open access.

Access to collections:

Opening hours: Mon–Fri 0930–1730. Public holidays closed.

Enquiries: By telephone, post, fax or e-mail.
Admission: Non-members are admitted for reference purposes (appointment required).
Lending: No.
Catalogue: None.
Classification: By subject.

Electronic facilities for non-members:

On-line search facilities: No.
CD-ROM facilities: No.
Internet access: Yes (appointment required).
Portable computers: Use permitted.

Other facilities for non-members:

Photocopying: Yes (payment required).

177 Zoological Society of London

The Library, The Zoological Society of London, Regent's Park, London NW1 4RY

Tel.: 020 7449 6293
Fax: 020 7586 5743
E-mail: library@zsl.org
WWW: http://www.zsl.org/core/library.html
Established: 1826

Librarian: Ann Sylph, BSc, MSc, MIInfSc

Collections:

The Society has one of the most important zoological libraries in the world, containing over 200,000 volumes and 5,000 periodical titles (of which 1,300 are current) on all aspects of zoology and animal conservation, and a collection of 30,000 photographs. An unquantified amount of material on the zoology of Latin America and the Caribbean is held. The collection is on open access.

Access to collections:

Opening hours: Mon–Fri 0930–1730. Public holidays closed.

Enquiries: By telephone, post, fax or e-mail.
Admission: Non-members are admitted for reference purposes (payment and proof of address required).
Lending: No.
Inter-library loans: Lends to other libraries.
Union record: BLDSC.
Catalogues: Author, title and classified subject card catalogue. EOSi automated catalogue.
Classification: Bliss Bibliographic Classification.

Electronic facilities for non-members:

Microcomputing facilities: No.
On-line search facilities: No.
CD-ROM facilities: Yes.
Internet access: No.
Portable computers: Battery-operated portable computers may be used.

Other facilities for non-members:
Photocopying: Yes (payment required).

MAIDSTONE

178 Horticulture Research International
Library, East Malling, Maidstone, Kent ME19 6BJ

Tel.: 01732 843833 ext. 341
E-mail: sarah.loat@hri.ac.uk
WWW: http://www.hri.ac.uk
Established: 1912 (1990 as Horticulture Research International)

Librarian: Sarah Loat, BA, ALA

Collections:

The Library is devoted to plant science (including plant physiology, pathology, entomology, breeding and genetics) for temperate and tropical fruits, ornamentals and woodland plants. Its total stock is 6,000 books, 30,000 volumes of journals and annual reports, and 80,000 pamphlets; 2,200 periodical titles are held, of which some 150 are current. Although no deliberate acquisition policy has been followed in relation to Latin America and the Caribbean, some of the Library's holdings are of relevance to the study of the area, including more than 35,000 pamphlets on tropical agriculture. The collection is on open access.

Access to collections:

Opening hours: Mon–Fri 0900–1700. Public holidays closed.

Enquiries: By telephone, post or e-mail.
Admission: Non-members are admitted for reference purposes (appointment with the Librarian required).
Lending: No.
Inter-library loans: Lends to other libraries.
Union record: BLDSC, BRISC (Biotechnology and Biological Sciences Research Council) libraries' consortium, COLALAS, LASER.
Catalogue: BRS automated catalogue.
Classification: Own classification.

Electronic facilities for non-members:
Microcomputing facilities: Yes.
On-line search facilities: No.
CD-ROM facilities: No.
Internet access: Yes.
Portable computers: Use permitted; power points available.

Other facilities for non-members:
Photocopying: Yes (payment required).
Microform holdings: Yes.
Reader-printer facilities: No.

MANCHESTER

179 Latin America Information Centre
St Margaret's Chambers, 5 Newton Street, Manchester M1 1HL

Address for correspondence: LAIC, PO Box 24, Manchester M7 4EX
Tel.: 0161 236 5906
Fax: 0161 236 5907
E-mail: laic@globalnet.co.uk
WWW: http://www.laic.co.uk/
Established: 1986 (Latin American News Service), 1989 (Latin America Information Centre)

Coordinator: John Warry

Collections:
The Latin American News Service (LANS) was established in 1986 to provide comprehensive news coverage of Central America. The service moved to its present site in Manchester in 1989 with the establishment of the Latin America Information Centre. In 1991 LANS news coverage was extended to include the whole of Latin America and the Caribbean; LANS also provides worldwide news coverage, with an emphasis on developing countries. The Centre has built up a library of several hundred books, periodicals and reports, and has an extensive collection of archival material on Latin America, spanning the past three decades. Material is also collected on global issues affecting the region, and there is a selection of fic-

tion by celebrated authors. The Centre produces *Weekly Newspacks* on all countries and regions of the world, sells books, periodicals, music materials, jewellery and handicrafts, and provides a travel service.

Access to collections:

Opening hours: Mon–Fri 1000–1700.

Enquiries: By telephone, post or e-mail.
Admission: Telephone in advance to make an appointment (limited space available).
Lending: No.
Inter-library loans: No.
Catalogue: Card catalogue (subjects, countries and regions).

Electronic facilities for non-members:

Microcomputing facilities: No.
On-line search facilities: No.
CD-ROM facilities: No.
Internet access: No.
Portable computers: Use permitted.

Other facilities for non-members:

Photocopying: Yes (payment required).

Publications:

Weekly Newspacks (prices on application; reduced subscription rates for students).
Regular booklists.
General leaflet.
Travel information.

180 University of Manchester

John Rylands University Library of Manchester, Oxford Road, Manchester M13 9PP

Tel.: 0161 275 3738. Admissions 0161 275 3789
Fax: 0161 273 7488
Telnet catalogue: library.man.ac.uk

Web catalogue: http://rylibweb.man.ac.uk/catalogue/
WWW: http://rylibweb.man.ac.uk/
Established: 1851 (Owens College), 1900 (John Rylands Library), 1972 (John Rylands Library merged with Manchester University Library)
Director and University Librarian: Christopher J. Hunt, BA, MLitt, ALA
Subject enquiries to: John F. Laidlar, BA, MA, PhD, Head of Administration and Staffing
Specialist's tel.: 0161 275 3742
Specialist's e-mail address: john.laidlar@man.ac.uk

Collections:

The Library has acquired material on Latin America since 1962 and has built up a collection of 20,000 books and 100 current and 50 non-current periodical titles, together with manuscripts and a small collection of microforms (including significant holdings of United States theses on Latin American literature, especially for the 1970s and 1980s); some 500 books, in addition to periodical parts, are added each year. The collection includes material on all countries of Latin America, but is particularly strong in its coverage of Brazil. The main subject strength is literature (particularly Brazilian literature), and this material, together with linguistics, is held in a specific Latin American collection. Other material is dispersed throughout the Library and there are significant collections on history and political science. Manuscripts, rare books, and those published before 1800 are held in the John Rylands Library, Deansgate, Manchester M3 3EH (tel.: 0161 834 5343; fax: 0161 834 5574). The collections in the Main Library are on open access, while those in the Deansgate building are on closed access.

Access to collections:

Opening hours: Main Library, Term: Mon–Sat 0900–2130, Sun 1200–2130. Vacation: Mon–Fri 0900–1730, Sat 0900–1300, Sun closed. Summer Vacation: Mon–Thurs 0900–1900, Fri 0900–1730, Sat 0900–1300, Sun closed. Public holidays closed, except for holidays in May, when the Main Library is open with limited services.
John Rylands Library, Deansgate: Mon–Fri 1000–1730, Sat 1000–1300. Public holidays closed.

Enquiries: By telephone, post, fax or e-mail.
Admission: Non-members are admitted for reference purposes. Payment is required for more than three visits per annum to the Main Library. The

Deansgate building is open to the general public, but readers are recommended to contact the Library in advance of a visit, as the material is on closed access.
Lending: No.
Inter-library loans: Lends to other libraries.
Union record: BLCMP, BLDSC, BUCLA, BUCOP, CALIM, COLALAS, CURL, NWRLS, UNITY.
Catalogue: BLCMP Talis automated catalogue.
Classification: Dewey Decimal Classification.

Electronic facilities for non-members:

Microcomputing facilities: No.
On-line search facilities: No.
CD-ROM facilities: No.
Internet access: No.
Portable computers: Use permitted; power points available.

Other facilities for non-members:

Photocopying: Yes (payment required).
Microform holdings: Yes.
Reader-printer facilities: Yes (payment required).

NEWCASTLE-UPON-TYNE

181 University of Newcastle upon Tyne
Robinson Library, University of Newcastle upon Tyne, Newcastle upon Tyne NE2 4HQ

Tel.: 0191 222 6000. Holdings enquiries 0191 222 7662. Admissions 0191 222 7670
Fax: 0191 222 6235
E-mail: library@ncl.ac.uk
Telnet catalogue: advance.ncl.ac.uk
Web catalogue: http://fulltext.ncl.ac.uk:8000/
WWW: http://www.ncl.ac.uk/library/
Established: 1871

University Librarian and Keeper of the Pybus Collection: Thomas W. Graham, MA, PhD, DipLib, ALA

Subject enquiries to: Jessica Plane, MA, ALA, Arts Liaison Librarian
Specialist's tel.: 0191 222 7656
Specialist's e-mail address: Jessica.Plane@ncl.ac.uk

Collections:

The Library acquires materials on Latin American history and literature in support of the University's teaching programme at the undergraduate and postgraduate levels. The collection now includes 4,000 books and 12 current and 3 non-current periodical titles. The best represented countries are Brazil, Mexico and Peru. The collection is on open access.

Access to collections:

Opening hours: Term: Mon–Fri 0900–2200, Sat 0900–1630, Sun 1100–1730. Vacation: Mon–Fri 0900–1700, Sat 0900–1300, Sun closed. Christmas, New Year, Easter and August Bank Holiday closed.

Enquiries: By telephone, post, fax or e-mail.
Admission: Non-members may be admitted for reference purposes (payment may be required).
Lending: Yes (payment required).
Inter-library loans: Lends to other libraries.
Union record: BLDSC, BUCLA, BUCOP, NRLS, OCLC.
Catalogue: Libertas automated catalogue.
Classification: Dewey Decimal Classification.

Electronic facilities for non-members:

Microcomputing facilities: Yes (payment required).
On-line search facilities: Yes (payment required).
CD-ROM facilities: Yes.
Internet access: No.
Portable computers: Use permitted; power points available.

Other facilities for non-members:

Photocopying: Yes (payment required).
Microform holdings: Yes.
Reader-printer facilities: Yes (payment required).

182 University of Northumbria

University of Northumbria Library, City Campus, Sandyford Road, Newcastle-upon-Tyne NE1 8ST

Tel.: 0191 227 4736
Fax: 0191 227 4563
E-mail: in.es@unn.ac.uk
Web catalogue: http://opac.unn.ac.uk/
WWW: http://www.unn.ac.uk/central/isd
Established: 1969

Director of Learning Resources: Jane Core
Subject enquiries to: G.J. Shields, BA, MPhil, DipLib, ALA, AIL, Information Specialist
Specialist's tel.: 0191 227 4133
Specialist's e-mail address: g.shields@unn.ac.uk

Collections:

The Library began collecting on Latin America in 1990. The material forms a minor part of the collection and consists of 6 current periodicals and about 2,000 books. Some 100–150 books (current material only) are added each year. Subject fields are in the social sciences — economics, geography, political science and social welfare — and in history and business/finance. The material is on open access.

Access to collections:

Opening hours: Term: Mon–Fri 0900–2100, Sat 0930–1700, Sun 1100–1700. Vacation: Mon, Wed–Fri 0900–1700, Tues, Thurs 0900–2100, Sat–Sun closed. Public holidays closed.

Enquiries: By telephone, post or e-mail.
Admission: Non-members are admitted for reference purposes (visitor's pass issued at enquiry desk).
Lending: May apply to become external borrower (payment required).
Inter-library loans: Lends to other libraries.
Union record: BLCMP.
Catalogue: BLCMP Talis automated catalogue.
Classification: Dewey Decimal Classification.

Electronic facilities for non-members:
Microcomputing facilities: Word-processing only.
On-line search facilities: No.
CD-ROM facilities: Yes (if licence permits).
Internet access: No.
Portable computers: Use permitted; power points available.

Other facilities for non-members:
Photocopying: Yes (payment required).
Microform holdings: No.
Reader-printer facilities: Yes (payment required).

NORWICH

183 University of East Anglia
University of East Anglia Library, Norwich, Norfolk NR4 7TJ

Tel.: 01603 592425/592407
Fax: 01603 259490
E-mail: library@uea.ac.uk
Telnet catalogue: library.uea.ac.uk or 139.222.192.1 (login: nepac)
Web catalogue: http://webpac.lib.uea.ac.uk/
WWW: http://www.lib.uea.ac.uk/
Established: 1962

Director of Library and Learning Resources: Jean Steward, BA, MA, ALA
Subject enquiries to: Kitty Inglis, BA, DipLib, Head of Resources
Specialist's tel.: 01603 592430
Specialist's e-mail address: k.inglis@uea.ac.uk

Collections:

The Library has a collection of 750,000 books and 2,000 periodical titles. Latin American material forms a minor part of the collection, with approximately 3,000 books, mainly in the field of history, together with some politics and economics. There are 3 current periodicals on Latin America. The collection is on open access.

Access to collections:

Opening hours: Term: Mon–Fri 0900–2100, Sat 0900–1700, Sun 1400–1900. Vacations: Mon–Fri 0900–1800, Sat–Sun closed. Christmas, New Year, Easter and August Bank Holiday closed.

Enquiries: By telephone, post, fax or e-mail.
Admission: Non-members may be admitted for reference purposes (application to the Librarian required).
Lending: Yes (payment required).
Inter-library loans: Lends to other libraries.
Union record: ANGLES.
Catalogue: Dynix automated catalogue.
Classification: Library of Congress Classification.

Electronic facilities for non-members:

Microcomputing facilities: No.
On-line search facilities: No.
CD-ROM facilities: Yes.
Internet access: Yes.
Portable computers: Use permitted at owner's risk; power points available.

Other facilities for non-members:

Photocopying: Yes (payment required).
Microform holdings: Yes.
Reader-printer facilities: Yes (payment required).

NOTTINGHAM

184 University of Nottingham
Hallward Library, University Park, Nottingham NG7 2RD

Tel.: 0115 951 5151. Holdings enquiries 0115 951 4514
Fax: 0115 951 4558
E-mail: library-comments@nottingham.ac.uk
Web catalogue: http://aleph.nottingham.ac.uk:4505/ALEPH
WWW: http://www.nottingham.ac.uk/library/
Established: 1881

Director of Library Services: Robert E. Oldroyd, BA, DipLib, ALA

Subject enquiries to: Deborah Bragan-Turner, BA, DipLib, Humanities Librarian
Specialist's tel.: 0115 951 4584
Specialist's e-mail address: Deborah.Bragan.Turner@nottingham.ac.uk

Collections:

The Library has been acquiring material on Latin American history and literature since the 1960s and now has a collection of over 5,000 volumes. The collection is held on open access.

Access to collections:

Opening hours: Term: Mon–Fri 0900–2145, Sat 0900–1645, Sun 0930–1645. Vacation: Mon–Fri 0900–2045, Sat 0900–1645, Sun 0930–1645. Christmas, New Year, Easter and August Bank Holiday closed.

Enquiries: By telephone, post, fax or e-mail.
Admission: Non-members are admitted for reference purposes.
Lending: Yes (payment required).
Inter-library loans: Lends to other libraries.
Union record: BLDSC, BUCOP, CURL, EMRLS.
Catalogues: Some pre-1985 material in card catalogue. Ex Libris Aleph automated catalogue.
Classification: Library of Congress Classification.

Electronic facilities for non-members:

Microcomputing facilities: No.
On-line search facilities: No.
CD-ROM facilities: No.
Internet access: No.
Portable computers: Use permitted; power points available.

Other facilities for non-members:

Photocopying: Yes (payment required).
Microform holdings: Yes.
Reader-printer facilities: Yes (payment required).

OLDBURY

185 Millbrook House Picture Library (*Railphotos*)
Unit 1, Oldbury Business Centre, Pound Road, Oldbury, West Midlands B68 8NA

Tel.: 0121 544 2970
Fax: 0121 253 6836

Subject enquiries to: David Johnson

Collections:

For the past 30 years Railphotos has been one of the largest specialist commercial picture libraries dealing with railway subjects worldwide, from 1896 to the present day. It has a collection of approximately 2,500 black-and-white and colour photographs of South American railways, mainly in 35mm format.

Access to collections:

Opening hours: Mon–Fri 1000–1600.

Enquiries: By post, telephone or fax.
Admission: By appointment.
Search/service fee: Negotiable. No commissions undertaken.
Lending: Yes.
Catalogue: None.
Classification: Images are filed by country.

Electronic facilities for non-members:

On-line search of images: No.
On-line delivery of images: No.
CD-ROM facilities: No.
Internet access: No.
Portable computers: Use permitted; power point available.

Other facilities for non-members:

Copying: None allowed on site.

OXFORD

186 Bodleian Law Library, University of Oxford
St Cross Building, Manor Road, Oxford OX1 3UR

Tel.: 01865 271463
Fax: 01865 271475
E-mail: law.library@bodley.ox.ac.uk
Telnet catalogue: library.ox.ac.uk
Web catalogue: http://library.ox.ac.uk
WWW: http://www.bodley.ox.ac.uk/guides/law/

Librarian: Barbara M. Tearle, LLB, MSt, ALA

Collections:

The Library receives material by copyright deposit and has substantial holdings on the Anglophone Caribbean from the eighteenth century to the present (especially from the 1920s onwards). Latin American acquisitions began about 1900 and form a minor part of the collection with over 1,000 books and 25 current periodical titles. The collections are on open access.

Access to collections:

Opening hours: Term: Mon–Fri 0900–2200, Sat 0900–1700, Sun 1100–1700. Vacation: Mon–Fri 0900–1900, Sat 0900–1300, Sun closed. Public holidays closed.

Enquiries: By telephone, post, fax or e-mail.
Admission: Non-members are admitted for reference purposes. A Form of Recommendation for Admission to the Bodleian Library must be completed (the form may be downloaded from the website) and presented to the Admissions Officer at the Bodleian Library; payment may be required.
Lending: No.
Inter-library loans: Lends to other libraries.
Union record: BUCLA, *Union List of Legal Periodicals* (IALS, no. 115), *Union list of Commonwealth and South African law* (IALS, no. 115), OLIS.
Catalogues: Abbreviations card catalogue (translates citations for legal serials and gives locations); Names card catalogue arranged by author and corporate body, with title entries for serials; Subject card catalogue arranged alphabetically by subject and sub-divided by jurisdiction and date; Geac

Advance OLIS automated catalogue contains entries for almost all the material and will eventually supersede the card catalogues.
Classification: Own classification.

Electronic facilities for non-members:

Microcomputing facilities: Yes.
On-line search facilities: Yes (payment required).
CD-ROM facilities: Yes (payment required).
Internet access: Yes.
Portable computers: Use permitted; limited power points available.

Other facilities for non-members:

Photocopying: Yes (payment required).
Microform holdings: Yes.
Reader-printer facilities: Yes (payment required).

187 Bodleian Library, University of Oxford
Broad Street, Oxford OX1 3BG

Tel.: 01865 277000. Holdings enquiries 01865 277161. Admissions 01865 277180
Fax: 01865 277182
E-mail: enquiries@bodley.ox.ac.uk
Telnet: library.ox.ac.uk
Web catalogue: http://library.ox.ac.uk
WWW: http://www.bodley.ox.ac.uk/
Established: The Library was founded in the mediaeval period, and re-established from 1598 to 1602

Director of University Library Services & Bodley's Librarian: Reginald P. Carr, BA, MA, MA, Hon. DLitt, FRSA
Subject enquiries to: Robert A. McNeil, MA, DipLib, Head, Hispanic Section
Specialist's tel.: 01865 277209
Specialist's e-mail address: robert.mcneil@bodley.ox.ac.uk

Collections:

The Bodleian Library has been acquiring books published on Latin America and the Caribbean since 1602. As a result it now has the best collection in

Great Britain outside the British Library. The number of volumes held on the area is in excess of 150,000, while periodicals total over 300 current and 1,100 non-current. Some 1,500 volumes are added to the collections each year. The various copyright privileges dating from 1610 have enabled the Library to receive nearly all books published in the United Kingdom and the United States on Latin America and the Caribbean since about 1820. Purchases were made in Spain in the seventeenth century, but donations brought in even more material. The Bodleian's collection of Mexican codices, which includes those now called Bodley, Laud, Mendoza and Selden, was received in this way. The Library's holdings of Latin American incunabula are also good. Dating from more recent times was the acquisition in 1870 of a large collection of Mexican Independence pamphlets, amassed in the 1860s by Henry Ward Poole. Purchasing declined because of lack of funds in the first half of the twentieth century, but revived in the 1960s. Special emphasis has been placed on the acquisition of material, both current and retrospective, in the humanities and social sciences, covering the Andean republics, Brazil, Mexico and the River Plate — though all areas of mainland Latin America and the Caribbean are covered in some depth. About ten per cent of acquisitions are of non-current material. The Library does not collect at all in the field of Latin American literature (except in American Indian languages); literature in Spanish and Portuguese is covered by the Taylor Institution Library (no. 199). While the Bodleian Library collects material on the Spanish-speaking, French and Dutch Caribbean, the history of the English-speaking Caribbean and former British colonial territories of Belize and Guyana is covered by Rhodes House Library (no. 194). Exchange agreements have been established with institutions and libraries in almost every Latin American country. The map section of the Bodleian has a large collection of maps of Latin America and the Caribbean, both historical and contemporary. Many manuscripts of Latin American interest, and all Oxford University theses, are held. See also Radcliffe Science Library (no. 193) and Rhodes House Library (no. 194).

Access to collections:

Opening hours: Term: Mon–Fri 0900-2200, Sat 0900–1300. Vacation: Mon–Fri 0900–1900, Sat 0900–1300. Closed from Christmas Eve to New Year's Day, from Good Friday to Easter Monday, on Encaenia Day (in June on the first Wednesday following the end of the Summer full term) and on August Bank Holiday Monday with the preceding Saturday.

Holdings enquiries: By telephone, post or e-mail.
Admission: Non-members may be admitted on written application (payment may be required). More detailed information is available from the Admission Office.
Lending: No.
Inter-library loans: Lends to other libraries.
Union record: BLDSC, BUCLA, BUCOP, COLALAS, CURL, OLIS, Oxford Union Catalogue of Latin Americana, *Serials in the British Library*.
Catalogues: Pre-1920 material on a CD-ROM, networked in the Library and published by Oxford University Press; subject access limited. Post-1920 material on Geac Advance OLIS union catalogue of books catalogued since early 1987 in all University of Oxford libraries.
Classification: None.

Electronic facilities for non-members:

Microcomputing facilities: Yes.
On-line search facilities: Yes.
CD-ROM facilities: Yes.
Internet access: Yes.
Portable computers: Use permitted.

Other facilities for non-members:

Photocopying: Yes (payment required).
Microform holdings: Yes.
Reader-printer facilities: Yes (payment required for printing).

Publications:

Colin Steele and Michael P. Costeloe, *Independent Mexico: a Collection of Mexican Pamphlets in the Bodleian Library* (London: Mansell, 1973).
The Bodleian Library pre-1920 Catalogue of Printed Books on Compact Disc (Oxford: Oxford University Press, 1993), 1 computer laser optical disk.

188 Department of Economics, University of Oxford
Manor Road Building, Manor Road, Oxford OX1 3UQ

Tel.: 01865 271093
Fax: 01865 271072
E-mail: library@economics.ox.ac.uk

Telnet catalogue: library.ox.ac.uk
Web catalogue: http://library.ox.ac.uk
WWW: http://www.ssl.ox.ac.uk/contact.html
Established: 1930s

Librarian: Margaret Robb, BS, MLS, MA, ALA

Collections:

The Library has collected economic material on Latin America and, to a lesser extent, on the Caribbean since the 1930s. There is now a large collection of material on the region, including over 100 periodical titles. Some material is held on microform. The collection is on open access.

Access to collections:

Opening hours: Term: Mon–Thurs 0900–2200, Fri 0900–1800, Sat 0930–1700. Vacation: Mon–Fri 0930–1800, Sat closed. Christmas, New Year, Easter and August Bank Holiday closed.

Enquiries: By telephone, post, fax or e-mail.
Admission: Non-members are admitted for reference purposes. Letter of introduction and payment may be required.
Lending: No.
Inter-library loans: Lends to other libraries.
Union record: BUCLA, BUCOP, COLALAS, CURL, OCLC, OLIS, Oxford Union Catalogue of Latin Americana.
Catalogues: Some earlier acquisitions are recorded only in the author and classified subject card catalogue. Geac Advance OLIS automated catalogue holds records for almost all the stock.
Classification: Library of Congress Classification (modified).

Electronic facilities for non-members:

Microcomputing facilities: Yes (payment may be required).
On-line search facilities: Yes (payment may be required).
CD-ROM facilities: Yes (payment may be required).
Internet access: Yes.
Portable computers: Use permitted; power points available.

Other facilities for non-members:

Photocopying: Yes (payment required).
Microform holdings: Yes.
Reader-printer facilities: Yes.

189 Department of Plant Sciences and Oxford Forestry Institute, University of Oxford

Plant Sciences Library (Forestry Collection), South Parks Road, Oxford OX1 3RB

Tel.: 01865 275082
Fax: 01865 275095
E-mail: enquiries@plantlib.ox.ac.uk
Telnet catalogue: library.ox.ac.uk
Web catalogue: http://library.ox.ac.uk
WWW: http://www.plantlib.ox.ac.uk/
Established: 1621, 1905 (Oxford Forestry Institute), 1996 (Plant Sciences Library)

Head, Library and Information Service: Roger A. Mills, MA, ALA

Collections:

The Library's forestry collections were built up in collaboration with the Forestry Department of CAB International (formerly Imperial Forestry Bureau, to 1951, and Commonwealth Forestry Bureau, 1951–) since the 1930s. The CABI–OFI Forestry Information Service is based on these collections. The Library is recognised by the International Union of Forestry Research Organisations as the western world's depository library for forestry literature in all languages and from all countries. Material is deposited on the understanding that it is permanently retained and made available for consultation without charge. Material on Latin America and the Caribbean has been collected since the early twentieth century. The collection is on open access.

Access to collections:

Opening hours: Mon–Fri 0900–1730. Public holidays closed.

Enquiries: By telephone, post, fax or e-mail (payment may be required).
Admission: Open to the general public for reference purposes.
Lending: No.
Inter-library loans: Lends to other libraries.
Union record: BLDSC, BUCOP, COLALAS, OLIS, SWRLS.
Catalogues: Material on forestry acquired before 1939 on microfilm catalogues. Forestry material acquired from 1939 indexed and abstracted on TREECD. Records for current acquisitions and much of the older material are on the Geac Advance OLIS automated catalogue.

Classification: Universal Decimal Classification and own classification.

Electronic facilities for non-members:

Microcomputing facilities: Yes (scanning, image-editing and word-processing).
On-line search facilities: No.
CD-ROM facilities: Yes.
Internet access: Yes.
Portable computers: Use permitted; power points available.

Other facilities for non-members:

Photocopying: Yes (payment required).
Microform holdings: Yes.
Reader-printer facilities: Yes (payment required).

Publications:

Agroforestry Abstracts (Wallingford: CABI, 1988–).
Forestry Abstracts (Wallingford: CABI, 1939–).
Forestry Products Abstracts (Wallingford: CABI, 1978–).
TREECD (London: SilverPlatter for CABI in cooperation with the Department for International Development and the Oxford Forestry Institute, 1991–).

190 International Development Centre, University of Oxford
International Development Centre Library, Queen Elizabeth House, 21 St Giles, Oxford OX1 3LA

Tel.: 01865 273590
Fax: 01865 273607
E-mail: sheila.allcock@qeh.ox.ac.uk
Telnet catalogue: library.ox.ac.uk
Web catalogue: http://library.ox.ac.uk
WWW: http://www2.qeh.ox.ac.uk/library/
Established: 1989

Librarian and Information Services Manager: Sheila L. Allcock, BSc

Collections:

The International Development Centre Library was formed in 1989 by the merger of two Oxford University departmental libraries, those of the Agricultural Economics Unit (formerly the Institute of Agricultural Economics) and the Institute of Commonwealth Studies. It therefore contains material published before this date. Latin American and Caribbean materials form a minor part of the collection, with greater geographical coverage of the Anglophone Caribbean than of other areas. Subjects covered include the economics of development, agricultural economics, environment, history, politics and rural sociology. There is a collection of press cuttings from the years 1950–95 covering developing countries. Theses and dissertations produced by Queen Elizabeth House students are held on closed access. Most of the collection (books, working papers and journals) is on open access.

Access to collections:

Opening hours: Term: Mon–Fri 0900–1800. Vacation: Mon–Fri 0900–1700. Christmas, New Year, Easter and August Bank Holiday week closed.

Enquiries: By telephone, post, fax or e-mail.
Admission: Non-members are admitted for reference purposes (application in advance to the Librarian required).
Lending: No.
Inter-library loans: Lends to other libraries.
Union record: BUCLA, BUCOP, COLALAS, CURL, OLIS, Oxford Union Catalogue of Latin Americana.
Catalogue: Geac Advance OLIS automated catalogue
Classification: Development Studies Classification.

Electronic facilities for non-members:

Microcomputing facilities: Yes.
On-line search facilities: Yes.
CD-ROM facilities: Yes.
Internet access: Yes; use of e-mail not permitted.
Portable computers: Use permitted on designated tables next to power points.

Other facilities for non-members:
Photocopying: Yes (payment required).

191 Modern Languages Faculty, University of Oxford

Modern Languages Faculty Library, Taylor Institution, St Giles, Oxford OX1 3NA

Tel.: 01865 278152
E-mail: library@mlfl.ox.ac.uk
Telnet catalogue: library.ox.ac.uk
Web catalogue: http://library.ox.ac.uk
WWW: http://users.ox.ac.uk/~mlflinfo/index.html
Established: 1959
Librarian: Gordon L. Robson, MA, DipLib
Subject enquiries to: Roger Shilcock, BA, Deputy Librarian
Specialist's tel.: 01865 278151
Specialist's e-mail address: roger.shilcock@mlfl.ox.ac.uk

Collections:

The Spanish and Portuguese sections joined the main library in the 1930s extension to the Taylor Institution (no. 199) in 1989. The collections are intended for undergraduates reading modern languages, but also contain material useful for graduate readers. There are 2,500 volumes and 3 periodicals on the literature of Latin America, and the collection's main strength is coverage of the Spanish American novel. There is a small collection of videos of Latin American feature films, which members may borrow; the Library has no viewing facilities. The collection is on open access.

Access to collections:

Opening hours: Term: Mon–Fri 0900–1800, Sat 0900–1300. Christmas and Easter Vacations: Mon–Fri 0900–1300, 1400–1730, Sat closed. Summer Vacation: Mon–Fri 0900–1300, 1400–1700, Sat closed. Public holidays closed, except May holidays (normal opening hours).

Enquiries: By telephone, post or e-mail.
Admission: Non-members may be admitted in exceptional circumstances. A letter of recommendation from a Professor, Reader or Lecturer of the

Modern Languages Faculty should be submitted to the Librarian; the application will then be considered by the Committee on Library Provision in Modern Languages.
Lending: No.
Inter-library loans: No.
Union record: BUCLA, OLIS, Oxford Union Catalogue of Latin Americana.
Catalogue: Geac Advance OLIS automated catalogue.
Classification: Own classification.

Electronic facilities for non-members:

Microcomputing facilities: No.
On-line search facilities: OxLIP.
CD-ROM facilities: Yes; access through OxLIP to networked CD-ROMs; a few locally-held CD-ROMs.
Internet access: Yes.
Portable computers: Use not permitted.

Other facilities for non-members:

Photocopying: Yes (payment required).
Microform holdings: Yes.
Reader-printer facilities: No.

192 Oxfam
Oxfam Library, 274 Banbury Road, Oxford OX2 7DZ

Tel.: 01865 313757
Fax: 01865 313770
E-mail: rbuck@oxfam.org.uk
WWW: http://www.oxfam.org.uk/atwork/history/library.htm
Established: 1942

Librarian: Rosalind Buck, BA, DipIM
Photo Library: Ros Goodway
Tel.: 01865 313767
E-mail: rgoodway@oxfam.org.uk

Collections:

Oxfam is a development, relief and campaigning organisation dedicated to reducing poverty and suffering around the world. The Library holds 12,500 books, reports and working papers, and 120 periodical titles. Latin American and Caribbean materials form a minor part of the overall stock; 451 books are relevant to the region and 10 of the Latin American titles published by the Economist Intelligence Unit are held. A collection of videos made by Oxfam or other agencies on development issues is available for viewing or loan. The Photo Library has a collection spanning most countries in which Oxfam operates, documenting projects and portraying the daily life of the communities concerned. Holdings are in excess of 30,000 slides and 20,000 prints, with over 3,000 slides relating to Latin America. Countries featured prominently include Bolivia, Brazil, El Salvador, Guatemala, Haiti, Honduras and Nicaragua.

Access to collections:

Opening hours: Mon–Fri 0900–1700.

Enquiries: By telephone, post, fax or e-mail.
Admission: Non-members are admitted for reference purposes (appointment required).
Lending: No.
Inter-library loans: No.
Catalogue: Idealist automated catalogue.
Classification: Own classification.

193 Radcliffe Science Library, Bodleian Library, University of Oxford

Parks Road, Oxford OX1 3QP

Tel.: 01865 272800. Admissions 01865 277180
Fax: 01865 272821
E-mail: rsl.enquiries@bodley.ox.ac.uk. Admissions: admissions@bodley. ox.ac.uk
Telnet catalogue: library.ox.ac.uk
Web catalogue: http://library.ox.ac.uk
WWW: http://www.bodley.ox.ac.uk/guides/rsl/
Established: 1749

Keeper of Scientific Books: Judith Palmer

Collections:

The Radcliffe Science Library is the scientific section of the Bodleian Library and holds extensive collections in scientific subjects, including physical sciences, medical and life sciences, and the history of science. The Library does not specifically collect scientific publications from Latin America and the Caribbean, but relevant material is found throughout the collections. This includes meteorological reports, geological and mining surveys, and naturalists' reports. Maps, particularly geological maps, are also collected. The material is on closed access.

Access to collections:

Opening hours: Term: Mon–Fri 0900–2200, Sat 0900–1300. Christmas and Easter Vacations: Mon–Fri 0900–1900, Sat 0900–1300. Summer Vacation: Mon–Fri 0900–1700, Sat 0900–1300. Christmas, New Year, Easter and August Bank Holiday week closed.

Enquiries: By telephone, post, fax or e-mail.
Admission: Non-members are admitted for reference purposes. A Form of Recommendation for Admission to the Bodleian Library must be completed (the form may be downloaded from the website) and presented to the Admissions Officer at the Bodleian Library; payment may be required.
Lending: No.
Inter-library loans: Lends to other libraries.
Union record: BLDSC, BUCLA, CURL, OCLC, OLIS, Oxford Union Catalogue of Latin Americana, *Serials in the British Library*.
Catalogues: Oxford University Union List of Serials on microfiche is occasionally useful. Geac Advance OLIS automated catalogue contains almost all serial titles. Some older works are on the Bodleian Library pre-1920 catalogue; all will eventually be included in OLIS. Theses from 1997 onwards are included in OLIS; earlier theses are recorded in the theses catalogue.
Classification: Own classification.

Electronic facilities for non-members:

Microcomputing facilities: No.
On-line search facilities: Yes (payment required).

CD-ROM facilities: Yes.
Internet access: Yes.
Portable computers: Use permitted; power points available.

Other facilities for non-members:

Photocopying: Yes (payment required).
Microform holdings: Yes.
Reader-printer facilities: Yes (payment required).

194 Rhodes House, University of Oxford

Rhodes House Library, South Parks Road, Oxford OX1 3RG

Tel.: 01865 270909. Admissions 01865 277180
Fax: 01865 270912
E-mail: rhodes.house.library@bodley.ox.ac.uk.
  Admissions: admissions@bodley.ox.ac.uk
Telnet catalogue: library.ox.ac.uk
Web catalogue: http://library.ox.ac.uk
WWW: http://www.bodley.ox.ac.uk/guides/pdf/rhl01.pdf
Established: 1929

Librarian: John Pinfold, MA, DipLib

Collections:

The Library was founded in 1929, but relevant material published after 1760 was transferred from the Bodleian. Geographically, the collections cover the British colonies, the USA and the Commonwealth. The subjects covered are history and the social sciences. Material on these areas received by the Bodleian through legal deposit is transferred to Rhodes House; older material is purchased to fill gaps in the collections and some relevant material published overseas is acquired. The Library has strong collections on the Anglophone Caribbean, including official publications, and on relations between the United States and Latin America. Manuscript collections include the Anti-Slavery Society. The collections are on closed access. During 2001 the United States holdings will be transferred to the new Vere Harmsworth Library in the Rothermere American Institute.

Access to collections:

Opening hours: Term: Mon–Fri 0900–1900, Sat 0900–1300. Vacation: Mon–Thurs 0900–1900, Fri 0900–1700, Sat 0900–1300. Christmas, New Year, Easter and August Bank Holiday week closed.

Enquiries: By telephone, post, fax or e-mail.
Admission: Non-members are admitted for reference purposes. A Form of Recommendation for Admission to the Bodleian Library must be completed (the form may be downloaded from the website) and presented to the Admissions Officer at the Bodleian Library; payment may be required.
Lending: No.
Inter-library loans: Lends to other libraries.
Union record: BUCOP, COLALAS, CURL, OLIS.
Catalogues: Card index for manuscripts. Author and periodical title card catalogue for material acquired before 1988. Subject catalogue on microfiche for material acquired before 1988. Bodleian Library Pre-1920 Catalogue of Printed Books does not give Rhodes House shelfmarks. Geac Advance OLIS automated catalogue for material catalogued since September 1988, and some earlier material.
Classification: Own classification.

Electronic facilities for non-members:

Microcomputing facilities: Yes.
On-line search facilities: Yes.
CD-ROM facilities: Yes.
Internet access: Yes.
Portable computers: Use is permitted at the enquiry desk end of the Reading Room.

Other facilities for non-members:

Photocopying: Yes (payment required).
Microform holdings: Yes.
Reader-printer facilities: Yes (payment required).

Publications:

Louis B. Frewer (comp.), *Manuscript Collections (Excluding Africana) in Rhodes House Library, Oxford* (Oxford: Bodleian Library, 1970).
Wendy S. Byrne (comp.), *Manuscript Collections (Africana and non-Africana) in Rhodes House Library, Oxford: Supplementary*

Accessions to the End of 1977, and Cumulative Index (Oxford: Bodleian Library, 1978).

Clare Brown (comp.), *Manuscript Collections in Rhodes House Library, Oxford: Accessions, 1978–1994* (Oxford: Bodleian Library, 1996).

195 Saint Antony's College, University of Oxford

Latin American Centre Library, 1 Church Walk, Oxford OX2 6LY

Tel.: 01865 274483
Fax: 01865 274489
E-mail: library@lac.ox.ac.uk
Telnet catalogue: library.ox.ac.uk
Web catalogue: http://library.ox.ac.uk
WWW: http://www.lib.ox.ac.uk/libraries/guides/LAC.html
Established: 1964

Librarian: Ruth Hodges, MA, DipLib
Librarian's e-mail address: ruth.hodges@lac.ox.ac.uk

Collections:

The Latin American Centre was established at the College in 1964 with the assistance of a grant from the Ford Foundation. In 1965, when Oxford University received national funding for Latin American studies, the Latin American Centre became the University's focal point for research on the region. The Library has a collection of 9,000 books, 220 boxes of pamphlets and offprints, 30 current periodical titles, 400 microforms and a collection of press cuttings. The main subject strengths are agriculture, economics, history and politics. The collection is on open access.

Access to collections:

Opening hours: Mon–Fri 0900–1245, 1400–1700. Christmas, New Year, Easter and August Bank Holiday closed. Closed for three weeks in August.

Enquiries: By telephone, post, fax or e-mail.
Admission: Non-members may be admitted for reference purposes. Application in advance to the Librarian required.
Lending: No.
Inter-library loans: Lends to other libraries.
Union record: BUCLA, BUCOP, COLALAS, CURL, OLIS, Oxford Union Catalogue of Latin Americana.

Catalogues: Oxford Union Catalogue of Latin Americana card catalogue. Author and subject card catalogue for material acquired before February 1991. Geac Advance OLIS automated catalogue for material acquired from February 1991.
Classification: Library of Congress Classification.

Electronic facilities for non-members:

Microcomputing facilities: No.
On-line search facilities: Yes.
CD-ROM facilities: No.
Internet access: Yes.
Portable computers: Permission must first be obtained from the Librarian.

Other facilities for non-members:

Photocopying: No.
Microform holdings: Yes.
Reader-printer facilities: No.

196 School of Anthropology and Museum Ethnography, University of Oxford

Balfour Library, Pitt Rivers Museum, School of Anthropology and Museum Ethnography, South Parks Road, Oxford OX1 3PP

Tel.: 01865 270939
Fax: 01865 270943
E-mail: mark.dickerson@prm.ox.ac.uk
Telnet catalogue: library.ox.ac.uk
Web catalogue: http://library.ox.ac.uk
WWW: http://www.lib.ox.ac.uk/libraries/guides/BAL.html
Established: 1940

Librarian: Mark R. Dickerson, BA, DipInfMan

Collections:

The Library collects material on archaeology, anthropology, ethnology, ethnomusicology, material culture and cultural ecology. Latin American and Caribbean material forms a minor part of a collection of 30,000 books and pamphlets, and 190 current and 110 non-current periodical titles. The collection on the region includes 750 books and pamphlets, and 5 current and 14 non-current periodical titles; 50–100 volumes are added each year. The material is on open access. Manuscripts, photographs, video recordings and musical recordings are held in separate collections in the Museum.

Access to collections:

Opening hours: Term: Mon–Fri 0900–1700. Vacation: Mon–Fri 0900–1230, 1400–1600. Christmas, New Year, Easter and the month of August closed.
Enquiries: By telephone, post, fax or e-mail.
Admission: Non-members may be admitted for reference purposes. Application in advance to the Librarian required.
Lending: No.
Inter-library loans: No.
Union record: CURL, OLIS.
Catalogues: Author and subject card catalogues for pamphlet collection. Author and partial classified subject card catalogues for material acquired before 1995. Geac Advance OLIS automated catalogue for material acquired from 1995 onwards.
Classification: Bliss Bibliographic Classification.

Electronic facilities for non-members:

Microcomputing facilities: No.
On-line search facilities: No.
CD-ROM facilities: Yes.
Internet access: Yes.
Portable computers: Use permitted; power points available.

Other facilities for non-members:

Photocopying: Yes (payment required).
Microform holdings: Yes.
Reader-printer facilities: No.

197 School of Anthropology and Museum Ethnography, University of Oxford

Institute of Social and Cultural Anthropology (ISCA), The Tylor Library, 51 Banbury Road, Oxford OX2 6PE

Tel.: 01865 274671
Fax: 01865 274630

E-mail: libisca@ermine.ox.ac.uk
Telnet catalogue: library.ox.ac.uk
Web catalogue: http://library.ox.ac.uk
WWW: http://www.lib.ox.ac.uk/libraries/guides/SCA.html
Established: Early 20th century

Librarian: Mike Morris, BA, MA, DipLib, ALA

Collections:

The Library collects social and cultural anthropology, with some sociology and linguistics. There are about 800 volumes dealing with the social anthropology of Amazonia, with some holdings in other areas. The collection is on open access.

Access to collections:

Opening hours: Term: Mon–Fri 0900–1730, Sat 0930–1230. Vacation: Mon–Fri 0900–1245, 1415–1700, Sat–Sun closed. Christmas, New Year, Easter and August closed.

Enquiries: By telephone, post, fax or e-mail.
Admission: Non-members are admitted for reference purposes (application in advance to the Librarian required).
Lending: No.
Inter-library loans: No.
Union record: OLIS.
Catalogues: Some material acquired before 1992 is recorded only in the author card catalogue. Records for material acquired from March 1992 and some earlier material are in the Geac Advance OLIS automated catalogue.
Classification: Own classification.

Electronic facilities for non-members:

Microcomputing facilities: No.
On-line search facilities: Yes.
CD-ROM facilities: No.
Internet access: Yes.
Portable computers: Reasonable use permitted.

Other facilities for non-members:

Photocopying: Yes (payment required).

198 School of Geography, University of Oxford
Library, Mansfield Road, Oxford OX1 3TB

Tel.: 01865 271912. Admissions 01865 271911
Fax: 01865 271929
E-mail: linda.atkinson@geog.ox.ac.uk
Telnet catalogue: library.ox.ac.uk
Web catalogue: http://library.ox.ac.uk
WWW: http://www.geog.ox.ac.uk/facilities/library/
Established: 1889
Librarian: Linda S. Atkinson, BSc, MSc, ALA

Collections:

The Library has collected material on Latin America and the Caribbean since its foundation, and now has 3,000 books, 2 current and 5 non-current periodical titles, 5 microforms, Mexican census material on CD-ROM, over 1,000 maps and 500 slides; some 30 books are added each year. In the older material the Andean countries are well represented; current acquisitions emphasise Mexico and the Caribbean. The Library has a worldwide collection of meteorological records. The collections are on open access.

Access to collections:

Opening hours: Term: Mon–Fri 0900–1800, Sat 1000–1300. Vacation: Mon–Fri 0900–1300, 1400–1700, Sat closed. Christmas, New Year, Easter and August Bank Holiday closed.

Enquiries: By telephone, post, fax or e-mail.
Admission: Non-members are admitted for reference purposes. Application in advance to the Librarian is preferred.
Lending: No.
Inter-library loans: Lends to other libraries.
Union record: BUCLA, BUCOP, COLALAS, CURL, OCLC, OLIS, Oxford Union Catalogue of Latin Americana.
Catalogues: Map card catalogue. Author and classified subject card catalogue for material acquired before 1990. Geac Advance OLIS automated catalogue for material acquired since 1990.
Classification: Own classification.

Electronic facilities for non-members:

Microcomputing facilities: No.

On-line search facilities: No.
CD-ROM facilities: No.
Internet access: No.
Portable computers: Use permitted after a safety check; power points available.

Other facilities for non-members:

Photocopying: Yes (payment required).
Microform holdings: Yes.
Reader-printer facilities: Yes (payment required).

199 Taylor Institution, University of Oxford
Taylor Institution Library, St Giles', Oxford OX1 3NA

Tel.: 01865 278154. Holdings enquiries 01865 278158
Fax: 01865 278165
E-mail: enquiries@taylib.ox.ac.uk
Telnet catalogue: library.ox.ac.uk
Web catalogue: http://library.ox.ac.uk
WWW: http://www.taylib.ox.ac.uk
Established: 1845

Librarian: Elizabeth A. Chapman, BA, MA, DipLib, FLA
Subject enquiries to: John E. Wainwright, MA, MLitt
Specialist's tel.: 01865 278141
Specialist's e-mail address: john.wainwright@taylib.ox.ac.uk

Collections:

The Taylor Institution Library is the University's main collection in modern and mediaeval European languages and literature, and the largest specialist library in this field in Britain. The Library has collected Latin American material since 1965 and now has over 20,000 books, and over 30 current and 80 non-current periodical titles; 600–700 volumes are added each year and approximately ten per cent of these are of non-current material. Some theses on microfilm are held. The collections cover Latin America and the Hispanic and Francophone Caribbean. The strongest holdings are of Argentine, Brazilian, Chilean, Colombian, Cuban and Mexican literature, and current acquisitions emphasise comprehensive coverage of the texts and of criticism of the major poets and novelists.

Studies of the Spanish and Portuguese languages as spoken in Latin America are also collected; indigenous languages of the Americas are not covered. The collection is on open access.

Access to collections:

Opening hours: October–June: Mon–Fri 0900–1900, Sat 0900–1300. July: Mon–Fri 0900–1700, Sat 0900–1300. August–September: Mon–Fri 1000–1300, 1400–1700, Sat 1000–1300. Christmas, New Year, Easter and August Bank Holiday week closed.

Enquiries: By telephone, post, fax or e-mail.
Admission: Non-members are admitted for reference purposes (advance application to the Librarian required).
Lending: No.
Inter-library loans: Lends to other libraries.
Union record: BLDSC, BUCLA, COLALAS, CURL, OCLC, OLIS, Oxford Union Catalogue of Latin Americana, RLIN.
Catalogue: Geac Advance OLIS automated catalogue.
Classification: Own classification.

Electronic facilities for non-members:

Microcomputing facilities: No.
On-line search facilities: Yes.
CD-ROM facilities: Yes.
Internet access: Yes.
Portable computers: Use permitted; power points available.

Other facilities for non-members:

Photocopying: Yes (payment required).
Microform holdings: Yes.
Reader-printer facilities: Yes (payment required).

PORTSMOUTH

200 University of Portsmouth
Frewen Library, Cambridge Road, Portsmouth PO1 2ST

Tel.: 023 9284 3222
Fax: 023 9284 3233

E-mail: library@port.ac.uk
Web catalogue: http://lib.port.ac.uk/
WWW: http://www.libr.port.ac.uk/
Established: 1869 (Portsmouth School of Science and Art), 1969 (Portsmouth Polytechnic), 1992 (Portsmouth University)

Librarian: Ian Bonar, BSc, ALA
Subject enquiries to: Anne Worden, MA, MA, ALA
Specialist's tel.: 023 9284 3243
Specialist's e-mail address: Anne.Worden@port.ac.uk

Collections:

The Frewen Library has collected Latin American material since 1969 and now has 10,000 books, and 38 current and 52 non-current periodical titles (with some material held on microform); 300 volumes are added each year. The main subject areas are history, linguistics, literature and the social sciences, with a geographical emphasis on Argentina, Brazil and Mexico. Collections on Central America and on gender studies are being developed. The Library holds the archive of the BBC Latin American Service, c. 1981–86 and the Lloyds Bank Latin American press cuttings collection from the 1980s. The collections are predominantly on open access.

Access to collections:

Opening hours: Term: Mon–Sun 0800–2400. Summer Vacation: Mon–Fri 0900–1730, Sat 1000–1600, Sun closed.

Enquiries: By telephone, post, fax or e-mail.
Admission: Non-members are admitted for reference purposes.
Lending: Yes (application in writing to the University Librarian and payment required).
Inter-library loans: Lends to other libraries.
Union record: BLCMP, BLDSC, BUCLA, COLALAS, SWRLS.
Catalogue: BLCMP Talis automated catalogue.
Classification: Dewey Decimal Classification.

Electronic facilities for non-members:

Microcomputing facilities: No.
On-line search facilities: No.
CD-ROM facilities: No.
Internet access: No.
Portable computers: Use permitted; power points available.

Other facilities for non-members:
Photocopying: Yes (payment required).
Microform holdings: Yes.
Reader-printer facilities: Yes (payment required).

READING

201 University of Reading
Main Library, Whiteknights, P.O. Box 223, Reading, Berks RG6 6AE

Bulmershe Library, Bulmershe Court, Earley, Reading RG6 1HY

Tel.: 0118 931 8770. Bulmershe Library 0118 931 8652
Fax: 0118 931 6636. Bulmershe Library 0118 931 8651
E-mail: library@reading.ac.uk
Web catalogue: http://www.unicorn.rdg.ac.uk/
WWW: http://www.rdg.ac.uk/libweb
Established: 1892

University Librarian: Julia Munro

Collections:

The Library has collected material on Latin America and the Caribbean since its foundation, and increasingly since the 1970s. There is now a collection of 2,000 books, 25 current periodical titles and 12 manuscripts; 50 volumes are added each year. The material is divided between the Main Library and the Bulmershe Library, with economics, environment, history, linguistics and sociology at the Main Library, and education, geography, film and sport at the Bulmershe Library. The collection is predominantly on open access.

Access to collections:

Opening hours: Main Library. Term: Mon–Thurs 0900–2215, Fri 0900–1900, Sat–Sun 1100–1700. Vacation: Mon–Fri 0900–1700, Sat–Sun closed.
Bulmershe Court Branch. Term: Mon–Thurs 0900–2100, Fri 0900–1800, Sat 0930–1230. Vacation: Mon–Fri 0900–1700, Sat closed.

Enquiries: By telephone, post, fax or e-mail.
Admission: Non-members are admitted for reference purposes.
Lending: Yes (payment required).

Inter-library loans: Lends to other libraries.
Union record: BLDSC, BUCLA, BUCOP, COLALAS, LASER.
Catalogues: Author and alphabetical subject card catalogues for material acquired before 1989. SIRSI Unicorn automated catalogue for material acquired since 1989 and for a substantial proportion of earlier stock.
Classification: Dewey Decimal Classification.

Electronic facilities for non-members:

Microcomputing facilities: No.
On-line search facilities: Yes (payment required).
CD-ROM facilities: Use of some stand-alone CD-ROMs is permitted.
Internet access: No.
Portable computers: Use permitted; a few power points in designated areas.

Other facilities for non-members:

Photocopying: Yes (payment required).
Microform holdings: Yes.
Reader-printer facilities: Yes (payment required).

RUGBY

202 Intermediate Technology
The Schumacher Centre for Technology and Development, Bourton Hall, Bourton-on-Dunsmore, Rugby, Warwickshire CV23 9QZ

Tel.: 01926 634400
Fax: 01926 634401
E-mail: itdg@itdg.org.uk
WWW: http://www.itdg.org/home.html
Established: 1967

Resource Centre Co-ordinator: Sandra M. Gibson, BA
E-mail address: sandrag@itdg.org.uk

Collections:

Intermediate Technology is an international development agency founded by Dr E.F. Schumacher (author of *Small is Beautiful*), specialising in appropriate technology transfer to rural communities in Africa, Asia and Latin America. Its aim is to enable poor people in the South to develop and use skills and technologies which give them more control over their lives and which contribute to the sustainable development of their communities. The Latin American holdings, which are on open access, constitute a minor part of the collection and include titles on appropriate technologies in relation to housing, energy, disaster mitigation and sustainable development, with a focus on Peru. IT maintains a Latin American regional office in Peru, IT Perú: http://www.itdg.org.pe, http://www.itdg.org.pe/cendoc (Centro de Documentación), http://www.infodes.org.pe (Proyecto InfoDes [Información para el Desarrollo]). ITDG has a publishing subsidiary: IT Publications, 103–105 Southampton Row, London WC1B 4HH (http:// www.itpubs.org.uk).

Access to collections:

Opening hours: Mon–Fri 0900–1300, 1400–1700.

Enquiries: By telephone or e-mail.
Admission: Open to the general public.
Lending: No.
Inter-library loans: No.
Catalogue: Inmagic automated catalogue.
Classification: Subject indexing based on appropriate technology and development issues.

Electronic facilities for non-members:

Microcomputing facilities: No.
On-line search facilities: Yes.
CD-ROM facilities: No.
Internet access: No.
Portable computers: Use permitted; power points available.

Other facilities for non-members:

Photocopying: Yes (payment required).

SAINT ANDREWS

203 University of St Andrews

University of Saint Andrews Library, North Street, St Andrews, Fife KY16 9TR, Scotland

Tel.: 01334 462281. Holdings enquiries 01334 462292. Admissions 01334 462283

Fax: 01334 462282
E-mail: library@st-and.ac.uk
Telnet catalogue: library.st-and.ac.uk
Web catalogue: http://138.251.116.3/
WWW: http://www-library.st-and.ac.uk/ (including link to Manuscripts page)
Established: 1413

Librarian: Neil F. Dumbleton, MA, MA

Collections:

The Library received material through copyright deposit between 1710 and 1836, but the acquisition of Latin American material started in about 1920. The collection now consists of 7,000 books and 30 current periodical titles; 100 volumes are added each year. The main subject strength of the collection is research material for the study of Amerindian languages and cultures; the Library cooperates with the Centre for Indigenous American Studies and Exchange in the development of the collection. In addition to works on anthropology and linguistics, the Library holds materials on education, environment, geography, history and sociology. The collection is on open access.

Access to collections:

Opening hours: Term: Mon–Thurs 0845–2200, Fri 0845–1800, Sat 0900–1700, Sun 1300–1900. Vacation: Mon–Fri 0900–1700, Sat 0900–1300, Sun closed.

Enquiries: By telephone, post, fax or e-mail.
Admission: Non-members are admitted for reference purposes.
Lending: Yes (payment required).
Inter-library loans: Lends to other libraries.
Union record: BLDSC, BUCLA, BUCOP, COLALAS, NLSLS, SCOL-CAP.
Catalogues: Manuscripts Catalogue: database available via telnet and the website. Periodicals Catalogue in three volumes: title catalogue. PAGE-CAT: author catalogue of Main Library material published before 1973. SAULCAT (Innopac) automated catalogue for material published in 1973 or later and material received in 1982 or later, regardless of publication date.
Classification: Library of Congress Classification.

Electronic facilities for non-members:
Microcomputing facilities: No.
On-line search facilities: No.
CD-ROM facilities: Yes.
Internet access: No.
Portable computers: Use permitted; power points available.

Other facilities for non-members:
Photocopying: Yes (payment required).
Microform holdings: Yes.
Reader-printer facilities: Yes (payment required).

SALFORD

204 University of Salford
Academic Information Services, Clifford Whitworth Building, The Crescent, Salford M5 4WT

Tel.: 0161 295 5846
Fax: 0161 295 5888
E-mail: advisor@ais.salford.ac.uk
Telnet catalogue: sais.salford.ac.uk
Web catalogue: http://sais.salford.ac.uk/
WWW: http://www.ais.salford.ac.uk/
Established: 1896 (1967 as University of Salford)

Director of Academic Information Services and University Librarian: Mark J. Clark, PhD
Subject enquiries to: Sue Slade, BA, ALA, Faculty Coordinator, Arts, Media and Social Sciences
Specialist's tel.: 0161 295 7246
Specialist's e-mail address: s.m.slade@salford.ac.uk

Collections:
The library has collected Latin American and Caribbean materials since the 1960s. The main subjects covered are economics, geography, history, linguistics, politics and sociology, with particular strengths in gender studies, the history of Brazil and industrial development. The material forms a

small part of the overall stock; 1,000 books are held, together with 2 current and 4 non-current periodical titles; 30 volumes are added each year. The collection is on open access.

Access to collections:

Opening hours: Term: Mon–Fri 0855–2100, Sat–Sun 1000–1600. Vacation: Mon–Fri 0855–1700, Sat–Sun closed. Public holidays closed.

Enquiries: By telephone, post, fax or e-mail.
Admission: Non-members are admitted for reference purposes.
Lending: Yes (payment required).
Inter-library loans: Lends to other libraries.
Union record: BLCMP, BLDSC, BUCLA, BUCOP, NWRLS.
Catalogue: BLCMP Talis automated catalogue.
Classification: Universal Decimal Classification to 1996. Dewey Decimal Classification from 1996.

Electronic facilities for non-members:

Microcomputing facilities: No.
On-line search facilities: Yes (payment required).
CD-ROM facilities: No.
Internet access: No.
Portable computers: Use permitted; power points available.

Other facilities for non-members:

Photocopying: Yes (payment required).
Microform holdings: Yes.
Reader-printer facilities: Yes (payment required).

SHEFFIELD

205 University of Sheffield
Main Library, Western Bank, Sheffield S10 2TN

Tel.: 0114 222 7204
Fax: 0114 222 7290
E-mail: library@sheffield.ac.uk
Web catalogue: http://library.shef.ac.uk/
WWW: http://www.sheffield.ac.uk/library/
Established: 1897

Director of Library Services and University Librarian: Michael S.M. Hannon, MA, DipLib, DMS, ALA
Subject enquiries to: Jacky Hodgson, BA, MA, ALA, Academic Liaison Librarian (Arts)
Specialist's tel.: 0114 222 7269
Specialist's e-mail address: j.d.hodgson@sheffield.ac.uk

Collections:

Latin American materials form a minor part of the overall stock of the Library and are mainly in the field of literature; there are over 4,000 books and 15 periodical titles. From 1965–67 the Library was one of the two British members of the Latin American cooperative Acquisitions Project (LACAP), through which it acquired material on economics, history, geography, archaeology and literature. The collection is on open access.

Access to collections:

Opening hours: Semester and Easter Vacation: Mon–Thurs 0900–2130, Fri–Sat 0900–1700, Sun 1400–1800. Christmas and Summer Vacations: Mon–Fri 0900–1700, Sat 0900–1230, Sun closed. Public holidays closed.

Enquiries: By telephone, post, fax or e-mail.
Admission: Non-members admitted for reference purposes (advance application to the Librarian required).
Lending: No.
Inter-library loans: Lends to other libraries.
Union record: BLCMP, BLDSC, BUCLA, BUCOP, COLALAS, CURL, RIDING, *Sheffield Union List of Serials*, YHJLS.
Catalogue: BLCMP Talis automated catalogue.
Classification: Dewey Decimal Classification.

Electronic facilities for non-members:

Microcomputing facilities: No.
On-line search facilities: No.
CD-ROM facilities: No.
Internet access: No.
Portable computers: Use permitted and may be connected to the mains after an electrical safety check.

Other facilities for non-members:
Photocopying: Yes (payment required).
Microform holdings: Yes.
Reader-printer facilities: Yes (payment required).

SOUTHAMPTON

206 Ordnance Survey
International Library, Technical Information and Support Services, Overseas Survey Directorate, Ordnance Survey, Romsey Road, Southampton, Hampshire SO16 4GU

Tel.: 023 8079 2659
Fax: 023 8079 2230
E-mail: rfox@ordsvy.gov.uk
WWW: http://www.ordsvy.gov.uk
Established: 1791

International Library Manager: R.D. Fox, BSc, ARICS

Collections:

The International Library of the Ordnance Survey includes 50,000 maps, 1.5 million aerial photographs, survey data from OS original surveys and map production records. The map collection aims to include all maps containing topographical information about the countries of interest to Ordnance Survey International. The Library's geographical coverage of Latin America and the Caribbean includes Belize, Guyana, the Falkland Islands and dependencies, the British Antarctic Territory, Bermuda and the Anglophone Caribbean. The collections are on open access.

Access to collections:

Opening hours: Mon–Fri 0900–1630. Public holidays closed.
Enquiries: By telephone, post, fax or e-mail (payment may be required for complex enquiries and for maps and aerial photographs).
Admission: Non-members are admitted for reference purposes (payment required).
Lending: No.
Inter-library loans: No.

Catalogue: A list of map and aerial photography holdings arranged by country on the website under Services: International Solutions.
Classification: Own classification for maps, survey data and aerial photographs.

Electronic facilities for non-members:

Microcomputing facilities: No.
On-line search facilities: No.
CD-ROM facilities: No.
Internet access: No.
Portable computers: Battery-operated portable computers may be used.

Other facilities for non-members:

Photocopying: Yes.
Microform holdings: Yes.
Reader-printer facilities: Yes.

207 Ordnance Survey

Ordnance Survey Library, Room C128, Ordnance Survey, Romsey Road, Southampton, Hampshire SO16 4GU

Tel.: 023 8079 2691
Fax: 023 8079 2879
E-mail: scaine@ordsvy.gov.uk
WWW: http://www.ordsvy.gov.uk
Established: 1791

Librarian: Sheila J. Caine, BSc, MInfSc

Collections:

The Ordnance Survey Library has a collection of 10,000 books, 300 periodicals, 2,000 photographs, 10,000 slides, 40,000 pamphlets, 200 microforms, 30 audio recordings and 200 video recordings, and 100 CD-ROMs. The Library's geographical coverage of Latin America and the Caribbean includes Belize, Guyana, the Falkland Islands and dependencies, the British Antarctic Territory, Bermuda and the Anglophone Caribbean. Material on these countries has been collected since 1945 and 300 books and 50 periodical titles on these countries are held. The subjects covered are geodesy, land survey, cartography, photogrammetry, and land and survey legislation. There is also some material on land tenure, international boundaries, and social and economic conditions in the countries covered. The collections are on open access.

Access to collections:

Opening hours: Mon–Fri 0930–1530. Public holidays closed.

Enquiries: By telephone, post, fax or e-mail to the Librarian.
Admission: Non-members are admitted for reference purposes.
Lending: No.
Inter-library loans: Lends to other libraries.
Catalogue: Author, alphabetical subject and classified catalogues on cards for material acquired before 1983. CALM 2000 automated catalogue for material acquired from 1983 onwards.
Classification: Universal Decimal Classification.

Electronic facilities for non-members:

Microcomputing facilities: By arrangement.
On-line search facilities: No.
CD-ROM facilities: No.
Internet access: No.
Portable computers: Battery-operated portable computers may be used.

Other facilities for non-members:

Photocopying: Yes.
Microform holdings: Yes.
Reader-printer facilities: No.

208 University of Southampton
Hartley Library, Highfield, Southampton SO17 1BJ

Tel.: 023 8059 2180
Fax: 023 8059 3007
E-mail: libenqs@soton.ac.uk
Web catalogue: http://www-lib.soton.ac.uk/
WWW: http://www.library.soton.ac.uk/
Established: 1914
University Librarian: Mark L. Brown, BA, PhD, DipLib, ALA

Subject enquiries to: Nick Graffy, BA, DipLib, ALA, Assistant Librarian, Arts
Specialist's tel.: 023 8059 6873
Specialist's e-mail address: ng@soton.ac.uk

Collections:

The Library has acquired material on Latin America and the Caribbean since its foundation and has fairly strong collections from the 1950s and 1960s, but acquisitions increased after 1983. Spanish Caribbean history, modern Brazilian literature and popular culture, and Brazilian and Mexican politics and political history are well represented, and there are some rare works on West Indian slavery. The collection now includes 10,000 books and 60 current periodical titles; there is some relevant manuscript material. The collection is predominantly on open access.

Access to collections:

Opening hours: Term and Christmas and Easter Vacations: Mon–Thurs 0900–2200, Fri 0900–1800, Sat 0900–1700, Sun 1200–2100. Summer Vacation: Mon–Fri 0900–1800, Sat 0900–1300, Sun closed. Christmas, New Year, Easter and August Bank Holiday closed.

Enquiries: By telephone, post or e-mail.
Admission: Non-members may be admitted for reference purposes (written application on the library's application form, addressed to the Librarian, required).
Lending: Non-members may apply for borrowing rights (payment may be required).
Inter-library loans: Lends to other libraries.
Union record: BLDSC, BUCOP, COLALAS, CURL, SWRLS.
Catalogue: SIRSI Unicorn automated catalogue.
Classification: Library of Congress Classification.

Electronic facilities for non-members:

Microcomputing facilities: No.
On-line search facilities: No.
CD-ROM facilities: Yes.
Internet access: No.
Portable computers: Use permitted after electrical safety check; power points available.

Other facilities for non-members:

Photocopying: Yes (payment required).
Microform holdings: Yes.
Reader-printer facilities: Yes (payment required).

STIRLING

209 University of Stirling
University of Stirling Library, Stirling FK9 4LA, Scotland

Tel.: 01786 467235. Holdings enquiries 01786 467220
Fax: 01786 466866
E-mail: library@stirling.ac.uk
Telnet catalogue: lib.stir.ac.uk
Web catalogue: http://webpac.stir.ac.uk
WWW: http://www.library.stir.ac.uk/index.html
Established: 1966

Director of Information Services and University Librarian: Peter Kemp MA, PhD

Collections:

The Library has collected material on Latin America and the Caribbean since its foundation. The main subjects covered are the history and literature of Latin America, with some economics, politics (including the relation of the state with the church and the military), and sociology. The collection includes 3,500 books and 7 periodical titles; about 50 volumes are added each year. The material is on open access.

Access to collections:

Opening hours: Term: Mon–Thurs 0900–2200, Fri 0900–1900, Sat 1100–1600, Sun 1200–1800. Vacation: Mon–Fri 0900–1700, Sat–Sun closed. Public holidays closed. Hours subject to variation; it is advisable to enquire before an intended visit.

Enquiries: By telephone, post, fax or e-mail.
Admission: Non-members are admitted for reference purposes.
Lending: Yes (payment required).
Inter-library loans: Lends to other libraries.

Union record: BUCLA, NLSLS.
Catalogue: Dynix automated catalogue.
Classification: Own classification.

Electronic facilities for non-members:

Microcomputing facilities: No.
On-line search facilities: No.
CD-ROM facilities: No.
Internet access: No.
Portable computers: Use permitted; power points available.

Other facilities for non-members:

Photocopying: Yes (payment required).
Microform holdings: Yes.
Reader-printer facilities: Yes (payment required).

STOKE-ON-TRENT

210 Staffordshire University
Thompson Library, College Road, Stoke-on-Trent, Staffordshire ST4 2XS

Tel.: 01782 294771
Fax: 01782 295799
E-mail: LLRS@staffs.ac.uk
Web catalogue: http://webpac.staffs.ac.uk/webpac/index.html
WWW: http://www.staffs.ac.uk/services/library_and_info/library.html
Established: 1970 (1992 as Staffordshire University)

Librarian and Head of Academic Services: Liz Hart, BA, DipLib, FLA, MIInFsc
Subject enquiries to: Debbie Roberts, Emma Stewart, Kathleen Morgan, Subject Librarians for the Social Sciences
Specialists' tel.: 01782 294809 or 01782 294770
Specialists' e-mail addresses: d.e.roberts@staffs.ac.uk, e.s.stewart@staffs.ac.uk, k.morgan@staffs.ac.uk

Collections:

The Library has collected on the region since the 1970s. The material, which forms a minor part of the overall stock, mainly relates to the Commonwealth Caribbean. The collection is on open access.

Access to collections:

Opening hours: Term: Mon–Thurs 0900–2200, Fri–Sat 0900–1800, Sun 1300–1800. Vacation: Mon–Fri 0900–1700, Sat–Sun closed. Public holidays closed.
Enquiries: By telephone, post, fax or e-mail.
Admission: Non-members may be admitted for reference purposes (application in advance to the Librarian required).
Lending: No.
Inter-library loans: Lends to other libraries.
Union record: WMRLS.
Catalogue: Dynix Horizon automated catalogue.
Classification: Dewey Decimal Classification.

Electronic facilities for non-members:

Microcomputing facilities: No.
On-line search facilities: No.
CD-ROM facilities: No.
Internet access: No.
Portable computers: Use not permitted.

Other facilities for non-members:

Photocopying: Yes (payment required).
Microform holdings: Yes.
Reader-printer facilities: Yes (payment required).

SWANSEA

211 University of Wales Swansea / Prifysgol Cymru Abertawe
Library and Information Centre, Singleton Park, Swansea SA2 8PP, Wales

Tel.: 01792 295697. Admissions 01792 295858
Fax: 01792 295891. Admissions 01792 295851
E-mail: library@swan.ac.uk. Admissions: m.price@swansea.ac.uk
Web catalogue: http://voyager.swan.ac.uk/
WWW: http://www.swan.ac.uk/lis/index.htm
Established: 1920

Director of Library and Information Services: Christopher M. West
Subject enquiries to: Ian Glen, MA, PhD, DipEd, MLib

Specialist's tel.: 01792 295030
Specialist's e-mail address: i.glen@swansea.ac.uk

Collections:

The Library has collected material on Latin America and the Caribbean since 1955, and now has a collection of over 2,000 volumes. The main subject areas covered are economics, geography, history, literature, politics and sociology, with Argentina, Cuba and Mexico the best represented geographical areas. Current acquisitions are mainly in support of the Department of Hispanic Studies and the Centre for Development Studies. The collections are on open access.

Access to collections:

Opening hours: Term: Mon–Fri 0845–2200, Sat 0900–1700, Sun 1200–2000. Vacations: Mon–Sat 0900–1700, Sun closed. Public holidays closed.

Enquiries: By telephone, post, fax or e-mail.
Admission: Non-members are admitted for reference purposes.
Lending: Yes (payment required).
Inter-library loans: Lends to other libraries.
Union record: BLDSC, BUCOP, CC–IW, WRLS.
Catalogue: Endeavor Voyager automated catalogue.
Classification: Library of Congress Classification.

Electronic facilities for non-members:

Microcomputing facilities: No.
On-line search facilities: No.
CD-ROM facilities: No.
Internet access: Limited access in Catalogue Hall.
Portable computers: Use permitted; power points available.

Other facilities for non-members:

Photocopying: Yes (payment required).
Microform holdings: Yes.
Reader-printer facilities: Yes (payment required).

WELWYN

212 Cat Survival Trust
Library, The Centre, Codicote Road, Welwyn, Hertfordshire AL6 9TU

Tel.: 01438 716873/716478
Fax: 01438 717535
E-mail: cattrust@aol.com and planetwise@aol.com (Library)
WWW: http://members.aol.com/cattrust and http://members.aol.com/planetwise
Established: 1976

Librarian: Judith Moore, BEd

Collections:

The Trust's original purpose was to promote the conservation of wild cats by breeding them in captivity and subsequently releasing them into suitable wild situations; it now concentrates on conserving the entire ecosystem — plants, animals and fungi — on which the cats and their prey depend. The Trust acquired a 10,000-acre reserve in Misiones, Argentina, an area of virgin forest with five species of cats (jaguarundi, ocelot, margay, puma and tiger cat), which was granted provincial park status and is managed in partnership between the Trust and the Argentine government. The Trust is in the process of securing a further 300,000 acres in Argentina, Chile and Costa Rica. The Trust has an extensive library which focuses on the environment and the flora and fauna of the world. It includes books, journals and newspapers (including the *Tico Times*, San José, Costa Rica), maps, and music and video material covering all aspects of life in Latin America. A worldwide database is maintained, containing details of 27,000 wildlife and environmental organisations, many of them in Latin America, supplemented by an extensive printed Internet extract library of home pages.

Access to collections:

Opening hours: Mon–Fri 0930–1730.

Enquiries: By telephone, post or e-mail.
Admission: By appointment.
Lending: No.
Inter-library loans: No.
Catalogue: Automated catalogue (Microsoft Access) with printed version.
Classification: Dewey Decimal Classification (modified).

Electronic facilities for non-members:
Microcomputing facilities: Yes.
On-line search facilities: Yes (payment required).
CD-ROM facilities: Yes.
Internet access: Yes (payment required).
Portable computers: Use permitted.

Other facilities for non-members:
Photocopying: Yes (payment required).

WOLVERHAMPTON

213 University of Wolverhampton
Harrison Learning Centre, St Peter's Square, Wolverhampton WV1 1RH

Tel.: 01902 322300
Fax: 01902 322194
E-mail: lib@wlv.ac.uk
Web catalogue: http://www.wlv.ac.uk/lib/systems/catalogue.htm
WWW: http://www.wlv.ac.uk/lib/
Established: 1969 (1992 as University of Wolverhampton)

Director of Learning Resources: Mary Heaney, BA, DipLib, MIInfSci
Subject enquiries to: Ann Edwards, MA, ALA, Academic Resource Librarian (Languages and European Studies)
Specialist's tel.: 01902 322314
Specialist's e-mail address: a.edwards@wlv.ac.uk

Collections:

Latin American material in the humanities and social sciences has been collected since the early 1970s in support of teaching in the School of Humanities, Languages and Social Sciences. There are now over 3,000 volumes and a small number of periodicals relating to the region. The countries best represented in the collection are Argentina, Brazil, Chile, Cuba, Mexico and Peru. The material is on open access.

In 1994 Professor Alistair Hennessy donated the Hennessy Collection of Cuban periodicals from the 1960s to the 1990s to the School of Humanities,

Languages and Social Sciences. In March 1998 the Forum for the Study of Cuba / Cátedra de Estudios sobre Cuba was inaugurated, in cooperation with the University of Havana. The Forum intends to develop research resources on Cuba by building on the foundation of the Hennessy Collection with the acquisition of books, press cuttings, papers, articles and tapes. The collection is on closed access.

Access to collections:

Opening hours: Term: Mon–Thurs 0900–2200, Fri 0900–1900, Sat–Sun 1330–1730. Vacations: Mon–Fri 0900–1715, Sat–Sun closed. Public holidays closed.

Enquiries: By telephone, post, fax or e-mail.

Admission: Non-members are admitted for reference purposes (advance application required). The Cuban Collection is viewed by appointment only (contact Dr A. Kapcia, tel.: 01902 322455; e-mail: a.kapcia@wlv. ac.uk).

Lending: Yes (in summer vacation only). The Cuban Collection is reference only.

Inter-library loans: Lends to other libraries.

Union record: BLCMP.

Catalogue: BLCMP Talis automated catalogue.

Classification: Dewey Decimal Classification.

Electronic facilities for non-members:

Microcomputing facilities: No.
On-line search facilities: No.
CD-ROM facilities: No.
Internet access: No.
Portable computers: Use not permitted.

Other facilities for non-members:

Photocopying: Yes (payment required).
Microform holdings: Yes.
Reader-printer facilities: Yes (payment required).

WOODBRIDGE

214 South American Pictures
48 Station Road, Woodbridge, Suffolk IP12 4AT

Tel.: 01394 383963/300423
Fax: 01394 380176
E-mail: morrison@south-american-pic.com
WWW: http://www.south-american-pic.com
Established: 1975, with experience dating from 1961

Subject enquiries to: Marion and Tony Morrison

Collections:

Tony and Marion Morrison are known for their photographic work and television film-making. They have written more than 50 books on Latin America, many illustrated with pictures from their commercial picture library, which contains photographs on a wide range of subjects on all countries of South and Central America, Mexico, Cuba, the Dominican Republic and Haiti. The collection is regularly expanded by contributions from associate photographers, some of whom are based in Latin America. Specialised topics include contemporary people and places, the environment, flora and fauna, Amazonia, the Nasca Lines and Carnival. A large proportion of the collection is devoted to archaeology, including sites and artefacts of the Maya, Aztec and Inca civilisations, and pre-Columbian cultures of the Ecuadoran and Peruvian coasts, El Dorado and the gold of Colombia, as well as lesser-known cultures throughout the continent. Recent additions include a major collection on Afro-Brazilian religion, evangelical churches and the people of Rio de Janeiro and the suburbs of São Paulo. There is an archive of black-and-white historical material. Colonial history is also extensively covered, including the Jesuit missions and churches of that period.

Access to collections:

Opening hours: Mon–Sun 0000–2400.

Enquiries: By telephone, post, fax or e-mail.
Admission: By appointment. Picture researchers welcome.
Search/service fee: £15–£25. Commissions considered.
Lending: None permitted.
Catalogue: An online catalogue is being developed on the website.

Electronic facilities for non-members:

Microcomputing facilities: No.
On-line search facilities: No.
CD-ROM facilities: No.
Portable computers: Use not permitted.

Other facilities for non-members:

Copying: Will be available online at low resolution for non-commercial purposes.

YORK

215 University of York
J.B. Morrell Library, Heslington, York YO1 5DD

Tel.: 01904 433865
Fax: 01904 433866
E-mail: libr1@york.ac.uk
Telnet catalogue: library.york.ac.uk or 144.32.172.1
WWW: http://www.york.ac.uk/services/library/
Established: 1962

Librarian: A. Elizabeth M. Heaps, BA, MA, DipLib, ALA

Collections:

Latin American materials form a minor part of the 750,000 volumes held in the Library. Collecting on the region began in 1964, and the Library now holds 2,500 books, 38 current and 12 non-current periodical titles, and small quantities of maps, microforms and music; 100 volumes are added each year. The Library collects in the humanities and social sciences, with special strengths in the politics and economics of Argentina, Brazil, Chile, Peru and Central America. The material is nearly all in English and is held on open access.

Access to collections:

Opening hours: Term: Mon–Fri 0900–2200, Sat 0900–1715, Sun 1400–1800. Christmas and Easter Vacations: Mon–Fri 0900–2100, Sat–Sun closed. Summer Vacation: Mon–Wed, Fri 0900–1715, Thurs 0900–2100, Sat–Sun closed. Christmas, New Year, Easter and August Bank Holiday closed.

Enquiries: By telephone, post, fax or e-mail.
Admission: Non-members are admitted for reference purposes.
Lending: Yes (application in writing to the Librarian and payment required).
Inter-library loans: Lends to other libraries.
Union record: BLDSC, BUCLA, COLALAS.
Catalogue: Dynix automated catalogue.
Classification: Own classification.

Electronic facilities for non-members:

Microcomputing facilities: No.
On-line search facilities: No.
CD-ROM facilities: No.
Internet access: No.
Portable computers: Use permitted; power points available.

Other facilities for non-members:

Photocopying: Yes (payment required).
Microform holdings: Yes.
Reader-printer facilities: Yes.

INDEX

Note: The index covers libraries and named collections by title, abbreviation, parent organisation and subject interest. Subject entries should be treated with reserve. For some collections, subject interest may imply little more than a statement of intent. On the other hand, since reference has normally been restricted to subjects (or their apparent synonyms) specifically mentioned in a library's entry, many excellent collections have doubtless been overlooked, particularly in the larger, general libraries. Entries are filed alphabetically, letter by letter.

References in the index are to entry numbers

Abolition of slavery, *see* Slavery
ActionAid, 72
Acton, J.E.E.D., *Baron*, Collection, 20
ACU, *see* Association of Commonwealth Universities
Administration, 34 (transport), 105
Admiralty Library, 146
Aerial photographs, 206
Aged, *see* Elderly
Agricultural Economics Unit, *see* International Development Centre, University of Oxford
Agriculture, 32, 45, 57, 85, 178, 195
   Aid programmes, 50
   Anglophone Caribbean, 32, 45, 96 190
   Brazil, 63 (photographs)
   Coffee, 128
   Economics, 190
   Forestry, 152
   Fruit, 178
   Mexico, 144 (photographs)
   Pests, 32, 45
   Rural sociology, 190
   Sugar, 61, 116, 133
   Tropical products, 32, 43, 45, 178
Agronomy, *see* Agriculture
AHRTAG, *see* Healthlink Worldwide
Aid,
   Development, 40, 50, 72, 89, 93, 192, 202

   Emergency, 40, 93, 192, 202
   see also Agriculture: Aid programmes; Medicine: Aid programmes
AIDS, 107
Albert Sloman Library, 33
Almanacs,
   Anglophone Caribbean, 13, 20
Amazonia, 53, 55 (flora and fauna), 158 (photographs), 197, 214 (photographs)
Amerindians, 22, 55, 75, 86, 143, 158, 168, 196, 197, 203
   Amazonia, 158 (photographs)
   Brazil, 63 (photographs)
   Catalogues, 158
   Codices, 33, 144 (photographs), 171, 187
   Linguistics, 8, 69, 86, 163, 187, 203
   Literature, 187
   Medicine, 171
   Photographs, 158
   Postcards, 158
   Pre-conquest civilisations, 22, 86, 143, 160 (architecture), 168, 171, 196, 214 (photographs)
   Religion, 7
Amnesty International, 73
Andean countries, 21, 187
   Drawings, 150
   Geography, 198
   History, 21

Humanities, 187
Manuscripts, 150
Politics, 21
Social sciences, 21, 187
Andersonian Library, 52, 54
Andes Press Agency, 74
Anglophone Caribbean, 20, 70, 71, 85, 94, 95, 96, 105, 106, 116, 171, 190, 194, 206, 207, 210
  Agriculture, 32, 45, 96, 190
  Almanacs, 13, 20
  Anthropology, 43
  Art, 20, 94
  Audio-visual material, 94
  Bibliographies, 94, 116
  Biography, 94
  Census data, 116
  Commerce, 16, 70, 96
  Constitutional law, 95
  Demography, 43
  Development plans, 96
  Directories, 94
  Economics, 20, 36, 43, 96, 116, 190, 194
  Education, 20, 76, 96, 116, 118
  Election reports, 95, 116
  Encyclopaedias, 94
  Environment, 96
  Foreign relations, 96
  Forestry, 189
  Gender, 96
  Geography, 20, 43, 94
  Handbooks, 13
  Health, 96
  History, 20, 29, 36, 43, 47, 70, 71, 94, 116, 168, 194
  Humanities, 43
  Insurance, 92
  Juvenilia, 94
  Land and survey legislation, 207
  Land law and tenure, 207
  Land survey, 207
  Law, 115, 186
  Literature, 20, 29, 36, 66, 71, 94
  Manuscripts, 43, 96, 116, 169, 194
  Maps, charts and atlases, 94, 187, 206
  Maritime and naval history, 146, 149
  Medicine, 43, 171
  Missions, 175
  Music, 79, 83
  Natural history, 20, 150
  Newspapers, 16, 84
  Official publications, 20, 76, 85, 95, 116, 194
  Pamphlets, 95, 116, 207
  Parliamentary practice, 95
  Periodicals, 20, 116
  Photographs, 20, 105, 155, 206 (aerial), 207
  Politics, 20, 43, 95, 96, 116, 194
  Posters, 94
  Press cuttings, 94, 95
  Pressure groups, 116
  Recorded sound, 207
  Science, 96
  Slavery, 20, 29, 60, 116, 157, 208
  Slides, 207
  Social sciences, 43, 71, 116, 194
  Statistics, 36, 96, 116
  Sugar, 61, 116, 133
  Tourism, 116, 165
  Trade, *see* Anglophone Caribbean: Commerce
  Trades unions, 116, 142, 166
  Travel, 94
  Video recordings, 94, 207
  Wallcharts, 94
  Women, 96, 116
  Yearbooks, 94
  Youth, 96
  see also Caribbean
Animal conservation, 55, 177, 212
Animal husbandry, 43
Animal products, 32
Antarctic, 28, 169, 206, 207
Anthropology and ethnology, 5, 8, 22, 37, 42, 43, 53, 65, 71, 86, 110, 111, 139, 140, 158, 168, 169, 171, 196, 197, 203
  Anglophone Caribbean, 43
  Argentina, 8, 65
  Bolivia, 8, 65, 72
  Brazil, 8, 65, 72, 168
  Chile, 8, 44, 65
  Colombia, 65, 72
  Cuba, 37
  Cultural anthropology, 86, 197

Dominican Republic, 72
Guatemala, 72, 143
Haiti, 72
Mexico, 37, 168
Nicaragua, 72
Paraguay, 8
Patagonia, 44
Periodicals, 27, 86
Peru, 8, 65, 72
Photographs, 158
Physical anthropology, 86
Social anthropology, 71, 86, 106, 140, 197
Uruguay, 8
Venezuela, 65
Antigua, 155 (photographs)
Anti-Semitism, 117
Anti-slavery, see Slavery
Anti-Slavery International, 75
Anti-Slavery Society, 194
Apiculture, 31, 57
Apis Club, 31
Appropriate Health Resources & Technologies Action Group, 107
Archaeology, 22, 86, 168, 171, 196, 205, 214 (photographs)
  Colombia, 214 (photographs)
  Ecuador, 168, 214 (photographs)
  Guatemala, 86, 143
  Mexico, 86, 144 (photographs), 168
  Periodicals, 27, 86, 168
  Peru, 168, 214 (photographs)
Architecture, 144 (photographs), 149 (naval), 160
Archive material, Guides to, 119
Archives, see Manuscripts
Archivo General de la Nación, Mexico, 20
Argentina, 17, 20, 33, 48, 139, 187, 200
  Antarctic territories, 28
  Anthropology, 8, 65
  Art, 148
  Civil engineering, 125
  Economic history, 61
  Economics, 36, 211, 215
  Environment, 212
  Flora and fauna, 212
  Geography, 211
  History, 20, 36, 48, 54, 61, 65, 200, 211

  Humanities, 48, 187, 213
  Jews and anti-Semitism, 117
  Law, 115
  Liberation theology, 8
  Linguistics, 54, 200
  Literature, 20, 36, 48, 54, 61, 65, 168
    (esp. fiction, poetry), 199, 200, 211
  Mechanical engineering, 126
  Misiones, 212
  Missions, 8
  Patagonia, 2, 4
  Photographs, 63
  Politics, 54, 211, 215
  Social history, 61
  Social sciences, 17, 65, 187, 200, 211, 213
  Social welfare, 8
  Statistics, 36
  Travel and exploration, 8
  Welsh (in Patagonia), 2, 4
  Wildlife, 212
Arms control, 129
Art, 20, 33, 70, 94, 103, 110, 120, 144 (photographs), 148, 170, 172, 173; see also paintings
Association of Commonwealth Universities, 76
ASTIC Research Associates, 37
Astorga Collection, 44
Astronomy, 85
Athenaeum, 69
Atlases, 33, 44, 94, 149, 159, 169; see also Maps
Audio tapes, see Recorded sound
Audio-visual material, 90, 174
  Anglophone Caribbean, 94
  see also Non-print material and Films, Photographs, Pictures, Recorded sound, Slides, Video recordings
Avon County Library, see Bristol City Libraries
Aztecs, 144 (photographs), 171, 214 (photographs)

Balfour Library, 196
Banana industry, 155 (photographs)
Banking, 77, 91, 97, 168
  Periodicals and reports, 77, 97
Bank of England, 77

Banners, 103
Barbados, 76, 150 (drawings, manuscripts), 155 (photographs); *see also* Anglophone Caribbean
Bates, H.W., papers, 150
BBC, *see* British Broadcasting Corporation
Bedford College, *see* Royal Holloway
Bees and bee-keeping, 31, 57
Belize, 94, 95, 206, 207
Bermuda, 206, 207; *see also* Anglophone Caribbean
BFI, *see* British Film Institute
Bibliographies, 10, 33, 119, 121, 169, 171
  Anglophone Caribbean, 94, 116
Biblioteca Latinoamericana Andrés Bello, 170
Biochemistry, 58
Biodegredation, 45
Biodeterioration, 45
Biodiversity, 45
Biographical dictionaries, 119
Biography, 88, 123, 139, 146, 149
  Anglophone Caribbean, 94
Biological control, 45
Biology,
  Periodicals, 27
Biomathematics, 57
Biotechnology, 45 (fungal), 85
BirdLife International, 19
Birds, 19
Birkbeck College, University of London, 78
Birmingham Central Library, 6
Birmingham Department of Leisure and Community Services, Library and Learning Division, 6
Birth control, 131
Black Media Archive, 36
Blake, Lady Edith, drawings, 150
Blanco White, José, Collection, 69
BLDSC, *see* British Library Document Supply Centre
Board of Inland Revenue, *see* Inland Revenue, International Division
Board of Trade, 5
Board of Trade, *see also* Department of Trade and Industry

Bodleian Law Library, 186
Bodleian Library, 187
  Radcliffe Science Library, 193
  Rhodes House Library, 194
Bolivia, 93, 192
  Anthropology, 8, 65, 72
  Demography, 72
  Economics, 74 (photographs)
  Education, 72
  Environment, 72, 74 (photographs)
  Geography, 72
  History, 65
  Liberation theology, 8
  Literature, 65
  Missions, 8
  Photographs, 63, 74, 113
  Politics, 72, 74 (photographs)
  Religion, 74 (photographs)
  Slides, 72
  Social sciences, 65, 74 (photographs)
  Social welfare, 8, 72
  Travel, 8, 74 (photographs)
Bolland Library, 18
Boole Library, 35
Booth Steamship Company, 70
Botanical illustrations, 58, 150
Botanists, 58, 150
Botany, 58, 85, 150
Boundaries, 159, 207
Bowen, E.G., Map Library, 3
Brazil, 21, 30, 33, 53, 67, 71, 93, 139, 187, 192, 200
  Agriculture, 63 (photographs)
  Amerindians, 63 (photographs)
  Anthropology, 8, 65, 72, 106, 168
  Architecture, 160
  Art, 148
  Birds, 19
  Chapbooks, 33
  Children, 75
  Civil engineering, 125
  Commerce, 63 (photographs)
  Culture, 63 (photographs)
  Demography, 30, 72, 102
  Development, 102
  Drawings, 58, 150
  Economic history, 61
  Economics, 30, 36, 53, 67, 74 (photographs), 102, 215

Education, 30, 63 (photographs), 72
Environment, 19, 30, 63 (photographs), 72, 74 (photographs), 102
Flora and fauna, 55, 63 (photographs)
Geography, 62, 67, 72, 168
Health services, 63 (photographs)
History, 20, 21, 54, 61, 62, 65, 67, 71, 134, 180, 181, 200, 204, 208
Humanities, 187, 213
Law, 30, 115
Liberation theology, 8
Linguistics, 25, 30, 54, 134, 200
Literature, 17, 20, 25, 30, 33, 54, 61, 65, 66 (twentieth-century), 70, 71, 134, 137 (twentieth-century), 180, 181, 199, 200, 208 (twentieth-century)
Manuscripts, 150
Microforms, 134
Missions, 8
Music, 83 (recorded sound)
Official publications, 85
Photographs, 63, 74, 113
Politics, 21, 53, 54, 62, 67, 72, 74 (photographs), 208, 215
Popular culture, 208
Poverty, 63 (photographs)
Religion, 63 (photographs), 74 (photographs)
Rubber, 132
Slavery, 75
Slides, 192
Social history, 61
Social sciences, 21, 53, 65, 71, 74 (photographs), 102, 180, 187, 200, 213
Social welfare, 8, 72
Statistics, 36
Tourism, 63 (photographs)
Transport, 63 (photographs)
Travel, 8, 74 (photographs)
Wildlife sounds, 83
Brighton Public Library, 13
Bristol City Libraries, 16
British Antarctic Territory, 28, 206, 207
British Architectural Library, 160
British Broadcasting Corporation, 79
British Broadcasting Corporation, Hulton Picture Library, *see* Hulton|Archive
British Broadcasting Corporation Latin American Service archive, 200
British Broadcasting Corporation, Music Library, *see* British Broadcasting Corporation
British Broadcasting Corporation Popular Music Library, *see* British Broadcasting Corporation
British Caribbean, *see* Anglophone Caribbean
British Film Institute National Library, 80
British Film Institute, National Film and Television Archive, 81
British Film Institute Stills, Posters and Designs, 82
British Geological Survey, 59
British Guiana, 150 (drawings, manuscripts); *see also* Guyana
British Institute of Recorded Sound, *see* British Library National Sound Archive
British Library Document Supply Centre, 10
British Library for Development Studies, 14
British Library Humanities and Social Sciences, *see* British Library, Reader Services & Collection Development
British Library Information Sciences Service, *see* British Library, Reader Services & Collection Development
British Library Lending Division, *see* British Library Document Supply Centre
British Library, Library Association Library, *see* British Library, Reader Services & Collection Development
British Library National Sound Archive, 10, 83
British Library, Newspaper Library, 84, 161
British Library of Political and Economic Science, 140
British Library, Reader Services & Collection Development, 85
British Library, Science Reference and Information Service, *see* British Library Reader Services & Collection Development
British Museum, Department of Ethnography Library, 86
British Museum (Natural History), *see* Natural History Museum

British Standards Institution, 87
British Trade International, 101
British Union Catalogue of Latin
    Americana, 121
Bromley, London Borough of, 135
Brotherton Library, 66
Brynmor Jones Library, 61
BSI, *see* British Standards Institution
BUCLA, *see* British Union Catalogue of
    Latin Americana
Building, 160
Bulmershe Library, 201
Business information, 44, 64, 77, 78, 85,
    91, 97, 101, 110, 138, 168, 182
Business Information Service, 85

CABI Bioscience UK Centre, 45
CAB International Institute of
    Parasitology, *see* CABI Bioscience UK
    Centre
CAB International Mycological Institute,
    see CABI Bioscience UK Centre
Caird Library, 149
CALA, *see* Contemporary Archive on
    Latin America
Cambridge Philosophical Library, *see*
    Scientific Periodicals Library,
    University of Cambridge
Cambridge University, *see* University of
    Cambridge
Cambridge University Library, 20
Cambridge University Museum of
    Archaeology and Anthropology, 104
Canning House Library, *see* Hispanic and
    Luso-Brazilian Council
Canon law, 109
Cardiff University, 30
Caribbean, 153 (photographs
    Banana industry, 155 (photographs)
    Economic history, 61
    Geography, 46 (human), 47, 62, 198
    History, 36, 47, 61, 62, 208
    Law, 115, 186
    Literature, 36, 61
    Medicine, 43, 171 (colonial)
    Manuscripts, 61
    Missions, 175
    Music, recorded sound, 48, 83
    Photographs, 113, 153
    Politics, 62

Recorded sound, 48, 86
Religion, 175
Slavery, 16, 157
Social history, 61
see also Anglophone Caribbean,
    Francophone Caribbean
Caribbean, Anglophone, *see* Anglophone
    Caribbean
Caribbean, Francophone, *see*
    Francophone Caribbean
Caribbean, Spanish, 208 (history)
Caribbean Studies Centre, Goldsmiths
    College, 106
Carnival, 214 (photographs)
Cartography, 159, 207
Catalogues, exhibition, 120, 148, 160,
    173
Catalogues, recorded sound, 83
Cátedra de Estudios sobre Cuba, 213
Catholic Central Library, 88
Catholic Institute for International Relations,
    89
Cat Survival Trust, 212
Cats, Wild, 212
Censorship, 176
Census data,
    Anglophone Caribbean, 116
    Mexico, 198
Central America, 200
    Anthropology, 86
    Economics, 215
    Geography, 47
    History, 47
    Manuscripts, 169
    Politics, 215
Central American Human Rights
    Committee collection, 121
Centre for Indigenous American Studies
    and Exchange, University of Saint
    Andrews, 203
Centre for Information on Language
    Teaching and Research, 90
Centre for Latin American Linguistic
    Studies, *see* Centre for Indigenous
    American Studies and Exchange
Centre for Missiology and World
    Christianity, University of
    Birmingham, 7

Centre for Research in Ethnic Relations, University of Warwick, 36
Centre for World Development Education, *see* Council for Education in World Citizenship
Centre of Latin American Studies, University of Cambridge, 21
CEWC, *see* Council for Education in World Citizenship
Chapbooks (Brazilian), 33
Chartered Institute of Bankers, 91
Chartered Institute of Transport, *see* Institute of Logistics and Transport
Chartered Insurance Institute, 92
Charts, 28, 159
  maritime, 146, 149, 169
  weather, 11
Chatham House Library, 161
Chatham House Press Library Collection, 84
Chichester, Sir Charles, archive, 61
Children, 72
  Health, 107
  Labour, 75
  Street children, 75
Chile, 8, 33
  Antarctic territories, 28
  Anthropology, 8, 44, 65
  Civil engineering, 125
  Drawings, 150
  Economic history, 61
  Economics, 36, 74 (photographs), 215
  Environment, 74 (photographs), 212
  Flora and fauna, 212
  History, 44, 54, 61, 65, 145
  Humanities, 213
  Jews and anti-Semitism, 117
  Liberation theology, 8
  Linguistics, 54, 145
  Literature, 54, 61, 65, 145, 199
  Manuscripts, 150
  Missions, 8
  Photographs, 63, 74, 113
  Politics, 54, 74 (photographs), 215
  Religion, 74 (photographs)
  Social history, 61
  Social sciences, 65, 74 (photographs), 145, 213
  Social welfare, 8
  Statistics, 36
  Travel, 8, 74 (photographs)
  Wildlife, 212
Chile Committee for Human Rights archive, 61
Chile Solidarity Campaign archive, 61
Christian Aid, 93
Christian church, *see* Church history
Christian sociology, 88
Church and state, 209
Church history, 7, 8, 109, 175
  Anglican, 8, 175
  New religious movements, 7
  Roman Catholic, 88, 109
Church Mission Society, 175
Church of England, 8, 175
CIIR, *see* Catholic Institute for International Relations
CILT, *see* Centre for Information on Language Teaching and Research
CILT Resources Library, 90
Cinema, 33, 71, 80, 81, 82; *see also* Films
City Business Library, 97
City development, 102
Civil engineering, 125, 160
Classical music, 79, 83, 169
Clifford Whitworth Library, *see* University of Salford, Academic Information Services, Clifford Whitworth Building
Climatology, 11, 113 (photographs)
Codices,
  Mexico, 33, 144 (photographs), 171, 187
Coffee, 128
Coleg Prifysgol Abertawe, *see* Prifysgol Cymru Abertawe
Coleg Prifysgol Cymru, Aberystwyth, *see* Prifysgol Cymru Aberystwyth
Coleg Prifysgol Cymru, Caerdydd, *see* Prifysgol Caerdydd
Coleg Prifysgol Gogladd Cymru, *see* Prifysgol Cymru Bangor
Coleg y Brifysgol Abertawe, *see* Prifysgol Cymru Abertawe
Coleg y Brifysgol Caerdydd, *see* Prifysgol Caerdydd

College of St Mark and St John, *see* Devon County Council
Colombia, 18, 93
　Anthropology, 65, 72
　Demography, 72
　Development, 102
　Drawings, 150
　Economics, 18
　Education, 72
　Environment, 72
　Geography, 72, 168
　Gold, 214 (photographs)
　History, 36, 65
　Literature, 36, 65, 199
　Manuscripts, 150
　Music, 83 (recorded sound)
　Photographs, 113
　Politics, 18, 72
　Social sciences, 18, 65
　Social welfare, 72
　Wildlife sounds, 83
Colonial history, British, 20, 29, 47, 105, 116, 194
Colonial legislation, British, 115
Colonial Office, *see* Foreign and Commonwealth Office
Colonial period of Latin America, 214 (photographs)
　Government documents, 171
　History, 85, 119, 134
　Medicine, 171
　Newspapers, 171
　Photographs, 214
Commerce, 16, 64, 70, 77, 85, 97, 101, 110, 128, 138, 151, 168
　Anglophone Caribbean, 16, 70, 96
　Brazil, 63 (photographs)
　Rubber, 132
　Statistics, 36, 43, 77, 97, 101
　Transport, 34
Commercial directories, 64, 85, 97, 101, 138
Commercial relations with Liverpool, 70
Commonwealth Agricultural Bureaux, *see* CABI Bioscience UK Centre
Commonwealth Bureau of Agricultural Economics, *see* International Development Centre
Commonwealth Bureau of Horticulture and Plantation Crops, *see* Horticulture Research International
Commonwealth Caribbean, *see* Anglophone Caribbean
Commonwealth Forestry Bureau, *see* Department of Plant Sciences and Oxford Forestry Institute
Commonwealth Institute, 94
Commonwealth Institute of Entymology, *see* CABI Bioscience UK Centre
Commonwealth Office, *see* Foreign and Commonwealth Office
Commonwealth Parliamentary Association, 95
Commonwealth Relations Office, *see* Foreign and Commonwealth Office
Commonwealth Resource Centre, 94
Commonwealth Secretariat, 96
Commonwealth Studies Library, *see* International Development Centre, University of Oxford
Communist parties, 142
Communities, Local, 89
Company information, 85, 97
Company law, 114
Company reports, 97
Conference proceedings, 10, 45, 123, 160
Conservation, 19, 58
　Animal, 55, 177, 212
　Birds, 19
　Plants, 58
Constitutional law, 140
　Anglophone Caribbean, 95
Consultants' reports, 102
Contemporary Archive on Latin America, 121
Conway, George Robert Graham, Collections, 1, 20
Cooperatives and the cooperative movement, 142
Copyright libraries,
　United Kingdom and Irish imprints, 2, 20, 39, 44, 85, 186, 187, 193, 194
　Newspapers, 84
　1710–1836, 203
Corporation of London City Business Library, 97

Corporation of London Guildhall Library, 98
Costa Rica
 Economics, 36
 Environment, 212
 Flora and fauna, 212
 Statistics, 36
 Wildlife, 212
Costume, 44, 82, 143, 144 (photographs)
Council for Education in World Citizenship, 99
Council of Foreign Bondholders, 98
Crane Library, 31
Creole dialectics, *see* Linguistics
Criminal law, 26, 140
Criminology, 26
Crop protection, 45, 57, 178
Crops, *see* Agriculture
Cuba, 142, 145
 Anthropology, 37
 Architecture, 160
 Art, 148
 Civil engineering, 125
 Economics, 53, 211
 Education, 37
 Geography, 37, 47, 211
 History, 17, 37, 47, 53, 145, 211
 Humanities, 213
 Linguistics, 37, 145, 213
 Literature, 17, 145, 199, 211
 Manuscripts, 213
 Music, 83
 Periodicals, 213
 Photographs, 153, 155, 214
 Politics, 37, 53, 211
 Press cuttings, 213
 Social sciences, 37, 53, 145, 211, 213
 Social welfare, 37
Culture, 63 (Brazil, photographs), 120, 153 (photographs)
 Popular, 208 (Brazil)
Cunninghame Graham, R.B., Collection, 139
Current affairs, *see* News sources, Press cuttings

Dance, 56
Darwin, Charles, archive, 58
Debt, *see* Economics
Defence, 129
Demerara, 150 (drawings, manuscripts)
Democracy, 40
Demography, 30, 43, 53, 102, 106, 131, 140, 151
 Anglophone Caribbean, 43
 Bolivia, 72
 Brazil, 30, 72
 Colombia, 72
 Dominican Republic, 72
 Guatemala, 72
 Haiti, 72
 Mexico, 30
 Nicaragua, 72
 Peru, 72
 Statistics, 101
 Welsh (in Patagonia), 2
Department for International Development, 50, 100
Department of Economics, University of Oxford, 188
Department of Ethnology and Pre-history, *see* School of Anthropology and Museum Ethnography
Department of Forestry, University of Oxford, *see* Department of Plant Sciences and Oxford Forestry Institute, University of Oxford
Department of Plant Sciences and Oxford Forestry Institute, University of Oxford, 189
Department of Theology, University of Birmingham, 7
Department of Trade and Industry, 101
Department of Trade and Industry, Statistics and Market Intelligence Library, 36; *see also* Department of Trade and Industry, British Trade International
Development and development plans, 12, 14, 40, 50, 96, 99, 100, 101, 102, 128, 152, 190, 192, 202; *see also* Economic development, Sustainable development, Town and country planning
Development and Project Planning Centre, University of Bradford, 12
Development Planning Unit, 102

Devon County Council, Devon Library and Information Services, 47
DFID, see Department for International Development
Dialects, 83
Diaries,
  Engineers', 125
  Missionaries', 8
Dictionaries, 33, 110, 121
  Amerindian, 8, 121, 163
  Anglophone Caribbean, 94
  Biographical, 119
  Technical language, 123
Diplomacy, see Foreign relations, International law
Directorate of Overseas Surveys, see Ordnance Survey
Directories, 121, 123
  Anglophone Caribbean, 94
  Commercial directories, 64, 85, 97, 101, 138
  Telephone directories, 101
Disability, 107
Disaster relief, see Aid: Emergency
Discs, see Recorded sound
Dissertations, see Theses
Documentary films, 81, 121 (video), 143
Documentary sound recordings, 83
Documents, Government, see Official publications
Dominica, 155 (photographs)
Dominican Republic, 72, 75
  Development aid, 89, 93
  Haitian migrant labour, 155 (photographs)
  Photographs, 153, 155, 214
DPPC, see Development and Project Planning Centre
DPU, see Development Planning Unit
Drama, 83
Drawings, 2, 58, 150, 160
Drugs, 99
Drugs trade, 71
Dublin City University, 38
Durham University, 42
Dutch-speaking Caribbean 187

Ealing College of Higher Education, see Thames Valley University

Earth science, 59, 85
East Malling Research Station, see Horticulture Research International
Ecclesiastical history, see Church history
Ecclesiastical law, 109
ECLAC, see Economic Commission for Latin America and the Caribbean
Ecological geography, 46
Ecology, 58, 71, 196 (cultural ecology), 212
Economic botany, 58
Economic Commission for Latin America and the Caribbean (ECLAC) publications, 128, 140, 161, 167
Economic development, 14, 50, 100, 116 (Anglophone Caribbean), 128, 152; see also Development and development plans, Town and country planning
Economic geography, 127, 134, 168
Economic history, 33, 61, 85, 140 (nineteenth and twentieth centuries), 168, 169
Economic reports and surveys, 36, 97, 101
Economics, 1, 4, 14, 18, 23, 30, 32, 33, 36, 38, 43, 50, 66, 77, 78, 85, 89, 100, 102, 105, 106, 110, 123, 139, 140, 151, 156, 161, 164, 166, 168, 169 (pre-1850), 182, 183, 188, 195, 201, 204, 205, 207, 209, 211
  Agricultural, 190
  Anglophone Caribbean, 20, 36, 43, 96, 116, 190, 194
  Argentina, 36, 211, 215
  Bolivia, 74 (photographs)
  Brazil, 30, 36, 53, 67, 74 (photographs), 102, 215
  Central America, 215
  Chile, 36, 74 (photographs), 215
  Coffee-producing countries, 128
  Colombia, 18
  Costa Rica, 36
  Cuba, 53, 211
  Defence, 129
  Development, 190
  Ecuador, 36
  Haiti, 36
  Jamaica, 36
  Mexico, 30, 36, 53, 67, 74 (photographs), 164, 211

Nicaragua, 18
Panama, 74 (photographs)
Periodicals, 23
Peru, 18, 74 (photographs), 154, 215
Photographs, 74, 153, 155
Press cuttings, 200
Reports, 36, 97, 101
Rubber, 132
Saint Lucia, 36
Saint Vincent, 36
Statistics, 43, 77, 101,
Transport, 34
Venezuela, 170
see also Individual commodities, industries and topics
Ecosystem, 212
Ecuador,
  Archaeology, 168, 214 (photographs)
  Birds, 19
  Development aid, 89
  Drawings, 150
  Economics, 36
  Environment, 19
  Manuscripts, 150
  Photographs, 113
  Statistics, 36
  Tourism, 165
Edinburgh University Library, 43
Education, 30, 40, 103, 107, 118, 201, 203
  Anglophone Caribbean, 20, 76, 96, 116, 118
  Barbados, 76
  Bolivia, 72
  Brazil, 30, 63 (photographs), 72
  Colombia, 72
  Cuba, 37
  Dominican Republic, 72
  Guatemala, 72
  Guyana, 76
  Haiti, 72
  Jamaica, 76
  Mexico, 30, 37
  Nicaragua, 72
  Periodicals, 118
  Peru, 72
  Statistics, 118
  Trinidad, 76
  Women, 103
Elderly, 108
El Dorado, 214
Election reports, Anglophone Caribbean, 95, 116
El Salvador, 93
  Development aid, 89, 192
  Human rights, 61
El Salvador Solidarity Campaign, archive, 61
Embajada de los Estados Unidos de Venezuela, 170
Emergency aid, see Aid, Emergency
Emigration
  Welsh (in Patagonia), 2, 4
Employment, 101 (statistics)
Encyclopaedias, 33, 121
  Anglophone Caribbean, 94
Energy, 85, 202
Engineering, 85
  Civil, 125, 160
  Mechanical, 126
Engravings, 112
Entomology, 45, 57, 150, 178 (plant)
Environment, 14, 19, 30, 32, 53, 71, 85, 102, 106, 123, 152, 165, 190, 201, 203, 212
  Anglophone Caribbean, 96
  Argentina, 212
  Bolivia, 72, 74 (photographs), 113 (photographs)
  Brazil, 19, 30, 63 (photographs), 72, 74 (photographs), 113 (photographs)
  Chile, 74 (photographs), 113 (photographs), 212
  Colombia, 72, 113 (photographs)
  Costa Rica, 212
  Dominican Republic, 72
  Ecuador, 19, 113 (photographs)
  Guatemala, 72
  Haiti, 72
  Mexico, 30, 74 (photographs), 113 (photographs)
  Nicaragua, 72
  Panama, 74 (photographs)
  Peru, 72, 74 (photographs), 113 (photographs), 154
  Photographs, 74, 113, 214
Ephemera, 36, 103, 116, 121, 168, 173
Epidemiology, 141, 151

Ethnography, 86, 111, 143 (Guatemala)
Ethnology, *see* Anthropology and ethnology
Ethnomusicology, 196
European Union publications, 140, 161
Eva Crane IBRA Library, 31
Exhibition catalogues, 120, 148, 160, 173
Expedition Advisory Centre, 159
Expedition reports, 141, 149, 150, 159
Exploration, *see* Travel and exploration
Export Market Information Centre, *see* Trade Partners UK

Faculty of Archaeology and Anthropology, University of Cambridge, 22
Faculty of Economics and Politics, University of Cambridge, 23
Faculty of History, University of Cambridge, 24
Faculty of Modern and Medieval Languages, University of Cambridge, 25
Falkland Islands and dependencies, 20, 28, 95, 206, 207
Family life, 103, 113 (photographs)
Family planning, 131
Fashion, 103
Fauna, 63 (photographs), 150; *see also* Flora and fauna
Fawcett Library: the National Library of Women, 103
FCO, *see* Foreign and Commonwealth Office
Feminism, 103
Fiction, *see* Literature
Films, 2, 11, 28, 80, 81, 82, 128, 149, 201
   Anglophone Caribbean, 94
   Costume designs, 82
   Documentary films, 81, 121 (video), 143
   Feature films, 9, 80, 81, 121 (video), 143, 191 (video)
   Periodicals, 80
   Posters, 82
   Press cuttings, 80
   Publicity materials, 80
   Set designs, 82
   Slides, 82
   Stills, 82
   see also Cinema
Finance, 77, 85, 91, 97, 98, 101 (statistics), 182
Fine arts, *see* Art
Fishing industry, 149
Flora and fauna, 55, 58, 63 (Brazil, photographs), 150, 212, 214 (photographs)
Folklore, 44, 85, 86, 104, 168
Folklore Society, 104
Food industries, 85
Food security, 40
Foreign and Commonwealth Office, 105
   Commonwealth Law Library, 115
Foreign relations, 3, 56, 96, 105, 129, 157, 161
   with the United States of America, 194
Foreign Research and Press Service press cuttings collection, 84
Forestry, 152, 189
Forum for the Study of Cuba, 213
Francophone Caribbean, 56, 187
   History, 36
   Linguistics, 56, 199
   Literature, 1 (twentieth-century), 29, 36, 199
   see also Caribbean
French West Indies, *see* Francophone Caribbean
Frewen Library, 200
Friends, Religious Society of, 157
Fruit, 178
Fungal biotechnology, 45
Fungal taxonomy, 45
Fungi, 45, 57, 212

Gascoigne Collection, 64
Gay studies, 85
Gender, 96, 120, 200, 204
Genealogy
   Welsh (in Patagonia), 2
Genetics,
   Plants, 58, 178
Geodesy, 207
Geography and topography, 9, 37, 42, 43, 46, 50, 52, 54, 62, 66, 67, 78, 106, 139, 149, 156, 159, 164, 168, 169, 182, 198, 201, 203, 204, 205, 211, 214 (photographs)

Andean countries, 198
Anglophone Caribbean, 20, 43, 94
Argentina, 211
Bolivia, 72
Brazil, 62, 67, 72, 168
Caribbean, 46 (human geography), 47, 62, 198
Central America, 47
Colombia, 72, 168
Cuba, 37, 47, 211
Dominican Republic, 72
Economic geography, 127, 134, 168
Guatemala, 72
Haiti, 72
Human geography, 46 (Caribbean), 168
Mexico, 37, 47, 62, 67, 164, 168, 198, 211
Nicaragua, 72
Periodicals, 27, 52, 54, 159
Peru, 62, 72
Photographs, 52, 153, 159, 214
Physical and ecological geography, 46
United Kingdom imprints, 47, 70, 135, 136
Geology, 59, 85, 193
Maps, 193
Periodicals, 27, 59
George Edwards Library, 56
German influence (post-1914), 117
Getty Conservation Centre, 81
Glaciology, 28
Glasgow City Libraries and Archives, 51
Godman, F.D., and O. Salvin, papers, 150
Gold, Colombian, 214 (photographs)
Goldsmiths' Collection, 169
Goldsmiths' College, 106
Government, *see* Politics
Government plans, 102
Government publications, *see* Official publications
Grammars, *see* Linguistics
Grenada, 150 (drawings, manuscripts), 155 (photographs)
Grey literature, 108, 152
Guatemala, 63 (photographs), 72, 93, 143, 192
Guatemalan Indian Centre, 143
Guerra, Francisco, Collection, 171

Guildhall Library, 98
Guyana, 76, 94, 95, 142, 158 (pictures), 206, 207
Civil engineering, 125
Education, 76
Mechanical engineering, 126
Missions, 175
Religion, 175

Habitats, 55
Hackney, London Borough of, 136
Haddon Library, 22
Haiti, 72, 75, 93, 192
Development aid, 89
Economics, 36
Migrant labour, 155 (photographs)
Statistics, 36
Handbooks, 13 (Anglophone Caribbean)
Harold Cohen Library, 71
Harold Turner Collection, 7
Harrison Learning Centre, 213
Hart, Richard, papers, 116
Hartley Library, 208
Healthlink Worldwide, 107
Health, Public, *see* Public health and preventive medicine; *see also* Health conditions and services
Health conditions and services, 40, 96, 107, 141, 151
Brazil, 63 (photographs)
Women, 103
Helminthology, 45
Helpage International, 108
Hennessy, Alistair, collection of Cuban periodicals, 213
Heythrop College, University of London, 109
Hispanic and Luso-Brazilian Council, 110
Hispanic literature, *see* Literature and literary criticism, Spanish-American; *see also under individual countries*
Hispanics in the United States, 37
History, 1, 3, 4, 5, 9, 15, 17, 20, 24, 33, 35, 36, 37, 43, 44, 46, 48, 53, 54, 61, 62, 64, 65, 66, 67, 68, 70, 71, 85, 88, 105, 106, 110, 119, 134, 139, 140, 145, 156, 159, 164, 168, 169, 180, 181, 182, 183, 184, 187, 190, 195, 200, 201, 203, 204, 205, 208, 209, 211

Andean countries, 21, 187
Anglophone Caribbean, 20, 29, 36, 43, 70, 71, 94, 116, 194
Argentina, 20, 36, 48, 54, 61, 65, 187, 200, 211
Bibliographies, 119
Bolivia, 65
Brazil, 20, 21, 54, 61, 62, 65, 67, 71, 134, 180, 181, 200, 204, 208
Caribbean, 36, 47, 61, 62, 208
Central America, 47
Chile, 44, 54, 61, 65, 145
Colombia, 36, 65
Colonial period, 85, 119, 134, 214 (photographs)
  Anglophone Caribbean, 20, 29, 47, 105, 116, 194
Cuba, 17, 37, 47, 53, 145, 211
Economic history, 33, 61, 85, 140, 168, 169
Guatemala, 143
Independence period, 47, 85, 147 (military aspects), 187 (Mexico)
Maritime, 146, 149
Medicine, 171
Mexico, 17, 20, 21, 36, 37, 47, 54, 61, 62, 67, 85, 164, 171, 181, 200, 211
Military, 64, 147
Patagonia, 2, 4
Periodicals, 119
Peru, 54, 62, 65, 71, 145, 181
Political history, 140 (nineteenth and twentieth centuries)
Social history, 33, 61, 168
Source materials, 119
Spanish Caribbean, 208
United Kingdom imprints, 47, 70, 135, 136
Uruguay, 20, 187
Venezuela, 36, 65, 170
Welsh (in Patagonia), 2, 4
Homerton Library, 136
Honduras, 93, 192
  Development aid, 89
Horniman Museum and Gardens, 111
Horticulture, 45, 58, 178
Horticulture Research International, 178
Housing, 102, 202

Hugh Owen Library, 3
Hull City Council, Hull Local Studies Library, 60
Hulton|Archive, 112
Hulton Getty Picture Collection, *see* Hulton|Archive
Human geography, 46 (Caribbean), 168
Humanitarian policy, 152
Humanities, 5, 30, 43, 44, 48, 53, 110, 139, 169, 187, 213, 215
  Andean countries, 187
  Anglophone Caribbean, 43
  Argentina, 48, 187, 213
  Brazil, 187, 213
  Chile, 213
  Cuba, 213
  Mexico, 187, 213
  Paraguay, 187
  Periodicals, 10, 85
  Peru, 213
  Uruguay, 187
Human rights, 40, 73, 175, 176
  Chile, 61
  El Salvador, 61
  Guatemala, 143
  Peru, 154
Hume Collection, 44
Hutchison Picture Library, 113
Hydrographical surveys, 146
Hydrographic Office, 146

IBRA, *see* International Bee Research Association
ILO, *see* International Labour Office
Incas, 171, 214 (photographs)
Incunabula, 85, 187
Independence struggle, 147 (military aspects)
Index on censorship, 176
Indians, *see* Amerindians
Indigenous peoples and languages, *see* Amerindians
Industrial mycology, 45
Industrial sciences, 85
Industry, *see* Economics
Information science, 85
Information technology, 85
inIVA, *see* Institute of International Visual Arts

Inland Revenue, International Division, 114
Inquisition, 20
Institute of Advanced Legal Studies, 115
Institute of Agricultural Economics, *see* International Development Centre, University of Oxford
Institute of Amerindian Studies, *see* Centre for Indigenous American Studies and Exchange
Institute of Arable Crops Research – Rothamsted, 57
Institute of Archaeology, *see* University College London
Institute of Bankers, *see* Chartered Institute of Bankers
Institute of British Geographers, 159
Institute of Commonwealth Studies, *see* International Development Centre, University of Oxford
Institute of Commonwealth Studies, University of London, 116
Institute of Contemporary History and Wiener Library, 117
Institute of Criminology, University of Cambridge, 26
Institute of Development Studies, 14
Institute of Economics and Statistics, University of Oxford, *see* Department of Economics, University of Oxford
Institute of Education, University of London, 118
Institute of Financial Services, *see* Chartered Institute of Bankers
Institute of Geography and Earth Studies, University of Wales Aberystwyth, 3
Institute of Historical Research, University of London, 119
Institute of Horticultural Research, *see* Horticulture Research International
Institute of International Visual Arts (inIVA), 120
Institute of Latin American Studies, University of Glasgow, 53
Institute of Latin American Studies, University of Liverpool, 71
Institute of Latin American Studies, University of London, 121
Institute of Linguists, 122
Institute of Logistics and Transport, 34
Institute of Naval Medicine, 146
Institute of Petroleum, 123
Institute of Race Relations, 124
Institute of Social and Cultural Anthropology, University of Oxford, 197
Institution of Civil Engineers, 125
Institution of Mechanical Engineers, 126
Institution of Mining and Metallurgy, 127
Insurance, 92, 97
Intermediate Technology, 202
International affairs, *see* Foreign relations
International Bee Research Association, 31
International Coffee Organization, 128
International Cooperation for Development, 89
International Development Centre, University of Oxford, 190
International Information Bureau press cuttings collection, 84
International Institute for Social History, 73
International Institute for Strategic Studies, 129
International Labour Office, 130
Publications, 75, 130
International law, 105
International Library, Ordnance Survey, 206
International organisations' publications, 12, 96, 140, 167, 172
Statistics, 50, 100, 140
International Planned Parenthood Federation, 131
International politics, *see* Foreign relations
International relations, *see* Foreign relations
International Rubber Study Group, 132
International Sugar Organization, 133
International Union for the Conservation of Nature and Natural Resources, 19
Interpreting, 122
Investment, 97
Irish imprints, 2, 20, 39, 44, 85, 187
IT Perú, 202

IUCN, *see* International Union for the Conservation of Nature and Natural Resources

Jamaica, 93, 142
  Drawings, 150
  Economics, 36
  Education, 76
  Manuscripts, 61, 150
  Newspapers, 16 (eighteenth-century)
  Statistics, 36
  Sugar, 61
  see also Anglophone Caribbean
James, C.L.R., Library, 136
James, C.L.R., papers, 116
James Hardiman Library, 49
Jazz, 83
J.B. Priestley Library, 12
Jesuits, 109, 214 (photographs)
Jewellery, Mexican, 144 (photographs), 179 (sales)
Jews, 20, 117 (since 1914)
John Rylands Library, 180
John Rylands University Library of Manchester, 180
Juvenile offenders, 26
Juvenilia, 6, 44
  Anglophone Caribbean, 94

Kew Gardens, *see* Royal Botanic Gardens, Kew
King's College London, 134
Kingston University, 62
Kirkpatrick, F.A., Collection, 20

Labour, 75, 101 (statistics), 103 (women), 130, 151, 155 (photographs), 166
Labour law, 140
Labour movements, 142
LACAP, *see* Latin American Cooperative Acquisitions Project
Land resource assessment, 32
Land Resources Development Centre, *see* Natural Resources Institute
Land survey, 207
Land tenure, 207
Language, *see* Linguistics
Languages, 25, 33, 90, 122, 145, 187, 191, 199, 200, 203, 204

Amerindian, 69, 163, 187, 203
  Chilean, 145
  Cuban, 145
  Dictionaries, 8, 33, 94, 110, 121, 163
  Dialects, 83
  Peruvian, 145
  Portuguese, 25, 90, 191, 199
  Recorded sound, 83
  Spanish, 25, 90, 191, 199
  see also Linguistics
Language Teaching Library, *see* CILT Resources Library
Lantern slides, 8, 52
Latin America Information Centre, 179
Latin American Business Archives, 168
Latin American Centre, University of Oxford, 195
Latin American Cooperative Acquisitions Project, 205
Law, 5, 30, 103, 105, 115, 146
  Anglophone Caribbean, 115, 186
  Argentina, 115
  Brazil, 30, 115
  Commercial, 97
  Company, 114
  Constitutional, 140
  Criminal, 26, 140
  Ecclesiastical, 109
  International, 105
  Labour, 140
  Land and surveying, 207
  Mexico, 30
  Periodicals, 115, 186
  Taxation, 114
  Urban bylaws, 102
  Venezuela, 170
League of Nations Intelligence Department press cuttings collection, 84
Leeds Library Service, 64
Legal materials and legislation, *see* Law
Legislation, *see* Law
León, Nicolás, Collection, 171
Liberation theology, 8, 89, 109, 175
Library and information science, 85
Life sciences, 32, 85, 193
Limehouse Library, 137
Linguistics, 5, 25, 30, 33, 37, 54, 56, 71,

85, 86, 90, 103, 110, 122, 134, 145, 156, 180, 197, 199, 200, 201, 204
  Amerindian, 8, 69, 86, 163, 187, 197, 203
  Argentine, 54, 200
  Brazilian, 25, 30, 54, 134, 200
  Chilean, 54, 145
  Cuban, 37, 145
  Francophone Caribbean, 199
  Mexican, 30, 37, 54, 200
  Peruvian, 54, 145
  Portuguese, 25, 39, 90, 199
  Spanish, 25, 39, 90, 199
  United Kingdom imprints, 70
  see also Languages
Literatura de cordel, 33
Literature and literary criticism, 1, 3, 5, 9, 15, 17, 20, 25, 30, 33, 36, 39, 42, 43, 48, 54, 61, 65, 66, 68, 70, 78, 85, 106, 134, 139, 145, 156, 168, 169, 179 (esp. fiction), 180, 181, 184, 191, 199, 200, 205, 209, 211
  Amerindian, 187
  Anglophone Caribbean, 20, 29, 36, 43, 66, 71, 94
  Argentina, 20, 36, 48, 54, 61, 65, 168 (esp. fiction, poetry), 199, 200, 211
  Bolivia, 65
  Brazil, 17, 20, 25, 30, 54, 61, 65, 66 (twentieth-century), 70, 71, 134, 137 (twentieth-century), 180, 181, 199, 200, 208 (twentieth-century)
  Caribbean, 36, 43, 61
  Chile, 54, 61, 65, 145, 199
  Colombia, 36, 65, 199
  Cuba, 17, 145, 199, 211
  Francophone Caribbean, 1 (twentieth-century), 29, 36, 199
  Mexico, 17, 20, 30, 36, 54, 61, 168 (esp. fiction, poetry), 181, 199, 200, 211
  Peru, 54, 65, 71, 145, 181
  Shakespeare translations, 6
  Spanish American, 1 (twentieth-century), 66 (twentieth-century), 70, 168 (esp. fiction, poetry), 191 (novel), 199
  Spoken, 83
  Travel, 78

United Kingdom imprints, 36, 70
Uruguay, 20
Venezuela, 36, 65, 170
Liverpool Libraries and Information Services, 70
Liverpool Record Office and Local Studies Department, 70
Liverpool's relations with Latin America, 70
Livesey, James, & Co., 126
Lloyds Bank Latin American press cuttings collection, 200
Llyfrgell Genedlaethol Cymru, 2
Logistics, 34
London Borough of Bromley, 135
London Borough of Hackney, 136
London Borough of Tower Hamlets, 137
London Chamber of Commerce and Industry, 138
London Guildhall University, 103
London Library, 139
London School of Economics, University of London, 140
London School of Hygiene and Tropical Medicine, University of London, 141
LSE *see* London School of Economics

Macdonald, Norman, press cuttings, 121
MAKE Resource, *see* Women's Art Library
Management, 34, 97, 138
Manufacturing, *see* Economics
Manuscripts, 1, 2, 8, 16, 20, 28, 43, 52, 58, 59, 61, 70, 73, 75, 85, 86, 96, 102, 103, 116, 125, 126, 144 (photographs), 148, 149, 150, 159, 168, 169, 171, 175, 179, 180, 187, 194, 196, 200, 201, 208
Manuscripts, Guides to, 119
Maps and atlases, 1, 2, 3, 6, 11, 20, 33, 44, 52, 58, 59, 85, 86, 128, 141, 146, 149, 150, 159, 168, 169, 172, 187, 193, 198, 206, 212, 215
  Anglophone Caribbean, 94, 169
  Antarctic and Southern South America, 28, 206
  Central America, 169
  Geological, 59, 193
  Guatemala, 143

Marine engineering, 146
Marine records, 11
Maritime history, 146, 149
Marketing data, 85
Market research, 101, 123
Marshall Library of Economics, University of Cambridge, 23
Marxism, 142
Marx Memorial Library, 142
Mathematics, 85
    Periodicals, 27
Mayas, 86, 143, 160 (architecture), 171, 214 (photographs)
Maya: the Guatemalan Indian Centre, 143
Mechanical engineering, 126
Media studies, 120
Medical entomology, 45
Medical mycology, 45
Medicine, 43, 85, 146, 162, 171, 193
    Aid programmes, 50
    Amerindian, 171
    Anglophone Caribbean, 171
    Caribbean, 171
    History, 171, 193
    Mexico, 171
    Periodicals, 162, 171
    Peru, 171
    Photographs, 113
    Theses, 43
    Tropical, 43, 45, 141
    Veterinary, 43
Mee, Margaret, Collection, 58
Merchant marine, 149
Mesoamerica, *see* Pre-conquest period
Metallurgy, 127
Meteorological Office Library, *see* National Meteorological Library and Archive
Meteorology, 11, 193, 198
Mexico, 20, 21, 30, 33, 36, 67, 71, 85, 139, 144 (photographs), 171, 187
    Agriculture, 144 (photographs)
    Anthropology, 37, 86, 168
    Archaeology, 86, 144 (photographs), 168
    Architecture, 144 (photographs), 160
    Archivo General de la Nación, 20
    Art, 144 (photographs), 148
    Aztecs, 144 (photographs)
    Census data, 198
    Civil engineering, 125
    Codices, 33, 144 (photographs), 171, 187
    Costume, 144 (photographs)
    Demography, 30
    Development, 102
    Economic history, 61
    Economics, 30, 36, 53, 67, 74 (photographs), 164, 211
    Education, 30, 37
    Environment, 30, 74 (photographs)
    Folklore, 104
    Geography, 37, 47, 62, 67, 164, 168, 198, 211
    History, 17, 20, 21, 36, 37, 47, 54, 61, 62, 67, 85, 164, 171 (colonial), 181, 187, 200, 211
    Humanities, 187, 213
    Incunabula, 85, 187
    Jewellery, 144 (photographs)
    Law, 30
    Linguistics, 30, 37, 54, 200
    Literature, 20, 30, 36, 54, 61, 168 (esp. fiction, poetry), 181, 199, 200, 211
    Manuscripts, 20, 144 (photographs)
    Medicine, 171
    Musical instruments, 144 (photographs)
    Official publications, 85
    Pamphlets, 187
    Photographs, 74, 113, 144, 214
    Politics, 21, 37, 53, 54, 62, 67, 74 (photographs), 164, 208, 211
    Religion, 74 (photographs), 144 (photographs)
    Slides, 144
    Social history, 61
    Social sciences, 21, 37, 53, 74 (photographs), 187, 200, 211, 213
    Social welfare, 37
    Statistics, 36
    Travel, 74 (photographs)
Mexicolore, 144
Microfiches, *see* Microforms
Microfilms, *see* Microforms

Microforms, 6, 7, 10, 11, 14, 16, 20, 28, 33, 37, 58, 61, 73, 75, 79, 84 (newspapers), 86, 98, 116, 118, 121, 131, 134, 142, 149, 161, 168, 180, 188, 195, 198, 199, 200, 207, 215
Middlesex University, 145
Migrant labour, 75, 155 (photographs)
Military affairs, 129, 147
Military and state, 209
Military history, 64, 147
Millbrook House Picture Library, 185
Minerals, 127
Mining, 127
Mining surveys, 193
Ministry of Defence, Admiralty Library, 146
Ministry of Defence, Whitehall Library, 147
Ministry of Overseas Development, *see* Department for International Development
Misiones, Argentina, 212
Missiology, 7
Missions, 8, 75, 109, 175
  Anglican, 8, 175
  Argentina, 8
  Bolivia, 8
  Brazil, 8
  Caribbean, 175
  Chile, 8
  Guyana, 175
  Jesuit, 109, 214 (photographs)
  Paraguay, 8
  Peru, 8
  Uruguay, 8
Mitchell Library, 51
MOD, *see* Ministry of Defence
Modern and Medieval Languages Faculty, University of Cambridge, 25
Modern Languages Faculty, University of Oxford, 191
Montserrat, 93; *see also* Anglophone Caribbean
Morrell Library, 215
Mountaineering, 52
Museum of Mankind Library, *see* British Museum, Department of Ethnography
Music, 2, 6, 10, 44, 79, 83, 85, 110, 111, 169, 172, 179, 196, 212, 215
  Books, 79, 169, 172
  Brazil, 83 (recorded sound)
  Caribbean, 48 (recorded sound), 79, 83 (recorded sound)
  Classical, 79, 83 (recorded sound)
  Colombia, 83 (recorded sound)
  Cuba, 83 (recorded sound)
  Ethnomusicology, 196
  Jazz, 83 (recorded sound)
  Musical instruments, 144 (photographs)
  Panama, 83 (recorded sound)
  Periodicals, 83
  Peru, 83 (recorded sound)
  Photographs, 113
  Popular, 79, 83 (recorded sound)
  Recorded sound, 79, 83, 169, 170, 172, 196
  Scores, 79, 169, 172
  Sheet music, 79, 110
Musicology, 111
Mycology, 45, 57

Nasca Lines, 214 (photographs)
National Art Library, 148
National Film and Television Archive, 81
National Lending Library, *see* British Library Document Supply Centre
National Library of Scotland, 44, 52
National Library of Wales, 2
National Library of Women, 103
National Maritime Museum, 149
National Meteorological Library and Archive, 11
National Sound Archive, British Library, 83
National University of Ireland, 49
Natural history, 44, 85, 111, 150
  Anglophone Caribbean, 20
Natural History Museum, 150
Natural resources, 19, 32
Natural Resources Institute, 32
Naturalists' reports, 150, 193
Naval architecture, 146, 149
Naval Historical Library, *see* Admiralty Library
Naval history, 146, 149
Naval science, 146

Navigation, 146, 149
Nazi influence, 117
Nematode taxonomy, 45
Nematology, 45, 57
New religious movements, 7, 71
Newspaper clippings, *see* Press cuttings
Newspaper Library, British Library, 84
Newspapers, 84, 97, 138, 161, 171 (colonial period), 212
  Guatemalan, 143
  Jamaican, 16 (eighteenth-century)
News sources, 40, 121, 154, 179, 213; *see also* Press cuttings
NGOs, *see* Non-governmental organisations
Nicaragua, 18, 72, 89, 93, 192
  Development aid, 89
Non-governmental organisations, 71, 121
Non-print material, *see* Films, Photographs, Pictures, Recorded sound, Slides, Video recordings
Northern Listening Service, 10
North Staffordshire Polytechnic Library, *see* Staffordshire University

OAS publications, *see* Organization of American States publications
ODI *see* Overseas Development Institute
Office of Population Censuses and Surveys *see* Office for National Statistics
Office for National Statistics, 151
Official publications, 12, 14, 20, 34, 85, 98, 102, 105, 140, 171
  Anglophone Caribbean, 20, 76, 85, 95, 116, 194
  Colonial period of Latin America, 171
  International organisations, 140, 161, 172
  Nineteenth-century, 20
  Statistical, 50, 71, 140
  United Kingdom, 172
  Venezuela, 170
Oil industry, 123
Oral history, 83
Ordnance Survey, 206, 207
Organisations, Regional, 14
Organization of American States publications, 73, 128, 140, 161

Overseas Development Administration *see* Department for International Development
Overseas Development Institute, 152
Overseas Geological Surveys, 59
Oxfam, 192
Oxford Forestry Institute, 189
Oxford University *see* University of Oxford

PAHO, *see* Pan American Health Organization
Paintings, 2, 110, 126, 159; *see also* Art, Pictures
Pamphlets, 7, 9, 20, 26, 28, 33, 44, 59, 64, 75, 76, 86, 95, 98, 103, 116, 117, 121, 123, 129, 131, 139, 140, 141, 142, 146, 149, 160, 161, 166, 168, 169, 178, 187, 195, 207
Panama, 74 (photographs), 83 (music)
Panama Canal, 74 (photographs)
Pan American Health Organization publications, 141
Panos Pictures, 153
Paraguay, 150 (drawings, manuscripts), 187
Parasitology, 45
Parliamentary Information and Reference Centre (Commonwealth), 95
Parliamentary practice, Anglophone Caribbean, 95
Partnership House Mission Studies Library, 175
Patagonia, 28
  Anthropology, 44
  Welsh settlement, 2, 4
Patents, 85
Pathology, Plant, 45
Pendle, George, press cuttings, 121
Penology, 26
Periodicals, 10, 20, 27, 33, 44, 85, 121, 168, 169, 180, 187
  Anglophone Caribbean, 20, 116
  Anthropology, 27, 86
  Archaeology, 27, 86, 168
  Architecture, 160
  Art, 120, 148
  Banking, 77, 91

Index

Biology, 27
Botany, 58
Cuba, 213
Development, 14
Economics, 23
Education, 118
Films, 80
Geography, 27, 52, 54, 159
Geology, 27, 59
History, 119
Humanities, 10, 85
Law, 115, 186
Mathematics, 27
Mechanical engineering, 126
Medicine, 162, 171
Mining, 127
Music, 83
Natural history, 150
Oil industry, 123
Science, 10, 27, 44, 85, 193
Social sciences, 10
Zoology, 177
see also Newspapers
Peru, 18, 71, 85, 93, 139, 154, 202
   Anthropology, 8, 65, 72
   Archaeology, 168, 214 (photographs)
   Architecture, 160
   Civil engineering, 125
   Demography, 72
   Development aid, 89
   Economics, 18, 74 (photographs), 154, 215
   Education, 72
   Environment, 72, 74 (photographs), 113 (photographs), 154
   Geography, 62, 72
   History, 54, 62, 65, 71, 145, 181
   Humanities, 213
   Human rights, 154
   Incunabula, 85, 187
   Liberation theology, 8
   Linguistics, 54, 145
   Literature, 54, 65, 71, 145, 181
   Manuscripts, 61
   Medicine, 171
   Missions, 8
   Music, 83 (recorded sound)
   News sources, 154
   Photographs, 63, 74, 113
   Politics, 18, 54, 62, 72, 74 (photographs), 154, 215
   Poverty, 154
   Press cuttings, 154
   Religion, 74 (photographs)
   Reports, 154
   Social sciences, 18, 65, 71, 74 (photographs), 145, 213
   Social welfare, 8, 72
   Sugar, 61
   Travel, 8, 74 (photographs)
Peru Support Group, 154
Pesticides, 45, 57
Pests, Agricultural, 32
Petroleum industry, 123
Philatelic collections, 85
Philip Wolmuth, 155
Philology, *see* Linguistics, Literature
Philosophy, 109
Photogrammetry, 207
Photographs, 2, 8, 40, 63, 74, 75, 112, 113, 142, 153, 155, 159, 160, 168, 192, 196, 214
   Aerial, 206
   Amazonia, 158, 214
   Amerindians, 63, 158
   Anglophone Caribbean, 20, 105, 155, 206 (aerial), 207
   Antarctic and Southern South America, 28, 206 (aerial), 207
   Anthropology, 158
   Antigua, 155
   Architecture, 144, 160
   Argentina, 63
   Barbados, 155
   Birds, 19
   Bolivia, 63, 74, 113
   Brazil, 63, 74, 113
   Caribbean, 113, 153
   Chile, 63, 74, 113
   Civil engineering, 125
   Climate, 113
   Colombia, 113
   Cuba, 153, 155, 214
   Dominica, 155
   Dominican Republic, 153, 155, 214
   Ecuador, 113

Environment, 74, 113, 214
Family life, 113
Geography, 52, 153, 159, 214
Geology, 59
Grenada, 155
Guatemala, 63, 143
Haiti, 155
Mechanical engineering, 126
Medicine, 113
Mexico, 74, 113, 144, 214
Music, 113
Panama, 74
Peru, 63, 74, 113
Puerto Rico, 155
Railways, 185
Religion, 74, 113, 153
Saint Lucia, 155
Trinidad, 155
Zoology, 177
Physical anthropology, 86
Physical sciences, 85, 193
Pictures, 28, 112, 149, 158, 159; see also Art, Drawings, Paintings, Prints
Pirates and piracy, 149
Pitt Rivers Museum, 196
Planning, see Development and development plans, Economic development, Regional development and planning, Town and country planning, Urban planning and development
Plantation crops, 45
Plant anatomy, 58
Plant breeding, 178
Plant diseases, 57
Plant ecology, 58, 212
Plant entomology, 178
Plant genetics, 178
Plant nematology, 45, 57
Plant pathology, 45, 178
Plant physiology, 178
Plant products, 32, 178
Plants, 55, 57, 58, 178, 212
Poetry, see Literature
Polar regions, 28, 52 (exploration)
Political history, 85, 140 (nineteenth and twentieth centuries), 208 (Brazil, Mexico)
Political parties, 116, 121

Politics, 1, 3, 4, 9, 14, 18, 33, 35, 37, 38, 43, 54, 62, 66, 67, 68, 85, 89, 98, 105, 106, 120, 129, 139, 140, 156, 161, 164, 169, 180, 182, 183, 190, 195, 204, 209, 211
Andean countries, 21
Anglophone Caribbean, 20, 43, 95, 96, 116, 194
Argentina, 54, 211, 215
Bolivia, 72, 74 (photographs)
Brazil, 21, 53, 54, 62, 67, 72, 74 (photographs), 208, 215
Caribbean, 62
Central America, 215
Chile, 54, 74 (photographs), 215
Colombia, 18, 72
Cuba, 37, 53, 211
Dominican Republic, 72
Ephemera, 116, 121
Guatemala, 72, 143
Haiti, 72
International, 3, 56, 96, 105, 129, 157, 161, 194
Mexico, 21, 37, 53, 54, 62, 67, 74 (photographs), 164, 208, 211
Nicaragua, 18, 72
Panama, 74 (photographs)
Peru, 18, 54, 62, 72, 74 (photographs), 154, 215
Photographs, 74, 153, 155
Venezuela, 170
Polytechnic, Wolverhampton, see University of Wolverhampton
Poole, Henry Ward, Collection, 187
Popular culture, 85, 208 (Brazil)
Popular music, 79, 83 (recorded sound)
Population, see Demography
Population censuses, see Census data
Population studies, 131
Ports and harbours, 125
Portsmouth Polytechnic see University of Portsmouth
Portuguese literature of Brazil, see Brazil, Literature
Postage stamps, see Philatelic collections
Postcards, 103, 158
Posters, 82 (film), 103
Anglophone Caribbean, 94
Poverty, 93, 102, 107, 192

Brazil, 63 (photographs)
Peru, 154
Pre-conquest period,
   Archaeology, 22, 27, 86, 143, 144 (photographs), 168, 171, 196, 205, 214 (photographs)
   Architecture, 160
Press cuttings, 28, 36, 40, 75, 80, 84, 98, 103, 121, 129, 161, 173, 190, 195, 200
   Anglophone Caribbean, 94, 95
   Antarctic and Southern South America, 28
   Art, 173
   Banking, 91
   Censorship, 176
   Cuba, 213
   Economics, 200
   Films, 80
   Finance, 91
   Guatemala, 143
   Human rights, 176
   Jews and anti-Semitism, 117
   Military affairs, 129
   Oil industry, 123
   Peru, 154
Pressure groups, 116 (Anglophone Caribbean)
Prifysgol Caerdydd, 30
Prifysgol Cymru Abertawe, 211
Prifysgol Cymru Aberystwyth, 3
Prifysgol Cymru Bangor, 4
Pring-Mill, Robert, 121
Prints, 2, 58, 112
Project Planning Centre for Developing Countries, see Development and Project Planning Centre
Prostitution, 75
Protestantism, 71
Psychology, 140
Public health and preventive medicine, 141; see also Health conditions and services
Publicity materials (films), 80
Puerto Rico, 155 (photographs)

Quakers, 157
Queen Elizabeth House, Oxford, 190
Queen Mary, University of London, 156
Queen Mother Library, University of Aberdeen, 1
Queen's University Main Library, 5

Race relations, 124
Racism, 124
Radcliffe Science Library, 193
Radzinowicz Library of Criminology, 26
RAI, see Royal Anthropological Institute of Great Britain and Ireland
Railphotos, 185
Railways, 98, 125, 168, 185 (photographs)
   see also Transport
Rainforests, 55, 83 (wildlife sounds)
Recorded sound, 2, 6, 10, 28, 48 (Caribbean), 58, 65, 79, 83, 90, 94 (Caribbean), 111, 131, 143, 169, 170, 172, 173, 196, 207, 213 (Cuba)
   see also Music
Recorded Sound Information Service, 83
Regent's College, 122, 131
Regional development and planning, 102
Regional organisations, 14
Relief programmes, see Aid, Emergency
Religion, 175
   Amerindian, 7
   Anglican, 8, 175
   Anglophone Caribbean, 175
   Bolivia, 74 (photographs)
   Brazil, 63 (photographs), 74 (photographs)
   Caribbean, 175
   Chile, 74 (photographs)
   Mexico, 74 (photographs), 144 (photographs)
   New religious movements, 7, 71
   Panama, 74 (photographs)
   Peru, 74 (photographs)
   Photographs, 74, 113, 153
   Roman Catholic, 88, 89, 109
   see also Church history
Religious Society of Friends, 157
Reports, 10, 31, 34, 36 (economic), 40, 45, 55, 72, 76, 77, 91, 97, 98, 101, 102, 115, 133, 141, 150, 154, 159, 160, 165, 179, 192
Research papers, 23, 31, 121, 152, 190, 192

Research Unit for New Religions and Churches, 7
Rhodes House Library, University of Oxford, 194
RIBA, see Royal Institute of British Architects
RIIA, see Royal Institute of International Affairs
River Plate, see Argentina, Paraguay, Uruguay
Rothamsted Experimental Station, see Institute of Arable Crops Research –Rothamsted
Rothermere American Institute, 194
Royal Anthropological Institute of Great Britain and Ireland, 86, 158
Royal Botanic Gardens, Kew, 58
Royal Commonwealth Society, see Cambridge University Library
Royal Geographical Society (with the Institute of British Geographers), 159
Royal Holloway, University of London, 46
Royal Institute of British Architects, 160
Royal Institute of International Affairs, 84, 161
Royal Naval Medical Service, see Admiralty Library
Royal Naval Museum, see Admiralty Library
Royal Scottish Geographical Library, 52, 54
Royal Scottish Geographical Society, 52
Royal Society of Medicine Library, 162
Rubber, 132
RUNERC, see Research Unit for New Religions and Churches
Rural policy, 152
Rural sociology, 190
Russian imprints, 33

Saint Antony's College, University of Oxford, 195
Saint Lucia, 155 (photographs)
  Economics, 36
  Statistics, 36
  see also Anglophone Caribbean
Saint Thomas, 150 (drawings, manuscripts)
Saint Vincent
  Drawings, 150
  Economics, 36
  Manuscripts, 150
  Statistics, 36
  see also Anglophone Caribbean
Salvador, El, see El Salvador
SAMS, see South American Mission Society
Scarlett Family archive, 61
School of Advanced Study, University of London
  Institute of Advanced Legal Studies, 115
  Institute of Commonwealth Studies, 116
  Institute of Historical Research, 119
  Institute of Latin American Studies, 121
School of Anthropology and Museum Ethnography, University of Oxford, 196, 197
School of Geography, University of Oxford, 198
School of Oriental and African Studies, University of London, 163
Schumacher Centre for Technology and Development, 202
Science, 44, 71, 85, 96, 103, 123, 146, 193
  History of science, 193
  Periodicals, 10, 27, 44, 85, 193
Scientific expeditions, 150
Scientific Periodicals Library, University of Cambridge, 27
Scientific reports, 150
Scores, 79, 169, 172
Scottish Science Library, 44
Scott Polar Research Institute, University of Cambridge, 28
Seafaring, 149
Security, 129, 161
Seeley Historical Library, University of Cambridge, 21, 24
Selly Oak Colleges, 7
Sex education, 107, 131
Sexuality, 103
Shakespeare Research Collection, 6
Sheet music, 79, 110

Ships, shipping and ship building, 146, 149, 168
Slavery, 16, 20, 29, 60, 75, 116, 157, 169, 194, 208
Slides, 6, 11, 65, 82, 128, 192, 198, 207
  Antarctic and Southern South America, 28
  Art, 120, 173
  Bees, 31
  Birds, 19
  Civil engineering, 125
  Environment, 19
  Geography, 52
  Guatemala, 143
  Lantern slides, 8, 52
  Mexico, 144
  see also Lantern slides
SOAS, see School of Oriental and African Studies
Social anthropology, 71, 86, 106, 140, 197; see also Anthropology and ethnology
Social conditions, 153 (photographs), 155 (photographs), 166, 207
Social development, 116 (Anglophone Caribbean)
Social history, 33, 61, 85, 146, 168
Social movements, 89, 142
Social sciences, 14, 15, 17, 18, 30, 33, 37, 43, 44, 49, 53, 65, 66, 85, 89, 102, 106, 110, 121, 139, 140, 145, 169, 182, 187, 197, 200, 201, 203, 204, 209, 211, 213, 215
  Andean countries, 21, 187
  Anglophone Caribbean, 43, 71, 116, 194
  Argentina, 17, 65, 187, 200, 211, 213
  Bolivia, 65, 74 (photographs)
  Brazil, 21, 53, 65, 71, 74 (photographs), 102, 180, 187, 200, 213
  Chile, 65, 74 (photographs), 145, 213
  Christian sociology, 88
  Colombia, 18, 65
  Cuba, 37, 53, 145, 211, 213
  Mexico, 21, 37, 53, 74 (photographs), 187, 200, 211, 213
  Nicaragua, 18
  Panama, 74 (photographs)
  Paraguay, 187
  Periodicals, 10
  Peru, 18, 65, 71, 74 (photographs), 145, 213
  Photographs, 74
  Sociology of development, 152
  Statistics, 101, 151
  Uruguay, 187
  Venezuela, 65
Social services, 151
Social statistics, 101, 151
Social welfare, 8, 14, 37, 72, 182
Socialist parties, 142
Society of Friends, 157
Sociology, see Social sciences
Sociology, Rural, see Rural sociology
Soil science, 57
Sound recordings, see Recorded sound
Source materials, 119
South American Mission Society, 8
South American Pictures, 214
Spanish American literature, see Literature and literary criticism, Spanish American
Spirituality, 88
Spoken literature, 83
Sport, 201
Spruce, Richard, archive, 58
Staffordshire University, 210
Standards, 87, 123, 160
Starr, Frederick, folklore collection, 104
Statistics, 36, 43, 50, 71, 97, 101, 123, 138, 140, 151
  Anglophone Caribbean, 76, 96, 116
  Argentina, 36
  Banking, 77
  Brazil, 36
  Chile, 36
  Commercial, 97, 101
  Costa Rica, 36
  Demographic, 101, 151
  Ecuador, 36
  Education, 76, 118
  Employment, 101
  Financial, 101
  Haiti, 36
  International organisations, 50
  Jamaica, 36
  Labour, 101

Mexico, 36
Oil industry, 123
Population, 101, 151
Production statistics, 43
Rubber, 132
Saint Lucia, 36
Saint Vincent, 36
Social, 101, 151
Sugar industry, 133
Statistics and Market Intelligence, *see* Trade Partners UK
Stephenson, Robert, 126
Stills, 82
Strategic studies, 129, 146, 147
Street children, 75
Study Centre for New Religious Movements in Primal Societies, *see* Research Unit for New Religions and Churches
Sue Cunningham Photographic, 63
Sugar, 61, 116, 133
Supply-chain management, 34
Survey data, 206
Surveys, Hydrographical, 146
Sustainable development, 19, 55, 202
Sydney Jones Library, 71

Taxation, 114
Taxonomy, 45 (fungal, nematode), 58
Taylor, Simon, papers, 116
Taylor Institution, 199
Technical legislations, 87
Technology, 85, 96, 103, 123
Technology transfer, 202
Telephone directories, 101
Television, 80
Templeman Library, University of Canterbury, 29
Textiles, 143
Thames Valley University, 164
Theology, *see* Religion
Theses, 2, 10, 31, 37, 86, 119, 121, 143, 168, 169, 173, 180, 187, 199
  Medicine, 43, 171
Thompson, Sir Eric, Library, 86
Three Continents Liberation Collection, 136
Tierra del Fuego, 28

Topography, *see* Geography and topography
Torrents, Nissa, Video Collection, 121
Tourism, 165
  Anglophone Caribbean, 116
  Brazil, 63 (photographs)
Tourism Concern, 165
Tower Hamlets, London Borough of, 137
Town and country planning, 102, 169; *see also* Economic development, Development and development plans
Trade, *see* Commerce
Trade marks, 85
Trade Partners UK, 101
Trades Union Congress, 166
Trades unions, 142, 166
  Anglophone Caribbean, 116
Translating, 122
Transport, 34, 85
  Brazil, 63 (photographs)
  see also Railways
Transport economics, 34
Travel and exploration, 13, 52, 64, 74 (photographs), 78, 105, 134, 139, 159, 168, 169, 171, 179, 214 (photographs)
  Early (pre–1900), 8, 25, 78, 168, 169
  Maritime, 146, 149
  Photographs, 153
  Polar, 52
  Scientific voyages and expeditions, 141, 150
  United Kingdom imprints, 71 (nineteenth-century), 135, 136
Treaties, 105
Trinidad,
  Civil engineering, 125
  Drawings, 150
  Education, 76
  Manuscripts, 150
  Photographs, 155
  see also Anglophone Caribbean
Trinity and All Saints College, 65
Trinity College Dublin Library, 39
Trócaire, 40
Tropical agriculture, *see* Agriculture
Tropical Development and Research Institute, *see* Natural Resources Institute

Tropical ecology, 46
Tropical medicine, 43, 45, 141
  see also Medicine
Tropical products, 32, 43, 178
Tropical Products Institute, see Natural
  Resources Institute
Tropics,
  Geography, 46
TUC, see Trades Union Congress
Turner, Harold, Collection, 7
Tylor Library, 197

Union Catalogue of Latin Americana,
  121
United Kingdom imprints, 2, 10, 20, 44, 51,
  71, 172, 215
  Copyright libraries, 2, 20, 39, 44, 84
    (newspapers), 85, 186, 187, 193,
    194, 203 (1710–1836)
  Economics, 23
  Geography and topography, 47, 135,
    136
  History, 36, 47, 70, 135, 136
  Linguistics, 70
  Literature, 36, 70
  Official publications, 85, 172
  Science periodicals, 10
  Travel and exploration, 13, 71 (nine-
    teenth-century), 135, 136
United Nations Information Centre, 167
United Nations publications, 75, 128,
  140, 161, 167, 172
United Society for the Propagation of the
  Gospel, see World Mission Association
United States imprints, 20, 172, 187
  Economics, 23, 36, 215
United States National Archives, 20
United States' relations with Latin
  America, 194
University College Cardiff, see Cardiff
  University
University College Cork, 35
University College Dublin, 41
University College London, 168
University College London,
  Development Planning Unit, 102
University College London, Folklore
  Society, 104

University College of Swansea, see
  University of Wales, Swansea
University of Aberdeen,
  Queen Mother Library, 1
University of Birmingham, 9, 175
University of Birmingham, Research Unit
  for New Religions and Churches, 7
University of Bradford, Development and
  Project Planning Centre, 12
University of Bristol, 17
University of Cambridge,
  Cambridge University Library, 20
  Cambridge University Museum of
    Archaeology and Anthropology, 104
  Centre of Latin American Studies, 21
  Faculty of Archaeology and
    Anthropology, Haddon Library, 22
  Faculty of Economics and Politics,
    Marshall Library of Economics, 23
  Faculty of History, Seeley Historical
    Library, 24
  Faculty of Modern and Medieval
    Languages, 25
  Institute of Criminology, Radzinowicz
    Library, 26
  Scientific Periodicals Library, 27
  Scott Polar Research Institute, 28
University of East Anglia, 183
University of Essex,
  Albert Sloman Library, 33
University of Exeter, 48
University of Glasgow, 53
University of Greenwich, Natural
  Resources Institute, 32
University of Hull, 61
University of Kent at Canterbury, 29
University of Leeds, 66
University of Leeds, Trinity and All
  Saints College, 65
University of Leicester, 67
University of Limerick, 68
University of Liverpool, 71
University of London,
  Birkbeck College, 78
  Goldsmiths College, 106
  Heythrop College, 109
  Institute of Advanced Legal Studies, 115
  Institute of Commonwealth Studies,
    116

Institute of Education, 118
Institute of Historical Research, 119
Institute of Latin American Studies, 121
King's College London, 134
London School of Hygiene and Tropical Medicine, 141
Queen Mary, 156
Royal Holloway, 46
School of Oriental and African Studies, 163
University College London, 168
University College London, Development Planning Unit, 102
University College London, Folklore Society Library, 104
University College London, Institute of Archaeology, 168
University of London Library, 169
University of Manchester, 180
University of Newcastle upon Tyne, 181
University of Northumbria, 182
University of Nottingham, 184
University of Oxford,
    Bodleian Law Library, 186
    Bodleian Library, 187
    Bodleian Library, Radcliffe Science Library, 193
    Department of Economics, 188
    Department of Plant Sciences and Oxford Forestry Institute, 189
    Institute of Social and Cultural Anthropology, 197
    International Development Centre, 190
    Modern Languages Faculty, 191
    Pitt Rivers Museum, 196
    Radcliffe Science Library, 193
    Rhodes House Library, 175, 194
    Rothermere American Institute, 194
    Saint Antony's College, 195
    School of Anthropology and Museum Ethnography, Balfour Library, Pitt Rivers Museum, 196
    School of Anthropology and Museum Ethnography, Tylor Library, Institute of Social and Cultural Anthropology, 197
    School of Geography, 198
    Taylor Institution, 199
University of Portsmouth, 200
University of Reading, 201
University of Saint Andrews, 203
University of Salford, 204
University of Sheffield, 205
University of Southampton, 208
University of Stirling, 209
University of Strathclyde, 52, 54
University of Surrey, 56
University of Sussex, 15
University of Sussex, Institute of Development Studies, 14
University of the West of England, 18
University of Wales Aberystwyth, 3
University of Wales Bangor, 4
University of Wales Swansea, 211
University of Warwick, 36
University of Wolverhampton, 213
University of York, 215
Urban bylaws, 102
Urban planning and development, 102
Uruguay, 8, 20, 33, 187
    Anthropology, 8
    Civil engineering, 125
    History, 20
    Humanities, 187
    Jews and anti-Semitism, 117
    Liberation theology, 8
    Literature, 20
    Mechanical engineering, 126
    Missions, 8
    Social sciences, 187
    Social welfare, 8
    Travel, 8
USA, *see* United States
UWE, *see* University of the West of England

Venezuela, 170
    Anthropology, 65
    Art, 170
    Economics, 170
    History, 36, 65, 170
    Jews and anti-Semitism, 117
    Law, 170
    Literature, 36, 65, 170
    Manuscripts, 61
    Mechanical engineering, 126

Official publications, 170
Politics, 170
Social sciences, 65
Venezuelan Embassy, 170
Vere Harmsworth Library, University of Oxford, 194
Veterinary entomology, 45
Veterinary medicine, 43
Veterinary mycology, 45
Victoria and Albert Museum, 148, 160
Video recordings, 2, 9, 28, 31, 36, 38, 40, 58, 65, 73, 75, 81, 90, 94, 110, 111, 121, 128, 131, 142, 143, 149, 165, 168, 170, 173, 191, 192, 196, 207, 212
Vital registration, 151
Voyages, 146, 149, 150

Wallace, Alfred Russel, archive, 58, 150
Wallcharts, 94 (Anglophone Caribbean)
Warren, Max, Collection, 175
War theory, 129
Weapons, 129
Weather charts, 11
Wellcome Library for the History and Understanding of Medicine, 171
Welsh settlement, Patagonia, 2, 4
West India Committee Library, 116
West Indies, *see* Anglophone Caribbean
Westfield College, *see* Queen Mary
Westminster City Libraries, 172
Wiener Library, 117
Wilberforce Collection, 60
Wild cats, 212
Wildlife, 55, 83 (recorded sound), 212
Women, 85, 103, 173
   Anglophone Caribbean, 96, 116
Women's Art Library, 173
Women's Library, 103
Working conditions, 142
Working papers, *see* Research papers
Worldaware, 174
World Mission Association, 175
World-Wide Fund for Nature–UK, 55
Writers and Scholars Educational Trust, 176
WWF–UK, *see* World-Wide Fund for Nature–UK

Yearbooks, 94 (Anglophone Caribbean), 133
Youth, 96 (Anglophone Caribbean)

Zoological Society of London, 177
Zoology, 85, 177

Printed in the United Kingdom
by Lightning Source UK Ltd.
773